Studies in Public Choice

Volume 32

More information about this series at http://www.springer.com/series/6550

Louis M. Imbeau · Steve Jacob
Editors

Behind a Veil of Ignorance?

Power and Uncertainty in Constitutional Design

Springer

Editors
Louis M. Imbeau
Department of Political Science
Pavillon Charles-De Koninck
Université Laval
Québec
Canada

Steve Jacob
Department of Political Science
Pavillon Charles-De Koninck
Université Laval
Québec
Canada

ISSN 0924-4700
Studies in Public Choice
ISBN 978-3-319-14952-3 ISBN 978-3-319-14953-0 (eBook)
DOI 10.1007/978-3-319-14953-0

Library of Congress Control Number: 2015930732

Springer Cham Heidelberg New York Dordrecht London

Printed on acid-free paper

Springer International Publishing AG Switzerland is part of Springer Science+Business Media
(www.springer.com)

Foreword

Constitutional political economy is one of the oldest fields in social science. It began in Athens during its Golden Age with careful analyses by Plato and Aristotle. Both analyzed fundamental macropolitical issues in civil and constitutional law. And, both developed categories and lines of reasoning that continue to be used today. Risk and uncertainty played a role in their designs, but mostly the risks associated with what today would be termed political agency problems. How likely would government leaders be to govern appropriately or inappropriately within the alternative designs considered, given the men who would occupy or select others for positions of authority? How can one construct a good, durable government out of persons who are not always good themselves?

The uncertainties that worried them most were those associated with mankind itself, both as government officials and as voters. They did not analyze how uncertainties might affect prospects for adopting particular institutions. Nor did they address the reasons why governments are necessary, perhaps because it seemed so obvious to them that they did not feel it necessary to articulate, or perhaps because governments were by then taken as facts of nature, rather than puzzles to be explained.

If the world were stable or predictable, a well-conceived legal system might be sufficient for most purposes, as suggested by Plato in his *Republic* and his dialog on the *Laws*. Similar conclusions seem to emerge from the contemporary law and economics literature as well. Given well-defined and tradable property rights, Pareto-efficient outcomes can be reached through exchange but for transaction costs.

Yet, there are more potential "property rights" than can be completely characterized by a static series of laws at a given point in time. As populations grow and technologies change, the matters over which rights must be defined also tend to change, as with the rights over hunting grounds, agricultural land, printed books, the electromagnetic spectrum, the bandwidth on the backbone of the Internet, and information stored on cell phones. What can be or should be owned is not always obvious, nor who should own it. Although core concepts of the civil law are remarkably robust, liability, contract, and property law are often adjusted at the margins through time and, in many cases, improved by those adjustments.

Moreover, there are problems and opportunities that emerge which can most effectively be addressed through coordinated responses of the sort that are not likely to emerge spontaneously from the uncoordinated behavior of individuals or families. An invasion may need to be blocked. Large-scale waterworks may be constructed to accommodate population pressures or environmental problems associated with greater population densities. A highway system may benefit from bridges and road signs. The production of such services may themselves be subject to surprises, technological advances, and variations in demand that require nearly constant adjustments.

Adapting to new opportunities and problems evidently requires ongoing decision-making procedures in order to modify and extend civil law, address emergencies, and provide services such as law enforcement, defense, highways, and social insurance.

Governments—in the sense of active policy making—can thus be said to be necessary because of uncertainty, because of the advantages of changing rules and policies to mitigate unanticipated problems and take advantage of new opportunities. Moreover, the same uncertainties that produce the demand for active governance also imply that governments—the standing procedures and authority to make public policies—are also likely to benefit from reform as new circumstances arise. Thus, formal and informal amendment procedures are normally included in constitutional documents.

As argued by Plato, Aristotle, and many others in the past two millennia, it is the risk that that authority will be abused that causes prudent men and women to favor vesting their governments with limited authority and for including standing procedures for replacing officeholders that ignore the constitution or poorly execute their duties, as with elections and procedures for impeachment.

Exactly what authority to delegate to government officials and deliberative bodies is, however, not entirely obvious. This is true of constitutions created "whole cloth" and those produced gradually through a series of reforms. As a consequence, responsibility for designing constitutions and reforming them are normally delegated to relatively small groups of relatively distinguished men and women who meet to negotiate the details, often in a single room. These same persons will often expect to occupy high office after a government or reform is adopted and so have pragmatic reasons to vest significant authority in the various offices created or amended. Yet which office will go to which man or woman is not always clear.

Many authors, including the editors of this volume, argue that uncertainty about who will subsequently occupy seats of authority tends to increase support for fine-grained characterizations of authority. Each constitutional committeeman may trust himself or herself to be an unconstrained president or prime minister but not all the others in the conference room or elsewhere who might come to office. Given the uncertainty about who will occupy positions of authority, a constitutional committee will tend to agree that their chief executive and parliament have a carefully limited authority, although each might prefer to have unbounded authority for himself or herself.

In this manner, some kinds of uncertainty can justify particular authorities, but others can justify bounding those authorities, while making agreements about the bounds more likely to occur. Thus it can be argued that constitutions are written and revised because of the risks and opportunities associated with uncertainty both inside and outside of government, and that such uncertainty makes formal constitutional documents more likely to be adopted.

This volume explores the dual of those direct implications of uncertainty. If uncertainty encourages constitutional reform and facilitates agreement for constrained authority, then the most detailed constitutions are adopted in situations in which uncertainty is the greatest. In that case, the specifications of political authority and civil liberties in constitutional documents can be used to determine the extent to which constitutional designers were operating behind a veil—a veil that combined uncertainty and ignorance.

To measure the opacity of that veil, a careful analysis of several important constitutions was undertaken by the contributors to this volume. They identify a surprising number of fine-grained power relationships in the constitutional documents examined, of the order of 500 power relationships are described in each case. Insofar as fine-grained details indicate uncertainty during the negotiation process, an index of the opacity of the veil can be constructed. That index, in turn, can be used to analyze the normative claims of Rawls, Buchanan, and many other contractarians—that agreements from behind relatively dense veils tend to better advance general interests and thus produce better constitutions.

The result is a very interesting research project that includes the most careful work on constitutional power and limits to authority of which I am aware. In general, the contributors find that constitutional negotiations normally took place in settings where uncertainty was considerable. They also find that the more detailed the characterization of power relationships, the more liberal and durable the democracy tends to be.

November 2014

Roger D. Congleton
BB&T Professor of Economics
West Virginia University

Contents

Chapter 1
Introduction

Louis M. Imbeau and Steve Jacob

This book addresses the issue of the impact of uncertainty in constitutional design. To what extent do constitution drafters and adopters make their decisions «behind a veil of ignorance»? More fundamentally, can we infer from constitutional texts the degree of uncertainty faced by constitution drafters and adopters?

A constitution is a *social contract* defining a set of rules by which the governed agree to be governed. As such a constitution ascribes power resources to governors while restraining the way they are expected to use them. But a constitution is also a *discourse* by the drafters and adopters about what let them to make their choices. Thus, behind the formal content of a constitution is hidden an informal statement about the very motivations of its creators. Looking at a constitution from each of these two viewpoints opens two different windows for uncovering the motivations that drove its drafters in the constitution-making process. The social-contract perspective tells us which institutions drafters and adopters agreed to put in place in order to reach their objectives. The discourse perspective helps reveal what these objectives actually were, in a context where uncertainty about future conditions was very high. This book adopts the second perspective. It looks at constitutions as discourses from which to infer the motivations of constitution drafters and adopters in the face of uncertainty.

The idea that constitutional choices are made under uncertainty and that this uncertainty determines the characteristics of such choices was first presented by James Buchanan and Gordon Tullock in their seminal work, *The Calculus of Consent*. They wrote:

> Recall that we try only to analyse the calculus of the utility-maximizing individual who is confronted with the constitutional problem. Essential to the analysis is the presumption that the individual is *uncertain* as to what his own precise role will be in any one of the whole chain of later collective choices that will actually have to be made. For this reason

L.M. Imbeau (✉) · S. Jacob
Département de science politique, Université Laval, Québec, Canada
e-mail: louis.imbeau@pol.ulaval.ca

S. Jacob
e-mail: steve.jacob@pol.ulaval.ca

L.M. Imbeau and S. Jacob (eds.), *Behind a Veil of Ignorance?*,
Studies in Public Choice 32, DOI 10.1007/978-3-319-14953-0_1

he is considered not to have a particular and distinguishable interest separate and apart from his fellows. This is not to suggest that he will act contrary to his own interest; but the individual will not find it advantageous to vote for rules that may promote sectional, class, or group interests because, by presupposition, he is unable to predict the role that he will be playing in the actual collective decision-making process at any particular time in the future. He cannot predict with any degree of certainty whether he is more likely to be in a winning or a losing coalition on any specific issue. Therefore he will assume that occasionally he will be in one group and occasionally in the other. His own self-interest will lead him to choose rules that will maximize the utility of an individual in a series of collective decisions with his own preferences on the separate issues being more or less randomly distributed (Buchanan and Tullock 1962: 78).

Buchanan and Tullock's perspective was positive as they wanted to describe how constitutional decisions were actually made. Following their lead, John Rawls (1971) then proposed his *maximin* criteria in a normative perspective. He saw a decision behind a «Veil of ignorance» (i.e., under uncertainty) as a thought experiment that could show how rational decision-makers should attend to the preferences of the least advantaged group in society when they are ignorant of their actual and future positions in society. We argue here for a return to the original positive perspective to assess the role of uncertainty in constitutional choice.[1]

Constitutional political economy distinguishes between constitutional choice and 'in-period' choice, or equivalently between choice *among* constraints and choice *under* constraints. The first refers to the choice *of* rules and the second to choice *within* rules (Brennan and Hamlin 2001: 120–127). Brennan and Hamlin argue that these two types of choice have important characteristics that differentiate them—motivational, informational, social-capital, and public-good characteristics. We focus here on motivational characteristics, i.e., on the degree decision-makers choose in their own private interest or in the general interest when making choices. In constitutional choice, rational decision-makers attend to the interest of the many. Because they do not know what their future position in society will be, their «individual interests fade into the background and are replaced by the general interest of all agents» (Ibid.: 120). Indeed,

«…the uncertainty introduced in any choice among rules or institutions serves the salutary function of making potential agreement more rather than less likely. Faced with genuine uncertainty about how his position will be affected by the operation of a particular rule, the individual is led by his self-interest calculus to concentrate on choice options that eliminate or minimize the prospects for potentially disastrous results» (Brennan and Buchanan 1985: 30).

However, 'in-period' choices are devoid of this type of ignorance as they are to last for a shorter period of time and as they are easier to change once adopted. In this context, decision-makers choose in their own interest. Assuming that a given

[1] For example, such a perspective has been applied to the analysis of the constitution-making process that followed the breakdown of the Soviet Empire in the early 1990s. Rowley (2008: 24) noted that «scholars recognized that Rawls's «veil of ignorance» played no role in [that] process».

constitutional document ensues from the constitutional level of decision-making[2], we may expect that it is submitted to the same motivational characteristic. Therefore, its content should reflect the general interest more than particular interests.

Thus, we may ask questions such as: Which constitution belongs to the constitutional level of decision-making and which does not? What explains the variation? Adopting a cognitive perspective, we read national constitutions as an indication of the motivations that their drafters had at the time of adoption so as to assess whether this constitution reflects their own private interests more than the general interest (Imbeau 2009; Imbeau and Jacob 2011).

The book proceeds in two parts. The first part (Chaps. 2–4) introduces to the intellectual filiation of the project and to its theoretical and methodological foundations. The second part (Chaps. 5–13) presents nine case studies built on the same structure: historical account of the making of the constitution, results of the content analysis of the constitutional text, and discussion of specific issues raised in the analysis. Chapter 14 concludes.

In Chap. 2, Stefan Voigt compares «two main veil notions regarding their value in explaining real world constitutional choices», John Rawl's 'veil of ignorance' and James Buchanan's and Gordon Tullock's 'veil of uncertainty.' Doing so, he surveys the political economics literature, looking at theoretical, experimental, and empirical approaches to evaluate how useful the notion of «veil» has been to explain the content of constitutions. He concludes «that the central conjectures of 'veilonomics' are unsatisfactory on theoretical grounds and refuted both experimentally and empirically».

Chapter 3 by Christine Rothmayr Allison nicely complements Voigt's chapter as it discusses the socio-legal literature. She shows how different explanatory approaches have developed over time, some close to Buchanan's idea of the role of uncertainty in constitution-making, and others radically different. The chapter first provides a brief overview on the general findings about the global spread of rights protection and then reviews the theoretical approaches, first discussing the literature that operates most closely with the concept of *uncertainty* and then by contrasting these approaches with alternative explanations that more or less ignore this concept. This allows the author to compare and contrast competing explanations of the empowerment of courts through constitutional change, in order to situate the role of *uncertainty* within the larger socio-legal literature on how and why constitutions change.

Chapter 4 by Louis Imbeau and Steve Jacob introduces the conceptual framework and the methodological apparatus developed in the Veil of Ignorance Project (VOIP) and presents some preliminary results. Imbeau and Jacob first expose the conceptual theoretical foundations of the project based on Buchanan's interaction approach and on the notion of power. Then, they describe the content analysis

[2] As Brennan and Hamlin argue, «capital-C Constitutions [i.e., Constitutional documents] are only a small part of the set of rules that govern 'in-period' choices. Equally, capital-C Constitutions often include elements that are not small-c 'constitutional' in our sense at all» (2001: 117).

method that was used to compare the discursive content of the constitutional texts analyzed in the following case studies. In the last section of their chapter, Imbeau and Jacob provide various measures of the opacity of the veil in 16 constitutions and test the validity of their results through a regression analysis.

In Chap. 5, Cristine de Clercy argues that «the American case surely constitutes a 'best case' scenario so far as aiming to probe the constitution-making process under conditions of deep and extensive uncertainty». She introduces the case by reviewing the founding of the American colonies and their move to declare independence from Great Britain. She then surveys the key events leading to the 1787 Constitutional Convention in Philadelphia, noting the position and interests of the Framers and the ratifying delegates. In the last section, she summarizes the results of the content analysis of the constitutional document concluding that the US constitution clearly reflects the general interest more than the drafters' private interests.

Chapter 6 by Louis Imbeau and Thomas Eboutou introduces the case study on Canada by insisting on the historical context, the «rising tide of modern constitutionalism» as they call it, in which the Canadian constitution was drafted in the 1860s. They first depict the economic and political situation in the former British North American colonies and describe the way the constitution was drafted and adopted, and then how it evolved through the twentieth century. Their second section gives the statistical results of the content analysis of the 39 constitutional texts forming the Canadian constitution. From the results of a regression analysis, they conclude that the content-analysis method developed by Imbeau and Jacob might be measuring two types of uncertainty, economic uncertainty, which significantly covaries with real GDP growth but is independent of time (uncertainty is higher when growth is lower), and political uncertainty which covaries with time but not with GDP growth (uncertainty is lower as we get further away from the founding date). The authors interpret this last finding to mean that constitution drafters seem to be less uncertain of their future as they get more experience in living together.

In Chap. 7, Nathalie Schiffino and Steve Jacob provide an overview of the making of the Belgian constitution in 1831, comparing the context in which it was drafted with the contemporaneous context of the 1993 constitution. Focusing on the change from a unitary regime in 1831 to a federal regime in 1993, they argue that domestic cleavages (catholic–liberal and bourgeoisie–working class in 1831; French–Flemish in 1993), consociationalism, and the international context (civil wars in Europe and foreign surveillance on the process of decolonisation from the Netherlands in 1831; EU membership in 1993) were important sources of uncertainty, in addition to the unframed process of devolution that has been going on in the more recent period. In the second part of their text, Schiffino and Jacob proceed to the content analysis of the two constitutional texts to conclude that constitution drafters worked behind an opaque veil of ignorance.

The following case study presented in Chap. 8 by Agnes Strauss describes in detail the making of the German «Basic Law» or *Grundgesetz*. It shows how, in the aftermaths of the military defeat in the Second World War, representatives from *Länder*, meeting at the Constitutional Convention at Herrenchiemsee in 1948 and at the Parliamentary Council in 1948–1949, interacted with Western allies (American, British, and French) to draft a constitution that would reflect the interests of the German drafters while pleasing the occupiers. In the second part of the chapter, the results of the content analysis of the *Grundgesetz* are presented. The author concludes that, because of the regular intervention of the Western Allies in the drafting process, «it is not easy to distinguish from the final constitutional text, to which degree the variables [identified in the content analysis] reflect the existence of a veil of ignorance and to which degree they reflect the compromises from the interests of the different veto players».

Chapter 9 by Emma Galli and Veronica Grembi applies Buchanan and Tullock's uncertainty hypothesis to the process of drafting the 1948 Italian constitution, especially with respect to the territorial organization of the Italian state. The chapter provides a vivid reconstruction of the main steps of the evolution of the relations between the central state and the periphery from the unification in the nineteenth century to the present time. Then, the authors compare the level of uncertainty relative to the design of the different levels of government, national, regional, and local. The results of their content analysis of the constitutional text show that uncertainty was significantly higher with regard to the regional level as compared to the national and to the local levels.

George Tridimas in Chap. 10 provides a wide overview of the constitutional history of Greece, surveying the six constitutions of 1844, 1864, 1911, 1927, 1952, and 1975, as well as the three revisions of 1986, 2001, and 2008. Then, he investigates the pattern of power relations in five post-WWII Greek constitutions in the period 1952–2008, a time span that covers the monarchical constitution of 1952 and the republican constitution passed in 1975 and its revisions. He records «an inexorable trend of increasing authority and instrumental and positive power relations». He concludes that «the hypothesis that constitutional writing in Greece was the result of disinterested framers designing institutions behind a veil of ignorance to cope with uncertainty receives less than solid support».

Is the Swiss constitution really constitutional? This is the question that Karin Ingold and Frédéric Varone raise in Chap. 11, arguing that Switzerland is a special case. After outlining the historical background of the Swiss constitution from its genesis in 1874, they proceed to the analysis of the results of the content analysis to assess the importance of uncertainty in the constitutional process in Switzerland. They conclude that their empirical results confirm that direct democratic instruments, such as mandatory referendum for constitutional amendments and popular initiatives, reduce uncertainty as citizens are part of the drafting and adoption process.

Chapter 12 looks at constitutional design during post-communist transition in Estonia. This period, Ringa Raudly argues, is particularly insightful for testing the veil of ignorance hypothesis as these countries were simultaneously moving from one-party to multi-party systems, from command to market economies, and from government unconstrained by laws to the rule of law. In a first section, the chapter gives an overview of the historical setting in which the Constitutional Assembly was convened, how the constitution was drafted, and what the motives and objectives of the framers were. A second section describes the content of the Estonian 1992 constitution in terms of the power relations framework, and a third section discusses the findings of the Estonian case study in the light the theoretical propositions presented in Chap. 4.

Thomas Eboutou builds Chap. 13 on the fundamental political economy premise that constitutional decisions are fundamentally different from in-period decisions, the former being characterized by higher uncertainty. He argues that the constitutions of Chad and Cameroon are more of an in-period than of a constitutional type of process as the Chadian and the Cameroonian presidents strongly controlled the drafting and adoption processes and therefore were pretty confident about the outcome. After telling the story of the two drafting processes, Eboutou turns to the analysis of the power relations in the two constitutional texts and concludes that the Chadian and Cameroonian cases reveal two weakness in the framework presented in Chap. 4, namely the absence of a measure of error and the importance of lawyers' legal writing style with regard to the third hypothesis which relates negative formulations to uncertainty.

In the conclusion, Cristine de Clercy reviews the comparative findings generated in the nine case studies and then considers these in light of the original theory concerning how uncertainty influences constitutional creation.

References

Brennan HG, Buchanan JM (1985) The reason of rules. Cambridge University Press, Cambridge

Brennan G, Hamlin A (2001) Constitutional choice. In: Shughart WF II, Razzolini L (eds) The elgar companion to public choice. Edward Edgar, Cheltenham, pp 117–139

Buchanan JM, Tullock G (1962) The calculus of consent: logical foundations of constitutional democracy. The University of Michigan Press, Ann Arbor

Imbeau LM (2009) Testing the «veil of ignorance» hypothesis in constitutional choice: a «walk-talk» approach. J Public Finance Public Choice 26(1):3–21

Imbeau LM, Jacob S (2011) Is the "Veil of Ignorance" in constitutional choice a myth? An empirical exploration informed by a theory of power. In: Marciano A (ed) Constitutional mythologies. Springer, Dordrecht, pp 53–69

Rawls J (1971) A theory of justice. Harvard University Press, Cambridge

Rowley CK (2008) Public choice and constitutional political economy. In: Rowley CK, Schneider FG (eds) Readings in public choice and constitutional political economy, Springer, New York, pp 3–29

Part I
Literature Reviews, Theory, and Method

Chapter 2
Veilonomics: On the Use and Utility of Veils in Constitutional Political Economy

Stefan Voigt

In reality, Constitutions are not written by social planners and veils of ignorance have large holes in them.

(Aghion et al. 2004: 578)

Abstract Time and again, discussions on "just" or "fair" constitutional rules are structured around the veil of ignorance (Rawls) or uncertainty (Buchanan). But how useful has this tool really been for identifying a set of rules large groups could agree to unanimously? Are thicker veils really connected with rules leading to more redistribution? This paper surveys the political economics literature broadly conceived and looks at theoretical, experimental, and empirical approaches. It concludes that the central conjectures of veilonomics are unsatisfactory on theoretical grounds and refuted both experimentally and empirically.

Keywords Veil of ignorance • Veil of uncertainty • Fair constitutions • Constitutional political economy

JEL Classification D63 • H11 • K10

1 Introduction

Constructing a direct link between principles for a "fair" or "just" society and the choice of a constitution appears straightforward. If a society's constitution contains the most basic rule set according to which members of society want to live together, then principles of fairness or justice should be reflected directly in this

S. Voigt (✉)
Institute of Law and Economics, University of Hamburg and CESifo, Johnsallee 35, 20148 Hamburg, Germany
e-mail: Stefan.Voigt@uni-hamburg.de

L.M. Imbeau and S. Jacob (eds.), *Behind a Veil of Ignorance?*,
Studies in Public Choice 32, DOI 10.1007/978-3-319-14953-0_2

document. John Rawls is often credited with having revived moral philosophy which was believed dead due to positivism and empiricism (e.g., Kersting 1993). His *Theory of Justice* inspires fellow philosophers even today (witness Sen's (2010) *Idea of Justice*).

Rawls famously draws on a veil of ignorance as an important precondition for the original position which is then used to derive his principles of justice. Rawls is explicitly engaged in normative and counterfactual reasoning. In contrast, representatives of Constitutional Political Economy are interested in explaining the choice of constitutional rules, among other issues. To make the two programs commensurable, this contribution tries to reformulate the central insights of the veil approach into positive hypotheses that are, at least in principle, testable. I then go on to ask a straightforward question: To what extent is the notion of the veil helpful in explaining the choice of constitutional rules?

The attempt to explain the content of constitutions drawing on the economic approach can be traced back to Buchanan and Tullock (1962). For decades, such a theory of endogenous constitutions was not picked up by anyone. Recently, this seems to have changed [see, e.g., the contributions by Aghion et al. (2004), Ticchi and Vindigni (2010), Hayo and Voigt (2013) survey the relevant literature.]. The central question dealt with in this paper can, hence, also be interpreted as part of this theory of endogenous constitutions.

As a survey-type article, this paper is primarily interested in providing some structure to the literature that relies on veil-type arguments. Some of the surveyed contributions develop their points in such a law-like manner that it seems justified to summarize them under the heading "veilonomics," hence the title of this paper.

Following the pertinent papers, questions such as whether thicker veils do increase the likelihood of constitutional agreement and whether the thickness of the veil can be discerned when analyzing the content of constitutions are discussed. Given that these questions can be answered in the affirmative, it is only a small step to inquire whether the thickness of the veil can be deliberately manipulated. This is a policy question and, hence, a far cry from the question that motivated Rawls.

A veil is per se something intransparent. Transparency has, however, been one of the catchwords of the entire discourse on governance. According to that debate, transparency is a crucial precondition for accountability and responsibility and, at the end of the day, for good governance. Thinking about deliberately increasing intransparency seems to be in marked contrast to that debate but can be entirely plausible within veilonomics.

The rest of the paper is structured as follows: Sect. 2 contains both a brief summary of the Rawlsian veil and a number of critical remarks. An attempt to translate arguments from moral philosophy into the world of real constitutional choices is being made in Sect. 3, largely along the lines of the veil of uncertainty as proposed by Buchanan and Tullock. Section 4 is a short section comparing the two approaches. Section 5 surveys contributions that have "tested" the notion of a veil in some way, namely (a) theoretically, (b) experimentally, and (c) empirically. Section 6 ventures possible steps beyond established veilonomics, and Sect. 7 concludes.

2 The Most Famous Veil: Rawls and Ignorance

The *Theory of Justice* is Rawls' most famous book, and he continued thinking about possibilities for its improvement for the rest of his life. In describing—and criticizing—the Rawslian notion of the veil, I rely, however, entirely on the *Theory of Justice*. Since I am not interested in the intricacies of political philosophy but rather in the relevance of some veil notion for constitutional choice, this seems justified.

Before Rawls introduces his veil proper, he describes the context for which this notion is needed (1971: 10f.):

> Thus we are to imagine that those who engage in social cooperation choose together, on one joint act, the principles which are to assign basic rights and duties and to determine the division of social benefits. Men are to decide in advance how they are to regulate their claims against one another and what is to be the foundation charter of their society. Just as each person must decide by rational reflection what constitutes his good, that is, the system of ends which it is rational for him to pursue, so a group of persons must decide once and for all what is to count among them as just and unjust.

A number of observations seem to be in order: First, the principles of justice claim eternal validity; they are not subject to any change. Second, Rawls envisages a grand and explicit agreement, no development in small steps. Third, there is no talk of any concrete society; hence, the issue of who exactly agrees on any principles is not explicitly dealt with.

In the sentence preceding the passage containing the explicit introduction of the veil, Rawls (1971: 1) describes the original position as a "purely hypothetical situation." I interpret this as Rawls being interested primarily—or even exclusively—in the derivation of some normative principles and not in the explanation of real-world choices of constitutional rules.

This is how Rawls introduces his veil (1971: 11):

> Among the essential features of this situation is that no one knows his place in society, his class position or social status, nor does any one know his fortune in the distribution of natural assets and abilities, his intelligence, strength, and the like. I shall even assume that the parties do not know their conceptions of the good or their special psychological propensities.

In other words, the actors behind the Rawlsian veil know nothing about their own identity; they are soulless automata.

Further, Rawls envisions a clear sequence of choices behind the veil (12). First, the actors behind the veil make the "choice of the first principles of a conception of justice which is to regulate all subsequent criticism and reform of institutions." Only in a subsequent step do they choose their constitution and in a third step the legislature and so on.

Binmore (1994: 329) interprets this not as a sequence of choices behind the veil but as four different veils. His interpretation is very convincing as the second choice will be made behind a veil that is already partially lifted in the sense that the "first principles of a conception of justice" have already been chosen. Binmore (ibid.) admits that he does not understand "precisely what Rawls intends that I remember and forget when I pass beyond his veil of ignorance."

Rawls' main interest seems to lie in deriving his famous two principles of justice.[1] He is explicitly disinterested in making the next step, namely in deriving constitutional rules that best incorporate these two principles (ibid., 14). "In particular, the content of the relevant agreement is not to enter a given society or to adopt a given form of government, but to accept certain moral principles." But a far-reaching consequence can be drawn from the Rawlsian premises: If the fundamental principles of justice can claim to be valid independent of time and place and form the basis for the choice of constitutional rules, then a universal ideal constitution ought to be derivable—even if Rawls never bothered to derive it himself. This does, however, not exclude that somebody else took up the question.[2]

According to Rawls, his two principles of justice hold independently of time and place. Although Rawls is explicitly not interested in deriving constitutional rules, an empirical follow-up question almost suggests itself: assuming that different societies might very well share different conceptions of fairness—and thus explicitly parting with Rawls' premises—do these lead to systematically different constitutional rules? An empirical analysis of the connection between first principles and constitutional contents can, of course, never refute Rawls' approach—as it is entirely normative. But if it could be shown that different conceptions of the normative, i.e., the fundamental principles, are reflected in differences in constitutional rules, then this would be an additional boost to the Rawlsian program. My hunch, however, is that constitutions are written by representatives of the elite whose preferences might substantially diverge from any fairness principles and such an exercise would, hence, be a blow rather than a boost to Rawlsians.

It has often been noted that Rawls attributes extreme risk aversion to his actors. The relationship between risk aversion and the principles actually chosen can be turned into a hypothesis: The higher the degree of risk aversion, the more should the chosen principles be pointing toward equality.

Rawls' theory is often attributed normative status. Shepsle (2006: 1035), for example, writes: "As a normative treatise, A Theory of Justice is a milestone of twentieth-century thinking about constitutional moments. As a basis for a historical or positive analytical treatment of actual constitution writing, it possesses problems." It might be useful to somehow qualify the status of the theory. Step one of his theory consists in a hypothetically positive claim: "Given that individuals know x and do not know y, they would choose fundamental principles 1 and 2."[3] Rawls himself describes this as "purely hypothetical." If one were mean, one could interpret this as an immunization

---

[1] To reiterate, they are (1) each person is to have an equal right to the most extensive basic liberty compatible with a similar liberty for others and (2) social and economic inequalities are to be arranged so that they are both (a) reasonably expected to be to everyone's advantage, and (b) attached to positions and offices open to all. The first principle always has precedence over the second; that is, they are ordered lexicographically.

[2] As far as I know, nobody has ever bothered to derive such a constitution in Rawlsian terms.

[3] One could argue that "step zero" of his theory was clearly normative. It would read: "You ought to forget y for the sake of this experiment." As was just pointed out, this imperative cannot be executed and the whole enterprise seems to be non-starter.

strategy. As we will see in Sect. 5 below, experimental researchers beg to differ. They try to emulate the conditions specified by Rawls in the laboratory and have real people choose their own fundamental principles.[4] Step two of Rawls' theory then is to claim validity for the derived principles for real-world situations. This is where his theory is clearly normative: "You (constitution-makers in the real world) should implement my two fundamental principles!"

Even if one believes that the fundamental principles derived at step one are correct (although most experiments have shown that real people choose different principles), the relevance of his normative advice is doubtful: Constitutional rules as the most basic layer of rules need to be self-enforcing. In other words, they need to constitute an institutional equilibrium. But what incentives do real-world constitution-makers have to follow the advice of a New England philosopher king?

Let me summarize. In this section, I have highlighted a number of queries regarding the notion of the veil underlying both Rawls' original position as well as his principles of justice derived behind that veil. I have also shown that Rawls' theory contains a nomological hypothesis that can be put to a test. The results of such tests will be reported in Sect. 5 below. Rawls' veil is clearly the most famous one, but he was definitely not the first to draw on this notion. The next section describes the veil as constructed by Buchanan and Tullock.

3 From Moral Philosophy to Real-World Constitutions: Uncertainty, not Ignorance

The *Calculus of Consent* by Buchanan and Tullock (1962) can be considered as the birthplace of Constitutional Political Economy. It is here that Buchanan and Tullock develop the argument that agreement on rules is scarce and that it is, hence, rational to economize on agreement by choosing rules adequately. It is here that Buchanan and Tullock develop their interdependence cost calculus, but it is also here that a version of a veil is presented which is completely different from the one developed by Rawls.[5] This is how the authors describe the necessity of uncertainty (ibid., 78): "Essential to the analysis is the presumption that the individual is uncertain as to what his own precise role will be in any one of the whole chain of later collective choices that will actually have to be made."

The Rawslian veil only works if societies are made up of actors who follow the imperative to forget who they are and deliberately walk through a veil of ignorance (however that can be done). In the Buchanan and Tullock version of the veil,

---

4 Rawls could, of course, claim that these experiments do not really depict what he had in mind.

5 But Buchanan and Tullock were not the first in developing a veil construction, either Harsanyi (1953, 1955) is an important precursor in the twentieth century. The notion of an "impartial spectator" can also be interpreted as a precursor of sorts, the notion going back at least to Adam Smith.

actors know very well who they are today, but are uncertain regarding their future positions. Unanimous agreement on constitutional rules will only be attained if the future is sufficiently uncertain. This likelihood will be higher the longer the constitution is expected to remain in force.

In a contribution jointly authored with Viktor Vanberg, Buchanan proposes to disentangle preferences into interests on the one hand and theories on the other. Regarding the choice of constitutional rules, one could, hence, distinguish between constitutional interests and constitutional theories. The interest component reflects the preferences of the individual, whereas the theory component reflects her hypotheses regarding possible cause–effect relationships.

	Interests	Theories
Corresponds more with what type of theory?	Contractarian	Deliberation
Status?	Evaluative	Cognitive
Falsifiability?	No (subjective)	Yes (objective)

Vanberg and Buchanan (1989: 53) intend to analyze constitutional choices that occur under realistic conditions, namely (1) people are not totally ignorant regarding their interests and are (2) not perfectly knowledgeable regarding their theories. The pleasant aspect about their approach is that empirically falsifiable hypotheses can be derived in a straightforward fashion. I shortly present the hypotheses contained in their contribution and add some comments.

Hypothesis 1 "As the veil's "thickness" increases so will the prospect of achieving agreement." (p. 54)

This is the core of the entire veil notion: The more uncertain I am regarding my future position in society, the more will I take the position of an impartial spectator. Since this reasoning applies to everybody, agreement on the content of the constitution becomes possible.

A number of follow-up questions immediately come to mind:

(1) How can the thickness of the veil be measured? Is it uni- or multidimensional?
(2) What is the functional form connecting the thickness of the veil with the prospect of agreement? Supposing the thickness of the veil could be measured, would the prospect of agreement be a linear function of the thickness? Would the prospect of agreement marginally decrease the thicker the veil becomes?
(3) If agreement is (normatively) striven for and the thickness of the veil increases prospects for agreement, then the question becomes can we deliberately manipulate the veil's thickness? To what degree can it be manipulated? Who has an interest in doing so—and who does not?

Hypothesis 2 "The degree of uncertainty is, in part, a function of the sort of rules that are under consideration. The essential dimensions here are the generality and the durability of rules. The more general rules are and the longer the period over which they are expected to be in effect, the less certain people can be about the particular ways in which alternative rules will affect them" (p. 54).

The hypothesis is straightforward and contains a partial answer to the second question formulated with regard to hypothesis 1 above: Yes, uncertainty—i.e., the thickness of the veil—can be deliberately increased by only allowing a certain type of rules, namely "general" ones; it is, hence, endogenous.[6] If participants at a constitutional convention are interested in achieving agreement and the hypothesis is correct, then we should observe constitutional conventions agreeing on some kind of meta-norm, namely that only "general" rules will be considered for inclusion in the constitutional draft.[7]

Further, the hypothesis implicitly assumes that generality and durability are complementary. Empirically, this can be true. Logically, it need not be true as the two belong to different dimensions: Whereas the generality of the constitutional rules agreed upon is entirely endogenous to the decisions of the constitutional convention, this is not the case with regard to the durability of rules. Their durability will be influenced by a host of factors not under the control of the constitutional convention. One can, however, argue that rules perceived as "fair" or "legitimate" would stand better chances of becoming durable rules. But this might lead to circular reasoning: The (expected) durability of rules increases the prospects of agreement. Having reached agreement increases the legitimacy of the rules which, in turn, increases their expected durability.

Empirically, a closely related kind of circular reasoning might, indeed, be relevant. It seems plausible to assume that the expectations of the delegates to a constitutional convention regarding the durability of their prospective constitution are formed on the basis of past experience of their own country. People in Haiti or the Dominican Republic are likely to expect their constitutions to remain in place only for the next eight or ten years. If most members of a constitutional convention assume a constitution to be short-lived, most of them will have fairly precise assumptions about their relative position over the expected life span of that constitution. If the entire veil argument is correct, then the likelihood that such countries will pass a draft unanimously (or might pass a draft at all) should be relatively low. Assuming that this gives the newly passed constitution only a limited amount of legitimacy and further assuming that legitimacy and longevity are connected, we have arrived at a self-fulfilling prophecy: If constitution-makers expect a constitution to be short-lived, they will act such that the constitution will, indeed, only be short-lived. Establishing this kind of causality empirically is, however, extremely difficult.[8]

---

6 This conjecture is also appealing because the generality or universalizability of rules has often been identified as one of the core ingredients of the rule of law (Kant 1797/1995; Hayek 1973; Buchanan and Congleton 1998).

7 It would be interesting to test whether any constitutional convention has agreed on such a meta-principle before agreeing on any substantial rules. Additionally, it would be interesting to know whether any constitutions themselves contain provisions requiring the generality of constitutional rules.

8 While writing their paper and reflecting upon durability, Buchanan and Vanberg might have had the US experience in mind. Elkins et al. (2009) show, however, that the median life span of all written constitutions produced since 1789 is below twenty years.

Hypothesis 3 "So far as the *interest dimension* is concerned, agreement is facilitated by whatever increases persons' uncertainty about the *particular* effects that alternative rules can be expected to have on them. ... So far as the *theory dimension* is concerned, prospects of agreement on desirable rules are enhanced not by creating uncertainty but, on the contrary, by raising the level of mutually shared information on the general working properties of alternative rules" (p. 60).

This is a modification of central hypothesis 1 and a consequence of splitting up the preferences into interests and theories. Regarding interests, nothing changes. Regarding theories, the exact opposite from the conventional result appears, however. Agreement will be more likely the lower the level of uncertainty. Note that it is completely irrelevant whether the theories are true in the sense of reflecting reality. As long as almost everybody believes them to hold true, this is sufficient for reaching agreement. In other words, this part of the conjecture deals more with beliefs than theories as conventionally conceived.

Putting this hypothesis to an empirical test is no mean feat as we need to have measures for both degrees of uncertainty regarding the individual interests and the degree of uncertainty regarding perceived theories.

Given that we are interested in agreement and that the thickness of the veil can be deliberately modified, we would want a very thick veil regarding the interest dimension and a completely transparent one regarding the theory dimension. To understand whether transparency regarding the theory dimension can be deliberately increased, we do not only need to know how members of society—or representatives in constitutional assemblies—acquire their theories.

The introduction of an interest and a theory component has a number of consequences. First, it moves the entire enterprise closer to Rawls which is amazing taking into account some of Buchanan's previous critique, e.g., (1977: 196): "... the Rawlsian framework as here interpreted must contain rather full information about alternatives for production and distribution available under cooperation,..." Robert Cooter (cited according to Buchanan 1977: 205) poignantly summarized the asymmetric assumptions regarding the information actors hold in the Rawlsian model: "..., an individual must know everything in general and nothing in particular." Now, Buchanan and Vanberg seem to wish for actors with exactly that asymmetrical information.

Second, it means that Buchanan—probably inspired by Vanberg—has become less pessimistic than in previous work: In *The Reason of Rules*, Brennan and Buchanan (1985: 140ff.) were rather pessimistic regarding the chances that rational actors could agree on deliberately increasing the thickness of the veil. Only four years later, Vanberg and Buchanan (1989: 54) wrote: "The variables that affect the veil's thickness, can, to some extent, be manipulated, and rational actors may take deliberate measures designed to put themselves behind a thicker veil, thereby entrancing the prospects of realizing potential gains from constitutional agreement."

Vanberg and Buchanan describe a possibility; they do not make a prediction. To turn this into a hypothesis, one would have to know the conditions under which constitutional conventions are predicted to increase the veil's thickness. From the point of view of contract theory, this is also interesting because it amounts to some sort of meta-rule. Staying within the Buchanan frame, this rule would need to be passed unanimously. Whether this is likely will be discussed—among other issues—in the next section.

4 Rawls or Buchanan: Ignorance Versus Uncertainty

This short section tries to compare the two main veil notions discussed so far regarding their value in explaining real-world constitutional choices. More than two centuries ago, Hume (1777/1987) vividly described the conditions under which new constitutions are often produced. He is rather critical concerning the relevance of unanimous agreement:

> ... and were one to choose a period of time, when the people's consent was the least regarded in public transactions, it would be precisely on the establishment of a new government. In a settled constitution, their inclinations are often consulted; but during the fury of revolutions, conquests, and public convulsions, military force or political craft usually decides the controversy.

Hume thus envisions a situation involving a very high degree of uncertainty. If the prevalence of uncertainty as such was sufficient for the passing of "fair" or "just" constitutions, then the resulting constitutional rules ought to be fair almost by definition.

We just saw that Vanberg and Buchanan consider the possibility that people choosing a new constitution might deliberately choose to increase the amount of uncertainty to increase the chances to agree unanimously. But if we imagine a Hume-like situation, the exact opposite seems a lot more intuitive: If general uncertainty is already high, people will strive to reduce uncertainty to be better able to build expectations regarding the future that has a high chance of turning out to be correct.

So how important is the distinction between Rawls and Buchanan at the end of the day? I propose to distinguish between two veil conjectures, one attached to Rawls and the other one to Buchanan. The Rawslian veil is used to derive two fundamental principles of justice, from which constitutional—and other—rules can be derived. I propose to call this the **substantive conjecture**. Buchanan's veil, in turn, is used to increase the likelihood of unanimous agreement. I propose to call this the **procedural conjecture**. In their comparison of the two different approaches toward the veil, Brennan and Hamlin (2002) point out that Rawls is interested in refining our ethical intuitions, whereas Buchanan is interested in politically feasible solutions.

5 Tests of the Veil Hypotheses

Scholars have picked up the veil notion in very different contexts. We propose to look at three of them in a little more detail here. The first one challenges veilonomics from a theoretical point of view. The second one is based on laboratory experiments, whereas the third and the last one are attempts to test some notion of the veil empirically.

5.1 Theoretical Challenges

In this subsection, I briefly present and discuss four issues that have been dealt with in the literature: (1) an attempt to introduce different kinds of uncertainty—instead of dealing with just one general and unspecified type. (2) Assuming that actors at the constitutional stage play a prisoners' dilemma game and further assuming the absence of risk aversion, agreeing on mutual cooperation should not be much of a problem; this is, at least, argued in one contribution. (3) Other contributions worry about preferences. The first one shortly presented here argues that representatives of constitutional political economy have been overly liberal in allowing any kind of preferences. Another contribution introduces expressive preferences and their possible consequences. These can, indeed, mean trouble for the entire approach. (4) Finally, attention is drawn to an approach that shows that public deliberation does not necessarily increase the likelihood of unanimous agreement. This has, of course, important implications for how to best set up a constitutional convention.

Mueller (2001) proposes to be more precise regarding the veil of uncertainty and distinguishes three kinds of uncertainty, namely (1) identity uncertainty, (2) numbers uncertainty, and (3) payoff uncertainty. Identity uncertainty is present if an individual at the constitutional stage knows everything about the future but not what type of person he or she will be himself or herself. Numbers uncertainty, in turn, is present if there are different types of players with different preferences—e.g., different ethnic groups—but the individual does not know how large these groups are. The choosing individual is, hence, unable to calculate any probability of what type he or she is likely to be. Finally, payoff uncertainty is present if the individuals at the constitutional stage are uncertain regarding the payoffs that various alternative choices will yield. A move from identity uncertainty to numbers uncertainty to payoff uncertainty implies a higher degree of uncertainty. Mueller assumes that "every individual at the constitutional stage can envisage the kinds of issues that will come up in the future" (ibid., 230). This is, of course, a very sweeping assumption. Instead, one might want to introduce a fourth kind of uncertainty, namely "issue uncertainty."

Mueller (ibid., 231) points out that when only identity uncertainty is present, then, following Knight (1921), no real uncertainty is present, but only risk. Mueller vividly describes the consequence of this assumption: "If in 20 or 100 years time, the threat of a flood would require the construction of a dike, the constitution framers could forecast this event, the future preferences of citizens, and determine their tax and effort obligations. These could then be written into the constitution. No second stage in the democratic process would be needed." It is not only the consequences that become clear but also the very unlikelihood that something like this might ever occur. At the other extreme (ibid., 235), if none of the uncertainties are lifted, then no procedure for making future collective choices can be written into the constitution stage.

Müller (1998) takes the Buchanan-type veil head on: Assuming that the coordination problem that individuals face when choosing constitutional rules is of a Prisoners' Dilemma type, he argues that the assertion that uncertainty increases the prospect of agreement is false. Rather, in the absence of uncertainty, actors would achieve both unanimity and fairness without problems. Unfortunately, this raises a subsequent problem: Given that his (theoretical) argument is convincing, why is it that representatives in constitutional assemblies so often fail to achieve unanimity?

Müller's argument is based on what Mueller (2001) calls "identity uncertainty": Players know the game they are playing (i.e., the payoffs) but do not know what specific role they will occupy (column or row). Given this uncertainty, they can choose cells. Choosing (C, C), e.g., would imply empowering a third party to enforce that solution. Müller (1998) argues that (D, D) is weakly dominated and the choice among the remaining cells boils down to a genuine coordination game.

In his comment on Müller, Kyriacou (1998) calls Müller's point an "interesting refutation" but sets out to qualify it by explicitly introducing some degree of risk aversion. Given risk aversion, a thick veil of uncertainty is shown to be conducive to the choice of fair rules. This qualification anticipates an important discussion between experimental economists, namely whether the idea of a veil is equivalent to the introduction of risk—or whether there is more to it. This discussion is summarized in the next section of the paper.

Witt and Schubert (2008) are also concerned with risk preferences, although they rely on them only as an example for the parsimony of preferences allowed in social contract models. According to them, these models are too parsimonious to allow for agreement on a social contract. Citizens' constitutional interests vary with their risk preferences. To find constitutional rules that are in everybody's interest and that are, hence, able to secure unanimous agreement, explicit assumptions concerning preferences are needed. They illustrate their point by referring to individuals' risk attitudes and their systematic change over an individual's life span. In a sense, they argue that the veil is too thick.

The usefulness of veilonomics and, indeed, the entire approach of constitutional political economy has come under attack from a pair of authors, namely Brennan and Hamlin (2002), *prima facie* unlikely to question the approach. They start from the observation that in post-constitutional democratic choices, expressive voting often plays a very important role: Voters know that their individual vote is not decisive, so they refrain from voting instrumentally and turn to express themselves. They are pushed to do so because the consequences of such behavior are basically costless. Brennan and Hamlin (ibid.) now argue that expressive voting might, relative to instrumental voting, become even more relevant regarding constitutional choices. But if this is the case, then it becomes not only unclear whether unanimity can ever be reached but, given that it does, whether the agreed-upon constitution is the best possible one the community could agree on in case that instrumental concerns did prevail.

How to get out of this conundrum? Do away with the approach of Constitutional Political Economy in its entirety? For Brennan and Hamlin, expressive voting can only take over instrumental voting due to the large numbers involved. In a sense, expressive voting is the consequence of the "veil of insignificance" (Kliemt 1986). So Brennan and Hamlin propose to lift this veil basically by delegating the power to write a constitution to a convention that is sufficiently small such that any individual member's vote is sufficiently important to keep instrumental and expressive voting in balance. Crampton and Farrant (2004) take issue with the solution proposed by Buchanan and Hamlin. They claim that "the expressive voting critique is devastating to the constitutional enterprise."

Stasavage (2007) is concerned with a different problem; in fact, the word "veil" does not even appear in his paper. Uncertainty in our context refers to lack of information regarding one's own position in society at some future date. Transparency, in turn, refers to information (or lack thereof) regarding the behavior of others acting on my behalf, e.g., representatives in a constitutional assembly. Transparency is, hence, important in principal agent relationships. Representatives of discourse theory such as Habermas usually argue that increases in transparency increase the chances of unanimous agreement. This issue is connected to our question because Vanberg and Buchanan (1989) claim that lower levels of uncertainty regarding theories are tantamount to a higher likelihood of reaching consensus.

Stasavage (2007) asks whether public deliberation is likely to lead to consensus. Drawing on game theory, he shows that public decision-making where citizens can observe both the vote of their representatives and the policy choice might increase, and not reduce, polarization. His formal result echoes the insights of Elster (e.g., 1995) who made this point with regard to constitutional assemblies a long time ago.

5.2 Laboratory Experiments

Experimental economics has been extremely successful over the last couple of decades; a number of Nobel prizes allocated to experimental economists attest to that. Experimental economics is closely related to behavioral economics as many experiments have shown that the traditional rationality assumptions used within economics are not reflected in how real people make real choices. But there have also been critical voices regarding the adequacy of the laboratory for testing conjectures regarding social contract theory. Binmore (1994: 184), e.g., who has carried out a number of experiments himself has this to say: "One cannot successfully mimic the real-life situations that matter to social contract discussions in the laboratory, but one can at least try to come as close as possible." Johansson-Stenman et al. (2002: 369) who have also conducted experiments involving the veil point out that preferences "revealed" via surveys or experiments might contain a good dose of moral thinking and thus not reveal the "true" preferences of the subjects.

For a long time, Frohlich et al. (1987) was the only experimental test of the veil hypothesis. It is a very broad experiment, setting out to test both the procedural and the substantive predictions made by Rawls. Frohlich et al. (1987: 4) describe the procedural predictions as (1) behind the veil, there will always be unanimous consent and (2) the principles chosen unanimously will always be the same. Rawls' substantial prediction is, of course, that actors will choose the difference principle that maximizes the lot of the worst off. Regarding substantive principles, subjects can choose from four different principles, namely (1) maximize the floor income (Rawls' difference principle), (2) maximize the average income, and two principles that Rawls would call "intuitionistic" because they constitute a mix of principles, namely (3) maximize the average income with a floor constraint and (4) maximize the average income with a range constraint. Before subjects decide collectively on their preferred principle of choice, they all have to pass a test making sure they have understood the four principles.

And here are the results: All groups (of five) were able to agree unanimously on a single principle. However, none of the (29) groups agreed on the Rawslian principle, whereas 25 agreed on the principle according to which average income ought to be maximized subject to a floor constraint (the remaining four groups chose to maximize average income *tout court*). Frohlich et al. also tested the individual popularity of the four principles by asking subjects to rank them. Rawls' principle reached the lowest number of first ranks (3) but the highest number of last place rankings (71).

Frohlich et al. does not only contain a careful discussion of the possibilities to put an ethical theory to an empirical test, but it is also very frank in admitting that not all of Rawls' hypothetical conditions can be met in the laboratory. They explicitly mention two, namely the size of the stakes and the information conditions and discuss possible limitations of their insights very openly.

Summing up their experiment, they did find some evidence in support of the procedural hypotheses (people could agree unanimously, and they agreed on the same principle across groups—at least in the overwhelming number of cases), but they were not even close to agree on Rawls' difference principle. The authors' main message seems to be that Rawls' one-dimensional principle does not reflect the complexity of human choices. The "intuitionistic principle" (maximize average income subject to a floor constraint) was not only much preferred but seems to be more human in the sense that we tend to have different goals which we try to reach by combining principles. It is, thus, not only the fact that Rawls' principle scored so badly that constitutes a problem but also the insight that people tend to trade off principles at the margin, much like economic goods (ibid., 21).

It almost seems as if the contribution by Frohlich et al. was so sweeping that one could not only get the impression that Rawls was dead but that, moreover, more experiments analyzing either the procedural or the substantive effects of the veil were all but superfluous.

Frohlich and Oppenheimer (1990) can be considered a direct continuation of Frohlich et al. (1987). Now, the question is whether consent to a distributive principle is stable over time. Overall, the authors answer "yes" to these questions. More precisely, Frohlich and Oppenheimer report (1) changes in the rankings of distributive justice principles over time, (2) the confidence of the subjects in their rankings, and (3) satisfaction with their choice having experienced taxation and redistribution. They conclude (1990: 473): "… when subjects participate in choosing the principle, their satisfaction is higher than when it is imposed upon them. When they participate and are required to choose *unanimously*, their confidence in the choice increases." Encouraging as these results may seem, the question of external validity might be especially severe here; the disutility from working is not very severe, and the real time over which an experiment extends is rather short. Whether an experiment such as this is adequate to identify the stability of one's choice regarding a distributive principle might be doubted.

More recently, Powell and Wilson (2008) have tried to mimic the Hobbesian Jungle in the laboratory. This is of relevance to our interest here because they also ask whether subjects agree unanimously to a constitutional contract to get out of the state of anarchy and whether—given that they have been able to agree on a contract unanimously—they then abide by it in subsequent rounds of the game. Of 32 situations in which a constitutional contract could have been concluded, only one was agreed upon unanimously. And alas, it was reneged upon only seconds after its conclusion and theft and plunder continued.

5.2.1 Using the Veil to Estimate a Social Welfare Function

We now move on to present a number of experiments that well deserve to be called "perverse" from a Rawlsian point of view. Remember that Rawls was a staunch opponent of utilitarianism with its teleological orientation. There are a variety of papers—mostly penned by Swedish authors—in which the veil is used to determine the shape of the social welfare function empirically. Usually, subjects are to choose between different societies that differ regarding average income and (or) the distribution of income (Johannesson and Gerdtham 1995 started that tradition). These papers are mentioned here because they also reveal some information on a critical assumption of Rawls', namely that actors are extremely risk averse. In addition, a more recent paper nicely separates between risk aversion on the one hand and preferences in favor of equality per se.

Johansson-Stenman et al. (2002) took up the lead and tried to use the veil to identify the relative importance of risk aversion on the one hand and the preference for relative standing on the other. The idea is that subjects are asked to choose the society they would want their (hypothetical) grandchildren to live in from a number of societies that differ regarding both mean income and income distribution (depicted as information on minimum and maximum income).[9] One

---

[9] Remember Mueller (2001) who uses exactly the same device to talk about identity uncertainty.

such society serves as a benchmark, and subjects are then asked to make pairwise comparisons with (in this case) eight other societies. The benchmark society has the highest average income but also the highest income inequality. Their choices reveal the relative risk premium (defined as the income they are willing to forego to live in a more equal society) and, implicitly, their relative risk aversion.

Remember that Rawls assumes subjects to be extremely risk averse. According to the results of Johansson-Stenman et al., less than 20 % of their subjects can be grouped into that category. At the same time, 17 % of their respondents were found not to display any risk aversion at all. The authors used the characteristics of their respondents to identify the determinants of risk aversion. They find that left-wing voters are significantly more risk averse than others, while business students appear to be least risk averse (ibid., 376).

Carlsson et al. (2003) is an almost perfect replica of Johansson-Stenman et al. (2002) with the important difference that it is being played in India which allows the authors to include at least two interesting twists: first, whether risk aversion is context dependent: After all, Swedish society is characterized by both less income inequality and higher average income than Indian society. Further, vertical mobility has been severely restricted in India due to the caste system. It turns out that risk aversion does not dramatically differ between Indian and Swedish students. The authors (ibid., 826) point out that among Indian students, there is a "somewhat higher fraction of the Rawlsian kind." In my reading of the results, the main difference is rather in the lower share of those who are not risk averse at all (4 % in India compared to 17 % in Sweden). The dummy for membership in "scheduled" (i.e., lower) casts was highly insignificant (with a *p*-value of 0.98).

Carlsson et al. (2005) introduce a distinction between "individual risk aversion" and "individual inequality aversion." The latter refers to a preference—and possibly a willingness to pay—to live in a more equal society per se. To disentangle the two, two experiments are played, in which the subjects decide what is best for the—still imaginary—grandchildren. The choice of a lottery refers to risk aversion, whereas the choice of a society refers to inequality aversion. In the latter experiment, the income of the grandchildren is always at the mean of society, but societies differ with regard to their income distributions. Carlsson et al. (2005: 384f.) find that females are both more risk and more inequality averse than males and that left-wing voters are also significantly more risk averse.[10]

Schildberg-Hörisch (2010) tackles with the same problem—how to distinguish simple risk aversion from genuine pro-equality preferences—but chooses to answer it via a different route. She draws on a dictator game with two additional features, namely (1) an efficiency loss for units transferred from the dictator to the receiver and (2) identity uncertainty: Participants decide how to divide the pie before they know whether they are the receiver or the dictator. She finds that social preferences differ depending on whether subjects decide from behind a veil or

[10] Brennan et al. (2008) are the first to test whether there is a systematic relationship between other regarding preferences and attitudes toward risk but fail to find any such relationship.

without such a veil. Women display more genuine preferences in favor of egalitarian outcomes than men, a result that has been found in many experiments (Croson and Gneezy 2009 is a survey).

These insights can be easily translated into a hypothesis which is empirically testable like "*ceteris paribus*, the higher the proportion of women in the constitutional assembly, the higher the degree of redistribution to be found in the constitutional document." Of course, the hypothesis can also be framed in terms of the ideological positions of the members of the constitutional assembly. But since being left-of-center is almost equivalent to being pro-redistribution, it would surprise nobody if it turned out to be confirmed by the data. As interesting as it is to learn something about the determinants of risk aversion, this is a far cry from the Rawlsian setting as those choosing the principles neither know their gender nor their ideological positions. But we might learn something on constitutional choices. Relatedly, Hayo and Voigt (2012) recently found that female leaders are more likely to increase the degree of constitutionally safeguarded judicial independence than their male counterparts.

Gerber et al. (2013) is an attempt to reveal preferences for redistribution as a function of uncertainty. The authors distinguish three different treatments that are run with a different degree of uncertainty—a veil with different degrees of thickness if you will—in this case regarding the productivity of the subjects. The treatments were called "no uncertainty" (in which subjects knew their own productivity), "full uncertainty" (in which they did not have any clue regarding their productivity) and "half uncertainty" (in which they received a noisy signal regarding their productivity). Compared to the theoretical benchmarks, subjects choose "too much" redistribution under half uncertainty and too little of it under full uncertainty. Interestingly, Gerber et al. did not find any gender effect in their experiment.

5.2.2 Introducing Behavioral Economics

Behavioral economists teach us that many of the standard assumptions regarding the rationality of actors are flatly wrong. Bukszar and Knetsch (1997) can be interpreted as the explicit contribution of behavioral economics to the discussion on the possibility to use veils for distilling people's preferences regarding redistribution. To do so, the authors rely on one of the central insights of behavioral economics, namely on reference points. Their main point is to show that preferences regarding redistribution are highly dependent on the concrete situation. Their claim is that these differences can be explained drawing on the different reference points subjects draw on when choosing a distribution principle. "Earning" one's endowments by a simple chance game, for example, significantly reduces the propensity to agree to redistribution rules as do differences in the input value to some sort of production. Their results can be interpreted to be at odds with those of Frohlich and Oppenheimer (1990) who found a high degree of stability in chosen principles.

Behavioral economics has taught us the importance of framing. One question to ask with regard to the experiments thus is how exactly they have been framed. Behavioral economics further teaches us that many actors do not have consistent and well-ranked preferences. To what degree can we assume that experiments on the veil can reveal valid information on participants' preferences if one central insight from behavioral economics is that actors do not have a set of stable preferences?

In Sutter and Weck-Hannemann (2003), the participants play a two-person game in which one person works and has to decide on the effort level, whereas the other person represents the tax authority and has the power to set the tax rate. Sutter and Weck-Hannemann are primarily interested in finding a Laffer curve effect experimentally. Their experiment is relevant in our context because the authors include a veil treatment in which subjects are uncertain *ex ante* as to whether they will be supplying labor or deciding on the tax rate. Following the terminology proposed by Mueller (2001), Sutter and Weck-Hannemann experiment with identity uncertainty. They do point out (ibid., 222) that their experiment does not reflect the veil setting in the usual sense as their subjects commit to specific actions once the veil has been lifted—and not to general rules—as is usually the case.

The results are a lot less clear-cut than expected: Average tax rates do not statistically differ from each other irrespective of whether they were chosen under uncertainty or not. The hypothesis that subjects are more likely to exert effort from behind the veil than under certainty conditions can only be confirmed for higher tax rates. Remarkably, with tax rates lower than 30 %, effort levels are even higher under the certainty than the uncertainty treatment.

Let us sum up: Almost all of the experiments draw on the Rawlsian version of the veil and, by implication, almost none on the Buchanan and Tullock version. With the exception of the Frohlich et al. (1987) piece, these studies show little interest in the "procedural veil" hypothesis (the conjecture that more uncertainty increases the likelihood of agreement), but almost all of them are interested in the substantial principles themselves. Following Rawls, "justice" or "fairness" is mostly being reduced to "distribution" or "redistribution" here. These experiments teach us that (1) people are unlikely to agree on the so-called difference principle but are more likely to agree on a principle according to which average income ought to be maximized subject to a floor constraint, (2) people are rarely as risk averse as assumed by Rawls, but a fifth or even a quarter of society might be as risk averse, (3) there is no consensus on whether agreement to a principle is stable (Frohlich and Oppenheimer 1990) or not (Bukszar and Knetsch 1997), and (4) the concept of the veil can be applied to disentangle attitudes toward risks from preferences in favor of equality per se.

This is an impressive list, but some caveats might be in order: (1) Most, but not all, experiments disregard the cost of redistribution. Preferences in favor of redistribution might be impacted by the costs to overall efficiency. (2) Recent research shows people not only underestimate the current degree of inequality, but they also state preferences in favor of redistribution that are at odds with their decisions at the voting booth [Norton and Ariely (2011), Schwartz (2011: 19) asks whether the authors have identified a new veil of ignorance behind which "people develop and express political preferences in ignorance of some of their own values."]. (3) Finally, the results of only two of these studies are directly comparable (Sweden vs. India). It is desirable to enlarge the number of countries for which similar results are available to see to what degree context influences both (a) the degree of risk aversion and (b) a preference in favor of equality per se.

For scholars interested in endogenous constitutional choice, many questions remain wide open. Is there any clear relationship between the degree of uncertainty members of a constitutional assembly are facing and the degree to which they include redistributive principles in the constitution? How can redistributive principles (not outcomes) be measured and compared across constitutions in the first place?

5.3 Empirical Tests

A serious challenge in testing the hypotheses spelled out in Sect. 3 above is that one needs to find a way to measure or estimate how thick the relevant veil is. As far as I know, this had never been explicitly attempted until the VOIP project was initiated by Louis Imbeau. In a 2009 paper, he describes the conceptual ideas of the project, whereas in Imbeau and Jacob (2011), the empirical approach is laid out in more detail. Their conceptual framework relies on power analysis and distinguishes between three distributions of power that decision-makers are interested in conserving—or modifying—through their choices. In a second step, they propose to carry out a detailed content analysis that is to reveal the various power relations embedded in constitutions. Their approach is described in more detail as Chap. 4 of this volume (Imbeau and Jacob 2015). The results of these analyses with regard to ten nation-state constitutions are also documented in this volume.

McGuire and Ohsfeldt have dealt with the choice of the US Constitution in a number of papers (e.g., 1986, 1989a, b, 1996) explicitly taking up the dichotomy between constitutional and post-constitutional choice introduced by Buchanan into Constitutional Political Economy. Although McGuire and Ohsfeldt never explicitly mention the veil, their papers are summarized here because they ask whether actors involved in constitutional choice make decisions more to the benefit of the general welfare than actors making post-constitutional decisions. One reason for this possibility could be the presence of "constitutional moments" à la Ackerman (1991), another one the higher degree of uncertainty prevalent regarding constitutional choice.

More particularly, McGuire and Ohsfeldt are interested in identifying the factors that led representatives of both the Philadelphia and the single-state conventions to vote in favor of—or against—a particular measure or the constitution in its entirety. They find that merchants, Western landowners, financiers, and large public securities holders supported the new constitution, whereas debtors and slave owners opposed the constitution (1989a: 175). They further find that there are important differences between the two phases of the ratifying procedure: Whereas for the delegates of the Philadelphia Convention, the interests of their constituents are a better predictor for their voting behavior than their own interests, the opposite is true for the delegates to the 13 state conventions.

McGuire and Ohsfeldt conceptualize the behavior of the representatives to the conventions within the realm of the principal agent model; that is, they differentiate between the interests of the representatives and those of their constituents. They further point to the fact that the ratification process can hardly be claimed to have taken place behind a veil of uncertainty à la Buchanan and Tullock and that it seems therefore justified to assign its ratification to the operational as opposed to the constitutional level (ibid., 184).

An ad hoc hypothesis for this difference could be that the Philadelphia delegates were more narrowly constrained in their voting behavior than those in the 13 states because the constitution would not have turned into effect if not at least nine of the 13 states had ratified it. Imbeau (2009: 5) argues that the difference in voting behavior between the drafting and the ratification stage might be due to differences in the thickness of the veil. This is, however, not saving the argument as McGuire and Ohsfeldt argue that in the latter, the representatives vote more in line with the interests of their constituents—and not the "general interest," however delineated.

Another literature is interested not in explaining the choice of entire constitutions but of some constitutional segments only. Ginsburg (2002), for example, is interested in explaining the different levels of Judicial Review found in many newly passed constitutions. He argues that strong Judicial Review can be interpreted as insurance: If I lose an upcoming election and the then majority wants to pass new legislation not in accordance with the constitution, the content of the constitution can be insured if it installs a neutral body endowed with the competence of Judicial Review. Ginsburg does not explicitly mention any kind of veil, but his theory is based on the degree of uncertainty prevalent at the constitutional stage; it thus seems perfectly compatible of the notion of the veil made prominent by Buchanan. In sum, the higher the degree of uncertainty at the constitutional stage, the higher the degree of constitutionally entrenched judicial review.

Ginsburg (2002) does set out to test his theory albeit on a very small scale. He proposes to measure the strength of judicial review by operationalizing three of its dimensions, namely (1) court size, (2) term length, and (3) access. These are his dependent variables. He proxies for political uncertainty at the time of constitutional design by constructing a variable "party strength" which is the difference in the first post-constitutional election between the seat shares of the strongest and second strongest parties or blocs of parties in the legislature. This is, of course, not unproblematic as one has to assume perfect foresight on the side of constitution-makers with regard to post-constitutional developments. It furthermore neglects the difference between plurality and proportional electoral systems: In plurality systems, it is highly likely that only two political parties will survive, whereas the number of "stable" parties in proportional systems can be a lot higher. Ginsburg interprets the bivariate correlations as showing that "party strength" is highly correlated with an index composed of all three variables proxying for judicial review.

The empirical test stands on problematic grounds. Not only is it a simple bivariate correlation, the number of observations is, moreover, confined to 18 countries in Eastern Europe that adopted new constitutions in the course of the 1990s. Hayo and Voigt (2012), drawing on a large sample of up to 100 countries and analyzing not only first-time constitutional choices of JR but also changes thereof over time, find only meager support for the insurance hypothesis. In other words, more uncertainty does not necessarily make politicians "buy" insurance in the sense of establishing a judiciary endowed with the capacity to refrain governments with different positions to reverse legislation passed by them.

To summarize, it is unclear whether—and if yes, to what degree—higher levels of uncertainty lead to a higher propensity for members of a society to agree unanimously on a basic set of rules. It is further unclear whether—and if yes, to what degree—higher degrees of uncertainty lead actors to be more risk averse and to choose, in turn, constitutional rules that contain more safeguards for the worst off, i.e., more redistribution. Relying on experimental evidence, there are quite a number of results indicating that the conjectures of both Rawls and Buchanan are not in line with how real people really behave. This sobering evidence is complemented by empirical evidence that is not in line with many of their predictions either.

6 Beyond Established Veilonomics

This section serves to go beyond established "veilonomics" and tries to connect the insights discussed so far with other strands of the literature. In Constitutional Political Economy, the veil is an instrument for making choices at the constitutional level. Vermeule (2001) argues that in historical, as opposed to purely hypothetical, situations, actors do know their identities such that a veil must be functioning differently under real-life conditions. To make his veil operational, he puts Rawls on his head (as Table 1 tries to show): Behind the Rawlsian veil, actors do not know their own identities, whereas behind the veil imagined by Vermeule, they know exactly who they are but are uncertain as to how exactly a certain choice will affect them personally. Vermeule does not only claim that such rules can be very useful for making post-constitutional choices but also that some of them found their way into the US Constitution.

Table 1 Putting Rawls' veil on its head

	Rawls	Vermeule
Certainty with regard to	Distributive consequences	Identity
Uncertainty with regard to	Identity	Distributive consequences

Vermeule believes veil rules to be only one means to countervail self-interested decision-making but reminds his readers that James Madison (in Federalist #10) argued that ambition should be counteracted by ambition via the separation of powers. Vermeule interprets veil rules as a supplement to the more established separation of powers. He identifies five different means ("tactics") to deliberately introduce uncertainty: (1) prospectivity (whereas retroactive legislation would be combined with certainty regarding identity, payoffs etc.), (2) generality, (3) durability, (4) delay, and (5) randomization, quickly adding that this last tactic has not been used very frequently but mentioning the selection of juries in the US as an example.

"Generality" and "durability" played already an important role in Vanberg and Buchanan (1989) discussed above. It is interesting to see that Vermeule interprets them as means (also) relevant for the post-constitutional level. An example of "delay" could be that heads of states agree on the introduction of a new common currency but decide that it will only become operative a number of years down the road. This was, actually, exactly the way the Euro was introduced.

Drawing on such "tactics" is, however, not without cost. Take the example of delay. To what degree is it plausible to assume that the politicians acting in t_0 are primarily concerned with the benefit of future generations? One could even assume the contrary: Perhaps the widespread use of "delay" indicates that politicians are particularly irresponsible? And even if they had the benefit of future generations in mind, how can one exclude that future generations do not have entirely different preferences? (see Holmes 1988 for a very similar argument).

Figure 1 is an attempt to depict and to put in context the veil rules discussed so far. The figure has two dimensions: The horizontal one can be interpreted as a sort of time line, whereas the vertical one depicts the respective level. In Constitutional Political Economy, a distinction is usually only made between constitutional and post-constitutional choice. Here, we propose to make a fourfold distinction: The first level refers to "pre-constitutional choice," i.e., the level on which decisions are made that will then be relevant for making constitutional choices proper. Remember that Rawls proposes to choose the basic principles first and the constitution only at a later stage. Rawls' veil is thus placed on this level. For empirical constitutional choice processes, it is on this level that criteria for members of the constitutional assembly are determined.

Vermeule's veil rules, as we just saw, come in only on the third level of Fig. 1 as he is interested in veil rules that are made part of the constitutional document and that are then used to make post-constitutional choices later on. If this covered the entire veil literature, we would be left with a curious gap that is depicted with the second box in Fig. 1, namely the degree of uncertainty—and attempts to manipulate it—during constitutional deliberations. It is on exactly this level that the VOIP enterprise aspires to make a contribution.

Elster (e.g., 1995) has actually worked a lot on this second level. He is, more specifically, concerned with the degree of transparency—or the thickness of the veil—between members of the constitutional assembly and society at large, making a distinction between public and secret deliberations of the constitutional assembly. In our context, we can interpret secret deliberations as implying a thick veil.

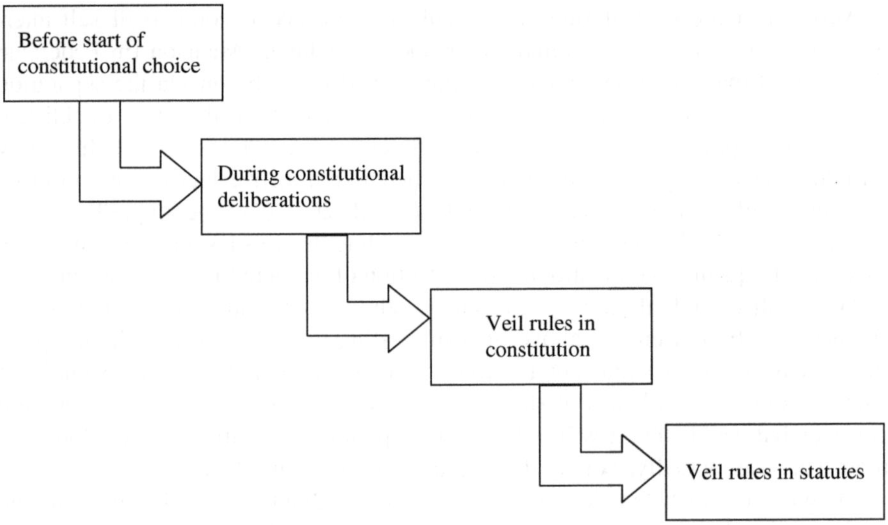

Fig. 1 Different veils at different stages

Elster asks under what conditions a norm against pronouncing purely self-interested claims can be expected to be strong and hypothesizes that it will be stronger in constituent assemblies than in ordinary legislatures. Secondly, the norm will have more impact in public settings than in cases in which discussions take place behind closed doors. He expects this to be the case because a broad public will not accept its representatives resorting to outright power games and calls this effect the "civilizing force of hypocrisy" (1991: 83ff.).

Note that we have just slipped in a different term—namely "transparency"—to paraphrase "the veil." A thick veil is to guarantee a low degree of transparency, and conversely, a high degree of transparency implies the absence of any veil. Yet the terms are not used as the direct inverse of the other: Whereas a veil refers to uncertainty regarding one's own position, lack of transparency refers to uncertainty regarding someone else's behavior. Transparency, hence, becomes relevant in principal agent situations in which I would like a delegate to a constitutional assembly to best represent my own interests. Two implications seem to follow: First, veil-type arguments implicitly assume that all decisions are taken by everyone concerned (direct participation) or that principal agent problems do not exist should decisions be taken by representatives. Neither seems convincing. Second, transparency arguments—concerned with the reduction of the principal agent problem—only make sense in the absence of uncertainty concerning the preferences of the principals.

Up until now, the fourth box of the figure has not been mentioned at all. It is to indicate the possibility that veil rules might not only be contained in constitutions that are to structure the law-making process later on, but also in statutory legislation. One means of randomization are lotteries. Examples for their use include the choice of jury members in the USA but also the choice of conscripts in some armies.

7 Conclusions and Outlook

We began this paper with a straightforward question, namely to what degree is the notion of the veil useful in explaining the choice of constitutional rules? Is there evidence that it is easier for groups of people to agree to a set of basic rules once they have been deprived of basic information regarding themselves? Is it true that—uncertain of one's own (future) self—people are more likely to be in favor of rules favoring redistribution? In this paper, we have surveyed much of the available constitutional economics literature on the use of veils in constitutional choice. We have seen that not all veils are alike and in particular that there are important differences between the notions of veils developed by Rawls on the one hand and Buchanan on the other. The literature dealing with veils has been structured into theoretical, experimental, and empirical contributions. Our overall conclusion is rather sobering: We found that the basic conjectures of veilonomics are not completely convincing in terms of theory, that neither the Rawls nor the Buchanan notion resonates well with experimental evidence, and that in the real world, the veil notion is not only said to be absent but even detrimental to the rational choice of constitutions. In their take on endogenizing constitutions, Ticchi and Vindigni (2010) explicitly define their "original position" as one in which any kind of veil is completely absent.

Throughout the paper, I suggested that a direct confrontation between the notion of the veil, on the one hand, and that of transparency, on the other, might lead to a helpful heuristic. As this paper is primarily a survey, the potential of this heuristic could only be hinted at here. Future contributions might ask under what conditions increases in transparency seem desirable and under what conditions the exact opposite, namely increasing the thickness of the veil, seems desirable.

Acknowledgments The author thanks Louis Imbeau for the suggestion to produce a survey of the use of veils in both Public Choice and Constitutional Political Economy. This paper was finished while I was a distinguished guest fellow at the Notre Dame Institute for Advanced Study. I thank my colleagues there for their hospitality and interesting discussions and Matthias Dauner, Nora El Bialy, Jerg Gutmann, Felix Horbach, Janina Satzer, and George Tridimas for helpful suggestions.

References

Ackerman B (1991) We the people, vol. 1: foundations. Belknap, Cambridge

Aghion Ph, Alesina A, Trebbi F (2004) Endogenous Political Institutions. Quart J Econ 119(2):565–611

Binmore K (1994) Game theory and the social contract volume I: playing fair. MIT Press, Cambridge

Brennan G, Buchanan J (1985) The reason of rules. Cambridge University Press, Cambridge

Brennan G, Hamlin A (2002) Expressive constitutionalism. Const Polit Econ 13:299–311

Brennan G, González L, Güth W, Levati V (2008) Attitudes toward private and collective risk in individual and strategic choice situations. J Econ Behav Organ 67:253–262

Buchanan J (1977) Freedom in constitutional contract—perspectives of a political economist. Texas A&M University Press, College Station/London

Buchanan J, Congleton R (1998) Politics by principle, not interest: towards nondiscriminatory democracy. Cambridge University Press, Cambridge

Buchanan JM, Tullock G (1962) The calculus of consent—logical foundations of constitutional democracy. University of Michigan Press, Ann Arbor

Bukszar E, Knetsch J (1997) Fragile redistribution choices behind a Veil of ignorance. J Risk Uncertainty 14:63–74

Carlsson F, Daruvala D, Johansson-Stenmann O (2005) are people inequality-averse, or just risk-averse? Economica 72:375–396

Carlsson F, Gupta G, Johansson-Stenman O (2003) Choosing from behind a veil of ignorance in India. Appl Econ Lett 10:825–827

Crampton E, Farrant A (2004) Expressive and instrumental voting: the scylla and charybdis of constitutional political economy. Const Polit Econ 15:77–88

Croson R, Gneezy U (2009) Gender differences in preferences. J Econ Lit 47(2):448–474

Elkins Z, Ginsburg T, Melton J (2009) The endurance of national constitutions. Cambridge University Press, Cambridge

Elster J (1991) Arguing and bargaining in the federal convention and the assemblée Constituante. Center for study of constitutionalism in Eastern Europe, School of Law, University of Chicago

Elster J (1995) Forces and mechanisms in the constitution-making process. Duke Law J 45:364–396

Frohlich N, Oppenheimer J, Eavey Ch (1987) Laboratory results on Rawls' distributive justice. Br J Polit Sci 17:1–21

Frohlich N, Oppenheimer JA (1990) Choosing justice in experimental democracies with production. Am Polit Sci Rev 84(2):461–477

Gerber A, Nicklisch A, Voigt S (2013) Strategic choices for redistribution and the veil of ignorance: theory and experimental evidence. Available at: http://papers.ssrn.com/sol3/papers.cfm?abstract_id=2271349

Ginsburg T (2002) Economic analysis and the design of constitutional courts. Theoret Inquiries Law 3:49–85

Harsanyi JC (1953) Cardinal utility in welfare economics and in the theory of risk-taking. J Polit Econ 61:434–435

Harsanyi JC (1955) Cardinal welfare, individualistic ethics, and interpersonal comparisons of utility. J Polit Econ 63(4):309–321

Hayek FA (1973) Law, legislation and liberty, vol. 1: rules and order. University of Chicago Press, Chicago

Hayo B, Voigt S (2012) Explaining constitutional change: the case of judicial independence. Available at: http://papers.ssrn.com/sol3/papers.cfm?abstract_id=2195492

Hayo B, Voigt S (2013) Endogenous constitutions: politics and politicians matter, economic outcomes don't. J Econ Behav Organ 88:47–61

Holmes S (1988) Precommitment and the paradox of democracy. In: Elster J, Slagstad R (eds) Constitutionalism and democracy. Cambridge University Press, Cambridge, pp 195–240

Hume D (1777/1987) Essays—moral, political, and literary, and with a foreword, notes, and glossary. In: Miller EF (ed) Liberty Classics, Indianapolis

Imbeau L (2009) Testing the 'veil of ignorance' hypothesis in constitutional choice: a 'walk-talk' approach. J Publ Financ Publ Choice 26(1):3–21

Imbeau LM, Jacob S (2011) Is the 'veil of ignorance' in constitutional choice a myth? An empirical exploration informed by a theory of power. In: Marciano A (ed) Constitutional mythologies. Springer, Dordrecht, pp 53–69

Imbeau LM, Jacob S (2015) Measuring the opacity of the 'veil of ignorance' in constitutions: theory, method and some results. In: Imbeau LM, Jacob S (eds) Behind a veil of ignorance? Power and uncertainty in constitutional design. Springer, Dordrecht

Johannesson M, Gerdtham U (1995) A pilot test of using the veil of ignorance approach to estimate a social welfare function for income. Appl Econ Lett 2:400–402
Johansson-Stenman O, Carlsson F, Daruvala D (2002) Measuring future grandparents' preferences for equality and relative standing. Econ J 112:362–383
Kant I (1797/1995) The metaphysics of morals. In: Gregor M (ed) Introduction, translation, and notes. Cambridge University Press, Cambridge
Knight F (1921) Risk, uncertainty, and profit. Hart, Schaffner, & Marx, Boston
Kersting W (1993) John Rawls zur Einführung. Junius, Hamburg
Kliemt H (1986) The veil of insignificance. Eur J Polit Econ 2(3):333–344
Kyriacou A (1998) A comment on Müller's "unveiling of the veil of uncertainty". Const Polit Econ 9:335–337
McGuire R, Ohsfeldt R (1986) An economic model of voting behavior over specific issues at the constitutional convention of 1787. J Econ Hist 46(1):79–111
McGuire R, Ohsfeldt R (1989a) Self-interest, agency theory, and political voting behavior: the ratification of the united states constitution. Am Econ Rev 79(1):219–234
McGuire R, Ohsfeldt R (1989b) Public choice analysis and the ratification of the constitution. In: Grofman B, Wittman D (eds) The federalist papers and the new institutionalism. Agathon, New York, pp 175–204
McGuire R, Ohsfeldt R (1996) The role of economic interest and ideology in Institutional choice: The ratification of the federal constitution in massachusetts, North Carolina. and Virginia, mimeo, University of Akron, OH
Müller C (1998) The veil of uncertainty unveiled. Const Polit Econ 9:5–17
Mueller D (2001) The importance of uncertainty in a two-stage theory of constitutions. Publ Choice 108:223–258
Norton M, Ariely D (2011) Building a better America—one wealth quintile at a time. Perspect Psychol Sci 6(1):9–12
Powell B, Wilson B (2008) An experimental investigation of Hobbesian jungles. J Econ Behav Organ 66:669–686
Rawls J (1971) A theory of justice. Belknap, Cambridge
Schildberg-Hörisch H (2010) Is the veil of ignorance only a concept about risk? An experiment. J Publ Econ 94(11–12):1062–1066
Schwartz B (2011) A new veil of ignorance? Commentary on Norton and Ariely (2011). Perspect Psychol Sci 6(1):19–20
Sen A (2010) The idea of justice. Penguin, London
Shepsle K (2006) Old questions and new answers about institutions—the riker objection revisited. In: Weingast B, Wittman D (eds) The oxford handbook of political economy. OUP, New York
Stasavage D (2007) Polarization and publicity: rethinking the benefits of deliberative democracy
Sutter M, Weck-Hannemann H (2003) Taxation and the veil of ignorance—a real effort experiment on the Laffer curve. Publ Choice 115:217–240
Ticchi D, Vindigni A (2010) Endogenous constitutions. Econ J 120:1–39
Vanberg V, Buchanan J (1989) Interests and theories in constitutional choice. J Theor Polit 1(1):49–62
Vermeule A (2001) Veil of ignorance rules in constitutional law. Yale Law J 111:399–433
Witt U, Schubert Chr (2008) Constitutional interests in the face of innovations: how much do we need to know about risk preferences? Const Polit Econ 19:203–225

Chapter 3
Law in Books Versus *Law in Action*: A Review of the Socio-legal Literature

Christine Rothmayr Allison

1 Introduction

The distinction between *law in books* and *law in action* is an important feature of socio-legal scholarship (Pound 1910). The focus on *law in action* distinguishes socio-legal scholarship from the approach taken in this edited and collaborative volume (Imbeau 2009; Imbeau and Jacob 2011, 2015). Legal interpretations develop and evolve over time without formal constitutional or other rule changing. Accordingly, socio-legal scholars are interested in how judges interpret and apply constitutional provisions, and how movements and interest groups turn to courts to protect their rights or to challenge current law and legal interpretation. Socio-legal scholarship also addresses the consequences of the mobilisation of law in everyday life. For example, constitutions are discussed in the light of their interpretability (Melton et al. 2013); they are compared in order to understand why some constitutional provisions empower social actors leading to policy change while others do not (e.g. Smith 2008; McCann 2009); their interpretation is analysed through theorising judicial behaviour (e.g. Epstein and Knight 1998; Segal and Spaeth 1993); or their impact on policy and social change—or lack thereof—is studied (Rosenberg 1991; McCann 1994, 1998). In short, formal constitutional change is not the primary focus of socio-legal scholarship as this is only one aspect of the understanding of constitutions in *action*.

As part of this focus on law in action, over the last few decades, scholars have been particularly intrigued by the increasingly important role of courts and judicial bodies in politics on the national and international level, in particular regarding the protection of rights. An important focus in this literature is the adoption of constitutional rules that delegate more power to independent courts through the introduction of constitutional review, i.e. empowering courts to invalidate legislation and governmental decisions if held unconstitutional or create more legal

---

C.R. Allison (✉)
Département de Science Politique, Université de Montréal, Montreal, Canada
e-mail: christine.rothmayr.allison@umontreal.ca

L.M. Imbeau and S. Jacob (eds.), *Behind a Veil of Ignorance?*,
Studies in Public Choice 32, DOI 10.1007/978-3-319-14953-0_3

opportunities by adopting new rights, i.e. in the form of a charter or bill of rights. Hence, with respect to the principal interest of this volume on constitution drafting, socio-legal research on "how and why constitutional change occurs" has mainly focused on the issue of "entrenching rights and empowering judiciaries" (Whittington 2008: 294).

Regarding the spread of constitutional review and rights protection around the globe, socio-legal scholarship addresses the following questions:

- Why do established democracies adopt written bills of rights or a rights catalogue and (newly) allow courts to review legislation with respect to its constitutionality?
- Under what conditions do new democracies establish independent constitutional courts and establish judicial review?
- What accounts for the spread of human rights and rights protection in national constitutions and on the international level around the globe?

This chapter discusses the socio-legal literature explaining the adoption of rights and rights catalogues and of judicial review through the courts in order to address the volume's topic of the role of uncertainty in constitution making. As the discussion below reveals, different explanatory approaches have developed over time (Ginsburg 2008), some close to Buchanan's idea of the role of uncertainty in constitution making and others again radically different. We proceed in two steps. A first section provides a brief overview on the general findings about the global spread of rights protection. In a second, more elaborate section, we review the theoretical approaches, by first discussing the literature that operates most closely with the concept of *uncertainty* and then by contrasting these approaches with alternative explanations that more or less ignore this concept. This will allow us to compare and contrast competing explanations of the empowerment of courts through constitutional change, in order to situate the role of *uncertainty* within the larger socio-legal literature on how and why constitutions change.

2 Waves of Constitutionalisation

Waves of democratisation (Huntington 1991) have been identified as crucial moments for constitution drafting. As Choudhry (2010) points out, there are however important differences in terms of constitutional content across waves:

> Huntington does not describe the important changes in the constitutional package associated with democratization from wave to wave. In the first wave, this package would have consisted of competitive, multiparty elections for a legislature, a politically accountable head of the executive that is either directly or indirectly elected, an independent bureaucracy, independent courts, a separation of the party and the state, etc. In the second and, decisively, in the third wave, this constitutional package came to include rights-based constitutionalism. A bill of rights that is entrenched and supreme over legislative and executive action, backed up by judicial review by independent courts, is now what we associate with a "normal" state .... (Choudhry 2010: 602–03)

As this citation illustrates, constitutionalisation contains two elements, an entrenched catalogue of constitutional rights *and* judicial review, two institutions that in most modern democracies go together despite variation in the form that judicial review takes—strong or weak—and in the types of rights that are constitutionally entrenched. Rights protection is evidently not exclusively the role of courts, but as the term "judicialisation" implies, nowadays the judiciary assumes in many democracies a central role in this respect. Some authors have focused more strongly on the spread of the institution of judicial review, while others were more interested in the adoption of bills of rights. Depending on the empirical focus, they arrived at different conclusions regarding the types of waves or scenarios to be distinguished.

In terms of the "global spread of constitutional review", Ginsburg (2008: 82–88) distinguishes between three waves of constitutionalisation, the first wave starting with the USA at the beginning of the nineteenth century. Various explanations compete for explaining the emergence of constitutional review in the USA, taking into account legal traditions, actors strategies or functionalist explanations pointing to the complementarities between federalism and judicial review (Ginsburg 2008: 83). The second wave is tied to the adoption of Kelsen's model of constitutional review in post-war Europe by several post-fascist countries and also encompasses countries that adopted constitutional review as part of decolonisation and the related drafting of new constitutions (Ginsburg 2008: 85–87). Finally, the third wave of spreading constitutional review follows the fall of the Berlin wall and the democratisation of east European communist regimes. Most post-soviet constitutions provide for judicial review. The democratisation of former east European communist countries was also accompanied by processes of democratisation and constitutionalisation on other continents (Ginsburg 2008: 87–88).

Hirschl proposes to distinguish between six "scenarios of constitutionalisation and the establishment of judicial review" (Hirschl 2004b: 7–8) which are linked to specific historical circumstances. Similar to Ginsburg, he identifies the "'reconstruction' wave" after the WWII (e.g. Germany, Japan) as a first type of scenario. Then, as a second scenario, he points to the independence scenario, where constitutionalisation and the introduction of judicial review are part of the decolonisation process (e.g. India, Ghana, Nigeria, Kenya). For a third scenario, the democratic transition scenario, he distinguishes further between a single transition scenario, where countries move from an authoritarian to a democratic regime (e.g. many southern European countries) and a fourth scenario, the dual transition scenario, where a country moves to a market economy and democracy at the same time as was the case for various post-communist countries. While these four scenarios are linked to situations of democratic transition or reconstruction and decolonisation, the fifth type of scenario occurs independently from any fundamental change of regime and processes of European integration. He coins it the "no apparent transition" scenario. Canada, Sweden, New Zealand or Israel constitute some examples falling into this category as they have all undergone a process of constitutionalisation since the beginning of the 1980s without any fundamental regime change. Finally, there is the sixth scenario, the "incorporation" scenario, where international norms, such as the European Convention of Human Rights (ECHR), are integrated into domestic law, as has been the case for various European countries, such as the UK.

The distinction of waves or scenarios of constitutionalisation is helpful for the analysis of constitution drafting in two different ways. They establish that there is an overall global trend towards constitutionalisation in the above-introduced sense and point to the fact that there are specific historical circumstances that are particularly conducive to constitutionalising rights protection. They also highlight the importance of the age of a constitution with respect to the type of rights and the extent to which human rights are incorporated into national constitutions. At the same time, the distinction among various scenarios indicates that there is great variation in the specific historical circumstances of constitutionalisation, reaching from established democracies, over supra-nationalisation to democratic transitions. Several theoretical approaches have been adopted to develop explanations of the occurrence of scenarios of constitutionalisation. We now turn to reviewing them.

3 Theoretical Approaches

One may readily identify three types of theoretical approaches that have been mobilised to make sense of the various waves of constitutionalisation. First of all, there are the approaches that operate with the concept of *uncertainty*. The *political insurance thesis* argues that the empowerment of independent courts through constitutional change aims at protecting those currently in power in case of a future loss to opposition forces (Ginsburg 2003). An alternative approach, the *political hegemonic thesis*, also emphasises uncertainty, but mainly argues that empowering courts through the adoption of fundamental right catalogues aims at securing the current political and economic elite's position in power (Hirschl 2004b). These approaches looking at the *uncertainty* of electoral democracy are the closest to Buchanan's emphasis on the role of uncertainty in rule adoption, and their findings support the basic theoretical assumptions underlying this volume.

To the contrary and secondly, *idea-based approaches* emphasise changing ideas and values about rights and point to the importance of lawyers and legal scholars, social movements and processes of diffusion of norms. The concept of uncertainty is not of importance to these approaches. This body of literature emphasises the importance of understanding and analysing how rights provisions and constitutional provisions are mobilised by various actors in politics and everyday life. Regarding constitutional changes, such a perspective proposes to tackle changing constitutional interpretation from a bottom-up perspective in order to understand how the mobilisation of legal norms influences judicial interpretation of rights provisions and other legal norms. Epp (1998, 2009) for example points to the importance of legal mobilisation for creating a "rights revolution". From this second perspective, using the distinction introduced by the editors in the theoretical framework, it is preceptorial rather than political or economic power that explains the spread of judicial review and rights protection.

Third, socio-legal scholars as well as international relation specialists are interested in the internationalisation of human rights regimes and courts. On the one hand, there is the challenge to understand why countries adhere or not to international human rights regimes. On the other hand, scholars are interested in studying how international human rights regimes influence constitution drafting on the national level. Again, we find approaches based on a strategic actor model and operating with some variation of the insurance thesis alongside explanations based on transnational networks, international organisations and various mechanisms of diffusion.[1] Some rely more on political and economic power relations and other on preceptorial power relations to explain the genesis and impact of international human rights regimes.

All three approaches are based on empirical analysis, ranging from case studies and small-N comparisons to large-N research designs—the latter being less developed. The large body of literature that discusses constitutionalism from a normative and conceptual point of view is not object of this chapter (see e.g. Whittington 2008). The research discussed below looks at well-established democracies, analyses processes of democratisation and is also interested in the supra- and international level, notably in human rights instruments and courts. Evidently, this interest in the global spread of rights protection is shared with various sub-disciplines of political science, in particular with comparative politics and international relations.

3.1 Political Insurance and Hegemonic Preservation

Political insurance and hegemonic preservation explanations mainly draw on domestic factors in order to explain the adoption of constitutional review and the introduction of a written catalogue of basic rights. Ramseyer (1994) pointed to the fact that judicial independence is tributary to electoral competition. Even though recent research on Eastern Europe (Popova 2012) arrives at the conclusion that this relationship does not hold in all cases, the idea that electoral competition might be an important factor for explaining judicial review—in terms of formal institutions as well as actual behaviour of the court, e.g. whether it is willing to strike down laws and hence assume its independence—inspired the *hegemonic preservation argument* proposed by Hirschl (2004b) and the *judicial insurance approach* developed by Ginsburg (2003) among others. Hirschl is interested in established democracies, while Ginsburg looks at scenarios of transition.

[1] Going beyond constitution making on the national level and adherence to international treaties, comparative research also analyses to what extent such changes in formal institutions make a difference in terms of actual right protection. This chapter, however, will not engage with this part of the debate as it is too far removed from the interest on constitution drafting and would request a thorough debate on theories of compliance in supra- and international law.

3.1.1 Established Democracies: Hegemonic Preservation

In his book, *Towards Juristocracy: The Origins and Consequences of the New Constitutionalism* (2004), Hirschl addresses the intriguing puzzle of why in *well-established* democracies, politicians would shift power from representative institutions to the judiciary through the constitutionalisation of rights. He focuses his research on what he calls the "'*no apparent transition*' *scenario*, in which constitutional reforms have been neither accompanied by nor the result of any apparent fundamental changes in political or economic regimes" (Hirschl 2004b: 8). He chooses a most similar case approach by comparing four cases, all sharing a Westminster political system and a common law tradition, Canada, New Zealand, Israel, and South Africa which have all undergone constitutionalisation of rights in the 1980s and 1990s. He starts out with the puzzle that for politicians to voluntary limit their own policy-making authority through shifting power to the courts through the adoption of a written bill of rights seems counterintuitive. His basic explanation is based on what he coins "self-interested *hegemonic preservation*", i.e. "…those who are eager to pay the price of judicial empowerment must assume that their position (absolute or relative) would be improved under a juristocracy" (Hirschl 2004b: 11). More concretely, in his empirical analysis, he demonstrates that it is the strategic interaction of three key elite groups, the political elite, the economic elite and the judges that allow us to explain, why and when constitutionalisation takes place and what form it takes. In fact, the empirical analysis, which also looks at the consequences of the constitutionalisation, demonstrates that political interests seek to protect and insulate their policy preferences (Hirschl 2004b: 12). The principal reasons evoked are that in situations where the political future of the elite is uncertain, because there are various challenges to their dominant social and political position, removing certain questions from electoral politics is perceived as preserving "the social and political status quo" (Hirschl 2004b: 213). As Garber (2006) reminds us, judicial power is politically constructed by various actors, and as Dahl already pointed out in the 1950s, elite views and values matter in this respect (Dahl 1957).

Hirschl (2000, 2002, 2004a, b) rejects the idea that constitutionalisation should be interpreted as elites simply adhering to progressive ideals by looking at what he calls the political origins of constitutionalisation. Rather, the ruling elite entrenches their preferences before their opponents might gain a majority. Thereby, the specific motivations differ among politicians, economic elites and judges. Judges seek generally to strengthen the power of their institution, while economic elites see strong rights protection going hand in hand with preventing too much government intervention (e.g. property rights). For political elites, the concrete motivations depend on the political struggles characterising a polity; for example, in the case of Canada, the issue of national unity is a key for understanding constitutionalisation under Trudeau according to Hirschl. Hirschl also points to the importance of

> sufficient level of certainty among those initiating the transition to juristocracy that the judiciary in general, and the Supreme Court in particular, are likely to produce decisions that will serve their interests and reflect their ideological preferences (Hirschl 2008: 65).

Last but not least, he also argues that constitutionalisation has not had the progressive economic and social effects desired in terms of redistributive effects, but rather that juristocracy has to be understood as part of a global trend, fuelled by economic liberalisation, to delegate power to independent bodies, that are not electorally accountable (Thatcher and Sweet 2002; Roberts 2010; Vibert 2007). His systematic review of constitutional rights jurisprudence in the four countries points to a trend to adopt

> …a narrow conception of rights, emphasizing anti-statist aspects of constitutional rights. Despite the open-ended wording of the constitutional catalogues of rights in Canada, New Zealand, Israel, and South Africa, the national high courts of all four countries tend to conceptualize the purpose of rights as protecting the private sphere (whether human or economic) from interference by the "collective" (often understood as the long arm of the encroaching state) (Hirschl 2005: 471).

In short, in the case of no apparent transition scenarios, the origins of constitutionalisation are strongly rooted in the specific, often existential political struggles of a polity, and essentially serve elite interests and preferences. Uncertainty serves to align these interests in order to foster delegation to institutions that might protect elite's interests in the future and to empower them through adopting a written catalogue of constitutionally guaranteed rights. Increased rights protection by the courts ultimately serves to protect existing political and economic power relations in the future.

3.1.2 Regime Transitions: Political Insurance

Ginsburg (2003, 2008) applies the idea of electoral uncertainty not to established democracies, but to situations of democratic transition. In his comparative study of the establishment of judicial review in China, Mongolia and Korea, he adds power relations and politics as explanatory factors to the conventional "demand"-side theory (Ginsburg 2008), which argues that the global expansion of judicial review and rights protection has to do with a globally increased "rights consciousness" (see below). Instead of simply assuming that there is a spread of judicial review that is linked to processes of democratisation around the globe, he wants to understand what motivates politicians to establish independent constitutional courts or to the contrary what motivates them not to render them independent. In sum, he explains "…the emergence of judicial review as a result of institutions and politics, rather than culture" (Ginsburg 2003: 15).

Ginsburg argues that "judicial review is a solution to the problem of political uncertainty at the time of constitutional design" (Ginsburg 2008: 90). Electoral uncertainty, the fact that winning parties will alternate in a democracy, makes it desirable for all parties involved in constitution drawing to "adopt judicial review as an alternative forum in which to challenge government policy as long as they perceive that there is some probability that a court will side against electoral winners" (Ginsburg 2004: 248). Hence, judicial review is seen as a form of insurance, and electoral uncertainty provides the thick veil of ignorance (without Ginsburg using this term) that helps parties to find common ground in constitution drafting with respect to delegating power to the courts (Ginsburg 2004: 248). The creation of independent courts for judicial review with broad competences and ease of access is less likely in situations where the constitution drafters expect to remain in power (Ginsburg 2004: 248). Electoral competition and uncertainty lead to all parties being willing to constrain future winners of election. These are, however, not the only motivations of constitution drawers. Other motivations have to do with protecting ethnic minorities—as judicial review provides a form of "minoritarian guarantee"—and with assuring investors of the protection of property rights, in other words an insurance against arbitrary state intervention (Ginsburg 2004: 248).

Ginsburg is not simply interested in the adoption of judicial review, and he also analyses how the highest court performs. As we know from the comparative literature on courts, similar formal review powers do not necessarily result in similar "behaviour", i.e. how willing the court is to strike down unconstitutional legislation and hence to provide "insurance" to use Ginsburg's term. As Ginsburg demonstrates, in Korea, competition among three parties with comparable strength led to the creation of an independent constitutional court (1988) that succeeded to assure its independence throughout various decisions in the first years after establishment. Also in Mongolia, the rise of a vital opposition favoured the creation of a relatively autonomous constitutional court (in 1992). To the contrary, Taiwan's party system was dominated by the hegemonic Kuomintang party and the constitutional court did not succeed in assuming its autonomy (Ginsburg 2008).

Ginsburg's book is part of a larger debate about the relationship between party competition and judicial independence of highest court. Various studies rely on intertemporal electoral uncertainty as a central explanation for the adoption of constitutional review but also for the effective independence of highest courts as expressed in their actual jurisprudence (Ramseyer 1994; Smithey and Ishiyama 2002; Chavez 2004; Finkel 2005, 2008). As explained in the introduction, the debate focuses on constitutional provisions (law in books) as well as actual behaviour of highest courts and other non-constitutional measures (law in action) to foster independence, i.e. whether they are willing and able to check governmental powers through judicial review. The logic behind the insurance thesis remains the same as discussed for Ginsburg. As Popova summarises, strategic actors engage in a cost-benefit calculation of the benefits and danger of independent highest courts. The greater electoral uncertainty, i.e. the stronger electoral competition is, the more likely is a ruling party to constitutionally establish and sustain independent highest courts in order to prevent future governments to persecute them once they are not in power any more (Popova 2012: 28–30).[2] The insurance thesis has become the most prominent approach for explaining the establishment of independent highest court in democratic transitions (Popova 2012: 29).

The discussion up to know has focused on approaches that we can consider to be related to Buchanan's idea about the role of uncertainty in constitution making

[2] Popova's research on post-communist countries, however, shows that this assumption does not work for lower courts (2012).

as they attribute an important place to electoral uncertainty to explain strategic behaviour leading to constitutionalisation in the form of written rights and delegation of rights protection to judicial institutions in established democracies as well as in situation of regime transitions. The following section contrasts these approaches with what has been termed "demand-side" explanations discussing the importance of ideas, civil society and various mechanism of diffusion for explaining the spread of the "rights revolution" (Epp 1998) around the globe.

3.2 Fragmentation of Power, Ideas and Legal Mobilisation

Traditionally, powerful courts have been associated with specific institutional features and legal traditions (Shapiro 1999). The federalism and separation of power thesis (Shapiro 1999: 196–199) proposes that judicial review particularly developed in countries with federal systems and systems of separation of power (presidential systems) on the governmental level. Lijphart (1999: 216–242) associates judicial review with other institutions of power division, such as federalism or bicameralism (for an update, see Vatter 2009). As comparative empirical studies have revealed, the fragmentation of power within political systems constitutes an important explanatory factor for explaining the development of a legalised and judicialised form of policy implementation, as Kagan (2001) and Kagan and Axelred (2001) for the USA and Kelemen (2011) have convincingly argued.[3] The separation of power thesis per se, however, cannot account for the spread of judicial review around the globe (Shapiro 1999), as judicial review has also flourished in unitary states and states where power is concentrated in the executive, as for example in Canada.

The legal tradition approach argues that English common law tradition emphasises more strongly the neutrality of judges and the ideal of limited government, and former English colonies are therefore more receptive for judicial review and show more judicial activism. As Shapiro (1999) and Helmke and Rosenbluth (2009), among others, have convincingly demonstrated, despite important difference in legal traditions between common and civil law regarding procedures and legal reasoning, the common law tradition is a weak predictor for strong judicial review and judicial independence.

In sum, institutional features and legal traditions cannot account for the global spread of constitutional review. The development of a human rights culture after WWII is the best contender for understanding the phenomenon. Shapiro (1994, 1999) essentially argues that advanced industrial democracies share a number of features that favour the development of judicial review and stronger rights protection not only for constitutional but also for administrative law. He points to

[3] The debate about the transformation of regulatory styles in the USA and Europe is not situated on the level of constitution drafting but rather on the level of policy formulation and implementation and will therefore not be discussed in more detail here.

the importance of increased delegation to independent agents along with the growing importance of the state in many domains of life after WWII to which citizens reacted with increased demands for transparency and accountability in modern democracies. According to Shapiro, therefore, the spread of judicial review and constitutionalisation of rights and rights protection around the globe essentially responds to social demand within a changing institutional context of delegation, liberalisation and raising welfare states.

There is a longstanding tradition and debate within socio-legal scholarship about the importance of social demand, but also social support for the spread of rights protection but also the actual impact of judicial review on policy making. There are different strands of literature that we can distinguish. There is the more human rights and international relations-oriented literature looking at the actual spread and diffusion of human rights and adherence to international rights regimes. From that approach, we can distinguish a more socio-legal tradition that looks at domestic legal mobilisation and the role of professionals for explaining the "rights revolution". Regarding the first stream of literature, there are competing explanations within this literature, some adopting a more strategic actor perspective based on how governments weigh the loss of sovereignty versus possible gains domestically and internationally, some focusing on civil society demands, mobilisation and processes of learning, and others again looking at mechanism of coercion. These various approaches from a diffusion perspective will be discussed further in Sect. 3.3. In this section, we concentrate on the socio-legal literature that looks at domestic factors explaining rights revolutions, namely the support by and mobilisation of civil society actors.

Within the socio-legal tradition, there is a longstanding debate about the importance of a written bill of rights for developing strong judicial review (Epp 1996; Songer 2008). Charles Epp has argued that a written bill of rights cannot per se explain the rights revolution that we can observe in several countries in the late twentieth century (Epp 1996, 1998, 2009). His analysis of the US case points to the fact that the expansion of judicially protected rights in the USA was the result of the mobilisation of civic actors and lawyers—rather than the change in formal institutions or the increased judicial activism by the judges. He points to three important elements in what he terms the "support structure" for the rights revolution: organised groups or movements that lobby and mobilise legally for better rights protection, lawyers that engage with the movements and civil rights actors, and third sufficient resources for litigating in court. In his well-known book, *The Rights Revolution*, Epp (1998), starting from the US case, compares Canada, India and Britain in order to test whether his theory about the importance of a support structure also holds from a comparative perspective. His comparison aims, among other things, at exploring "…the contingent conditions that shape the development of constitutional rights and judicial power in practice" (1998: 198). His comparison arrives at the conclusion that "…rights are conditioned on the extent of a support structure for legal mobilization" (1998: 198). It is hence the demand and pressure of civil society actors disposing of broad support in society that leads to expanding rights and rights protection. While written bills of rights and responsive judges also played a role, it is the sustained and broadly supported pressure from below with the support of lawyers (Sarat and Scheingold 2006; Kagan 1996) that created what he terms the right revolution.

Others share Epps's perspective that the "rights revolution" needs to be explained through a combination of factors attributing a prominent place to civil society pressure and changing values. In his book, *Delegating Rights Protection*, David Erdos studies the adoption of Bills of Right in Westminster systems by comparing Canada, New Zealand, the UK and Australia, which have all adopted bills of rights in the 1980s and 1990s with the exception of Australia. While there are specific political triggers for each of the cases that explain why the change occurred (or failed to happen) at a specific moment in time, ideas and changing values are the crucial background factors explaining the move to written bills of rights within a family of systems traditionally considered to provide a less favourable institutional environment compared to other, non-Westminster parliamentary systems. He arrives at the conclusion that

> Postmaterialization has constituted the most important background factor behind BORI [Bill of Rights] projects in countries such as Canada, the United Kingdom, New Zealand, and Australia (Erdos 2010: 149).

The rise of post-materialist values with its greater emphasis on civil liberties and equality led to the growth of a "post-materialist rights constituency" that mobilised for a greater formalisation and hence protection of civil liberties and equality directly or at least provided generalised support for such demands by specific civil society groups (Erdos 2010: 24–27).

For demand-side explanations, i.e. the hypothesis that the spread of judicial review together with an increased rights protection and rights culture is a response to social forces (Ginsburg 2008: 89), uncertainty does not enter into the explanation. In contrast to the strategic model of behaviour by elites, which is at the centre of the political insurance and the political hegemony thesis, changing values and bottom-up mobilisation rely more strongly on a sociological than an economic model of behaviour and take a bottom-up perspective to constitutional rights, not limiting their analysis strictly to constitution drafting. From a different angle and closer to the interest of this volume, Blount et al. (2012) comparative empirical research on participation in constitution making show that there is an association between public involvement and rights: "Processes involving a referendum produce constitutions that are more likely to have virtually every category of right" (2012: 54). However, they are correct to be prudent to draw conclusions on the causality at work, as "the problem of endogeneity is endemic in efforts to tie process to outcomes" (2012: 57). As the authors point out, further research on the genesis of public participation in the constitution-making process will have to sort out whether such participation results from pressure and demand by the civic society or rather is part of an elite strategy or agreement in order to decrease uncertainty in terms of the acceptance, legitimacy but also constitutional endurance. As we know from research by the same authors, public participation in constitution making, in form of a referendum or the election of a constitutional assembly, increases the lifespan of a constitution in democratic systems (Elkins et al. 2009).

So far, the results produced by the Comparative Constitutions Project per se do not allow favouring the elitist over the popular account or vice versa. In addition, as the following section argues, the focus on national processes of constitution making needs to be complemented through an analysis of the emergence of international and supra-national rights regimes and concurring processes of diffusion.

3.3 The Internationalisation of Human Rights Regimes

Socio-legal scholars are also interested in international human rights regimes and courts. Over the last few decades, we can observe a proliferation of international judicial institutions. This proliferation went along with a fundamental change in the form of international courts. Such institutions are increasingly addressing cases between individuals and states or between private actors instead of settling conflict between nation states; their jurisdiction is more often compulsory, and most importantly, access rules have changed, hence allowing individuals to challenge their own states' decisions or policies before an international court (Alter 2006; Keohane et al. 2000). It is the "…empowerment of individual citizens to bring suit to challenge the domestic activities of their own government" (Moravcsik 2000: 217) that radically distinguishes international human rights regimes and courts from previous generations of international adjudication and international law. Hence, not only socio-legal scholars, but also international relations and European integration specialists address the multilevel characteristics of rights regimes and rights protection in their work from various theoretical angles. This section first discusses approaches in line with the political insurance thesis discussed above. Alternative explanations, based on various diffusion mechanisms and emphasising the ideational mechanism at work in this proliferation process, are discussed after. The focus will thereby be on the impact that international human rights regimes exert on national constitutions, i.e. how they influence their content. The literature on international human rights regimes is also interested in the question of whether the spread of rights and rights protection mechanism around the globe actually makes a difference regarding the actual protection and guarantee of human rights, e.g. whether they contribute to reduce the prevalence of rights violation. As this debate is more removed from the focus of this volume, this section only discusses the question of adhering to international rights regimes and their impact on the content of constitutions even though from a socio-legal perspective human rights in action need as much to be studied as formal human rights provisions on the international and national level.

3.3.1 European Convention of Human Rights and Other International Rights Regimes

By emphasising the aspect of delegating power to an independent international actor, Moravscik (2000) states a research puzzle comparable to the work by

Ginsburg and Hirschl discussed above in order to explain the creation of international human rights regimes in post-war Europe:

> Why would any government, democratic or dictatorial, favour establishing an effective independent international authority, the sole purpose of which is to constrain its domestic sovereignty in such an unprecedentedly invasive and overtly nonmajoritarian manner? (Moravscik 2000: 219)

Adherence to international human rights regimes is interpreted as a mean for governments to protect their democratic institutions from possible, undemocratic future challenges, "...thereby enhancing their credibility and stability vis-à-vis nondemocratic political threats" (Moravscik 2000: 220). Political uncertainty plays a crucial role in his argument of how governments ponder the potential benefits against the "negative" impact on their sovereignty. In fact, he proposes that those governments, who face greater uncertainty regarding their democratic future, will more likely accept the limitations that come with adhering to an international rights regime. New democracies will favour human rights regimes as a form of *insurance*, while well-established democracies see the loss in sovereignty to outweigh potential benefits. For new democracies, the creation of an international court to enforce the human rights will set constrains on future governments by creating a judicial body responsible for enforcing a human rights regime.

Empirically, Moravscik analyses the positions of European governments towards the creation of the ECHR. Based on the analysis of the negotiations, he distinguishes between those governments in favour of strong enforcement mechanism, i.e. compulsory jurisdiction and the possibility for individual petitions, from those opposing such mechanism (Moravskik 2000: 231). He finds support for his thesis in that new democracies (defined as democracies only since a date between 1920 and 1950) were those that supported strong enforcement mechanism (Austria, France, Italy, Iceland, Ireland and Germany), while established democracies were rather opposed. In short, theoretically and empirically, Moravscik's work emphasises the importance of uncertainty in how countries define their positions and, as is the case for Ginsburg and Hirschl, conceptualises the delegation of rights protection to international bodies as a form of insurance against future possible backlashes against the transition to (liberal) democracies.

In a different institutional context, for the International Criminal Court (ICC), Simmons and Danner (2010: 233) also argue that governments weight sovereignty costs against the possible gains through tying their hands by adhering to the ICC. In their research, they show that the states that are the most vulnerable to future prosecution through the ICC together with states that are the most unlikely to find themselves before the ICC are the ones that adhered the most readily:

> In fact, other factors being equal, unaccountable autocracies are more likely to commit themselves to the Court than are democratic countries with a recent history of such conflicts (Simmons and Danner 2010: 227).

In this case, the credible commitment has the function to *reduce political uncertainty* in terms of future violence, and signal to the domestic forces and opposing rebels, the credible commitment of the government to end the spiral of violence because it risks to be prosecuted through the ICC. And indeed, the authors find empirical evidence of positive effects on peace processes of such early commitment. Again, political uncertainty is used to explain the puzzle of delegating more power to courts, in this case on the international level.

For both types of supra-national and international institutions, we can conclude that political uncertainty is an important—but not the only—factor explaining actor's strategy of promoting and adhering to an international institution promoting rights protection through the creation of a convention and enforcement institutions with the power to legally pursue violations. The following paragraphs discuss a different theoretical take on the same phenomenon of increased rights protection and delegation to courts on the international level, which operates with a more sociological model of human behaviour.

Civil society actors in general and social movements more specifically have been shown to be the important actors influencing rights and rights discourses. The literature on international human rights in particular points to the importance of social movements and civil society actors in the establishment of international human right regimes after the Second World War. As Tsutsui et al. (2012) in a literature overview show, there are many studies pointing to the important influence of specific movements and civil society actors in the push for establishing international human rights after the Second World War, in particular for the Universal Declaration of Human Rights (adopted in 1948, UDHR), but also in the further development of human rights regimes later on, starting from basic civic rights, over human rights, to women rights, indigenous rights to genocide and torture, etc. In particular, they also emphasise the importance of social movements for translating human rights into actual practice, while drawing attention to the limits of the mobilisation for human rights in terms of influencing actual practice.[4] Reviewing this mainly, IR focused literature on the genesis of international human rights regimes would demand a chapter on its own. Research from a socio-legal perspective is of more immediate interest to the purpose of this volume. Madsen (2007) proposes an interesting, more law focused account of the genesis of the ECHR.

Regarding the ECHR discussed above, Madsen (2007) takes ideas and legal actors centre stage for explaining its genesis and institutionalisation:

> …the objective is a sociology …that centers on the *circulation* of ideas and models – how competing ideas and models were being promoted by a host of actors using their specific national and international resources, expertise, and other capitals, and how these exchanges helped produce European law and institutions… (Madsen 2007: 139).

His historical analysis highlights the importance of legal actors and ideas in the genesis of ECHR. His analysis reveals that besides political factors initiating and spurring Europeanisation, legal actors and diplomats with legal careers were crucial in creating and circulating ideas from the national to the European level and back, ultimately generating a "novel doctrine" of autonomous human rights law

[4] As international relations scholars are well aware of, there is abundant debate between such more constructivist traditions of research versus realist approaches in IR. However, this is not the object of this chapter.

(Madsen 2007: 156) and creating new opportunities for national actors to simultaneously engage on national and supra-national arenas. This process created a forth and back of exporting and importing ideas on human rights across political levels and ultimately through EU enlargement beyond the initial borders of European integration (Madsen 2007: 157).

The literature cited to illustrate a more bottom-up and stronger socio-legal take on the emergence of supra-national human rights instruments does not apply a rational actor model in the sense of Buchanan, and uncertainty does not have any explanatory power. Specific historical circumstances create opportunities and also contribute to mobilise civil society actors promoting ideas and formulating demands as the literature overview by Tsutsui et al. (2012) explains. Madsen further emphasises the importance of elite legal actors in these processes and hence points to the importance of legal expertise and entrepreneurs in shaping supranational institutions and their evolution. On the international level, "constitutionalisation" can thus be explained in rather parallel terms to what we observed for national processes, a combination of social demand and legal expertise and support—at least from a socio-legal perspective and within a constructivist approach to international relations. For national constitution drafting, the more important question is nevertheless whether and to what extent international human rights regimes influence the content of national constitutions.

3.3.2 Diffusion and Convergence in National Constitutions

There is a longstanding interest in "constitutional borrowing" (Epstein and Knight 2003) fostered by processes of globalisation (Slaughter 2000, 2003). Various aspects are studied under the label of constitutional borrowing, reaching from emulation of other nations' constitutions to citing foreign precedent (Epstein and Knight 2003: 196–197). Recent large-N research is particularly interested in the influence of international factors on the content of national institutions, and this will be the main focus of the literature reviewed in this section. Evidently, within this literature, various explanations compete in terms of the mechanism explaining diffusion, as Dobbin et al. (2007) distinguish: social construction, coercion, competition and learning. The following discussion will not review this debate, but rather concentrate on the empirical results: Are constitutions converging because of international human rights institution and globalised legal communities (Slaughter 2000, 2003)?

Beck et al. (2012) analysed to what extent "…modern national constitutions adapt to the global human rights movement…" (2012: 487) and test a straightforward hypotheses stating that the most recent constitutions and the constitutions of the most recent democracies incorporate human rights the strongest. Theoretically, they assume that the international environment, i.e. how prominent the human rights discourse is at the time of the adoption of the constitution, has an impact on the incorporation of human rights into the national constitution in addition to more traditional citizen rights. Their multivariate regression shows that while regime characteristics and history are relevant, the ratification of human rights treaties and the global human rights discourse are strong predictors for the incorporation of human rights language into national constitutions.

Elkins et al. (2013) are also interested in the "role of international human rights documents in coordinating state behaviour with regard to national constitution making" (Elkins et al. 2013: 63). They notably want to verify the claim that we can observe a convergence among nation states in terms of human rights constitutionally guaranteed. Theoretically, they do not privilege one theoretical explanation for the convergence over another, but point to the fact that "theories 'on acculturation and socialisation'" (Elkins et al. 2013: 68) imply that the internationalisation of human rights would lead to some convergence in national constitutions. Empirically, they look at 680 "constitutional systems" from 1789 to 2006. Their data document that the number of countries with rights provisions in their constitution has increased over time. At the same time, constitutions include a greater number of rights over time (Elkins et al. 2013: 71). Not all rights have had the same degree of success though:

> Some rights – for example, freedom of expression and freedom of religion – appear to be so central that almost nine of every ten contemporary constitutions include them. The vast majority of rights, however, have penetrated fewer than half of contemporary constitutions and appear to be optional constitutional features (Elkins et al. 2013: 72).

There seems to be a difference between the trajectories of first- and second-generation rights, where first-generation rights such as freedom of expression, freedom of association or freedom of religion have become almost universal, which is not the case for second-generation rights such as economic and social rights (Elkins et al. 2013: 73). In terms of the role of international human rights instruments, they point to the importance of the UDHR and International Covenant on Civil and Political Rights (ICCPR) for the proliferation of rights in national constitutions:

> Constitution writers working under the umbrella of international rights treaties are more likely to pattern their documents after the international instruments, but they are even more likely to do so if their country has ratified the instrument. These findings are consistent with a view in which international instruments provide a focal set of norms for constitution makers" (Elkins et al. 2013: 91–92).

Go (2003) came to a similar conclusion in terms of the importance of international human rights for the content of national constitution in post-colonial states. Like Elkins et al., he rejects the convergence thesis. Even though isomorphism increased after 1990s, he also observes a complexification and differentiation:

> Thus, if globalizing constitutionalism has emerged at all, it is one wracked with divergence as much as convergence, a differentiation in content as much as a homogenization in form (2003: 90).

This might be the result of various different mechanisms of diffusion being at play at the same time, not to forget the importance of past constitutions and legal heritage for drafting new constitutions. As Goderis and Versteeg argue, which rights are constitutionally entrenched is influenced by other countries' constitutions in particular those with similar legal traditions and the same former colonising power (2013: 33). Economic dependence also is crucial as countries tend to emulate the constitutions of their principal aid donors (2013: 33). Hence, there might be learning, acculturation and coercion processes at work at the same time in order to explain transnational influence on rights provisions in constitutions.

Within the literature discussed in this section, national constitution making is not independent anymore from international and transnational processes, even though the precise mechanisms at work in these processes of diffusion remain contested. Furthermore, it would be erroneous to think that processes of emulation and diffusion in constitution drafting are a fairly recent phenomenon, mainly concerning constitution drafting related to the waves of decolonisation and democratisation after the Second World War. Elkins has convincingly argued that the diffusion perspective is also useful for explaining the first wave of democratisation and constitution drafting in the nineteenth-century Europe (Elkins 2010).

4 Conclusion

The preceding literature review shows that a large part of socio-legal scholarship is focusing on the mobilisation and interpretation of constitutional norms and not on constitution drafting per se. Recently, there has been more research on constitution drafting given greater efforts to collect comparative data on constitutions (see the work by Elkins, Ginsburg and others cited above). By emphasising the importance of law in action, this research reminds us of the fact that constitution making is not limited to times of constitution drafting but represents a continuous process through which constitutional norms evolve—sometimes in important ways without any formal changes at all. Recent research has also made additional efforts to connect national episodes of constitution drafting to international processes of generating and reinforcing international human right regimes. The literature on the proliferation of human rights reveals that the focus on the national level provides a too limited perspective. Processes of diffusion are important in terms of the types of rights and the extent to which human rights are entrenched in national constitutions.

The literature review points to an ongoing debate between demand and supply, between bottom-up perspectives and top-down elite-driven explanations. Uncertainty enters mainly into the latter approach in order to explain the decision of political elites to adopt judicial review and entrench written rights in the national constitution or in order to understand why national governments are willing to tie their own hands by adhering to international rights institutions. Electoral uncertainty is used to explain why elites would transfer power to other institutions through judicial review and entrenching rights. In this perspective, the spread of constitutional review and rights protection around the globe needs to be primarily explained on the basis of an analysis of political and economic power relations at the national and international level. Demand-side and bottom-up explanations do not negate the important role of elites in these processes, but emphasise preceptorial power and how changing ideas and values ultimately allow for explaining the global spread of rights protection.

It seems fair to conclude that a good part of the literature takes Rawl's veil of ignorance seriously in the opposite sense: actors interpreting or making constitutions are never stripped of their roles and positions in history and society. Research therefore asks how their position in society and history influences their ideas, their interest and behaviour in the interpretation and mobilisation of constitutional provisions or in the formulation of such provisions. Legal ideas and expertise, thereby, constitute an important source of knowledge as socio-legal research demonstrates.

References

Alter KJ (2006) Private litigants and the new international courts. Comp Polit Stud 39(1):22–49

Beck CJ, Drori GS, Meyer JW (2012) World influences on human rights language in constitutions: a cross-national study. Int Sociol 27(4):483–501

Blount J, Elkins Z, Ginsburg T (2012) Does the process of constitution-making matter. In: Ginsburg T (ed) Comparative constitutional design. Cambridge University Press, Cambridge, pp 31–65

Chavez RB (2004) The rule of law in nascent democracies: judicial politics in Argentina. Stanford University Press, Stanford

Choudhry S (2010) After the rights revolution: bills of rights in the postconflict state. Ann Rev Law Soc Sci 6:301–322

Dahl RA (1957) Decision-making in a democracy: the supreme court as a national policy-maker. J Publ Law 6:279–295

Dobbin F, Simmons BA, Garrett G (2007) The global diffusion of public policies: social construction, coercion, competition, or learning? Ann Rev Sociol 33:449–472

Elkins Z, Ginsburg T, Melton J (2009) The endurance of national constitutions. Cambridge University Press, New York

Elkins Z (2010) Diffusion and the constitutionalization of europe. Comp Polit Stud 43:1–31

Elkins Z, Ginsburg T, Simmons BA (2013) Getting to rights: treaty ratification, constitutional convergence, and human rights practice. Harvard Int Law J 54(1):61–95

Epp CR (1996) Do bills of rights matter? The Canadian charter of rights and freedoms. Am Polit Sci Rev 90(4):765–779

Epp CR (1998) The rights revolution. lawyers, activists, and supreme courts in comparative perspective. University of Chicago Press, Chicago

Epp CR (2009) Making rights real: activists, bureaucrats, and the creation of the legalistic state. University of Chicago Press, Chicago

Epstein L, Knight J (1998) The choices justices make. CQ Press, Washington

Epstein L, Knight J (2003) Constitutional borrowing and nonborrowing. Int J Const Law 1(2):196–223

Erdos D (2010) Delegating rights protection: the rise of bills of rights in the Westminster world. Oxford University Press, Oxford

Finkel J (2005) Judicial reform as insurance policy: Mexico in the 1990s. Latin Am Polit Soc 47(1):87–113

Finkel JS (2008) Judicial reform as political insurance: Argentina, Peru, and Mexico in the 1990s. University of Notre Dame Press, Indiana

Ginsburg T (2003) Judicial review in new democracies: constitutional courts in Asian cases. Cambridge University Press, Cambridge

Ginsburg T (2008) The global spread of constitutional review. In: Whittington K, Kelemen RD, Caldeira GA (eds) Law and politics. Oxford University Press, Oxford

Go J (2003) A globalizing constitutionalism? Views from the postcolony, 1945–2000. Int Sociol 18(1):71–95

Goldstein LF (2004) From democracy to juristocracy—review essay. Law Soc Rev 38(3):611–629

Graber MA (2006) Foreword: from the countermajoritarian difficulty to juristocracy and the political construction of judicial power. Maryland Law Rev 65(1):1–14

Helmke G, Rosenbluth F (2009) Regimes and the rule of law: judicial independence in comparative perspective. Annu Rev Polit Sci 12:345–366

Hirschl R (2000) The political origins of judicial empowerment through constitutionalization: lessons from four constitutional revolutions. Law Soc Inq 25:91–149

Hirschl R (2002) Resituating the judicialization of politics: Bush V. Gore as a global trend. Can J Law Jurisprud 15(2):191–218

Hirschl R (2004a) "Juristocracy"—political, not juridical. Good Soc 13(3):6–11

Hirschl R (2004b) Towards juristocracy: the origin and consequences of the new constitutionalism. Harvard University Press, Massachusetts

Hirschl R (2005) Reply—constitutionalism, judicial review, and progressive change: a rejoinder to McClain and fleming. Tex Law Rev 84:470–507

Hirschl R (2008) The judicialization of politics. In: Whittington KE, Kelement DR, Caldeira GA (eds) The Oxford handbook of law and politics. Oxford University Press, Oxford, pp 119–141

Huntington SP (1991) The third wave. Democratization in the late twentieth century. University of Oklahoma Press, Norman and London

Imbeau LM (2009) Testing the 'Veil of Ignorance' hypothesis in constitutional choice: a 'walk-talk' approach. J Publ Financ Publ Choice 26(1):3–21

Imbeau LM, Jacob S (2011) Is the 'Veil of Ignorance' in constitutional choice a myth? An empirical exploration informed by a theory of power. In: Marciano A (ed) Constiutional mythologies. Springer, Dordrecht, pp 53–69

Imbeau LM, Jacob S (2015) Measuring the opacity of the 'Veil of ignorance' in constitutions: theory, method and some results. In: Imbeau LM, Jacob S (eds) Behind a veil of ignorance? Power and uncertainty in constitutional design. Springer, Dordrecht

McCann MW (1998) Law and political struggles for social change: puzzles, paradoxes, and promises in future research. In: Schultz DA (ed) Leveraging the law. Using the courts to achieve social change. New York, Peter Lang, pp 319–349

Kagan RA (1996) American lawyers, legal culture, and adversarial legalism. In: Friedman LM, Scheiber HN (eds) Legal culture and the legal profession. Westview Press, Boulder, pp 7–51

Kagan RA (2001) Adversarial legalism. The American way of law. Harvard University Press, Cambridge

Kagan RA, Axelred Lee (eds) (2001) Regulatory encounters. Multinational corporations and American adversarial legalism. University of California Press, Berkeley

Kelemen RD (2011) Eurolegalism: the transformation of law and regulation in the European Union. Harvard University Press, Cambridge

Keohane RO, Moravcsik A, Slaughter AM (2000) Legalized dispute resolution: interstate and transnational. Int Org 54(03):457–488

Lijphart A (1999) Patterns of democracy. Government forms and performance in thirty-six countries. Yale University Press, New Haven

Madsen MR (2007) From cold war instrument to supreme European court: the European court of human rights at the crossroads of international and national law and politics. Law Soc Inq 32(1):137–159

McCann M (1994) Rights at work. Pay equity reform and the politics of legal mobilization. Chicago University Press, Chicago

McCann MW (2009) Interests, ideas, and institutions in comparative analysis of judicial power. Polit Res Q 62(4):834–839

Melton J, Elkins Z, Ginsburg T, Leetaru K (2013) On the interpretability of law: lessons from the decoding of national constitutions. Br J Polit Sci 43(02):399–423

Moravcsik A (2000) The origins of human rights regimes: democratic delegation in postwar Europe. Int Org 54(02):217–252
Popova M (2012) Politicized justice in emerging democracies: a study of courts in Russia and Ukraine. Cambridge University Press, Cambridge
Pound R (1910) Law in books and law in action. Am Law Rev 44:12–36
Ramseyer JM (1994) The puzzling (in) dependence of courts: a comparative approach. J Legal Stud 23:721–747
Roberts A (2010) The logic of discipline: global capitalism and the architecture of government. Oxford University Press, Oxford
Rosenberg GN (1991) The hollow hope: can courts bring about social change?. University of Chicago Press, Chicago
Sarat A, Scheingold SA (eds) (2006) Cause lawyers and social movements. Stanford University Press, Stanford
Segal J, Spaeth H (1993) The supreme court and the attitudinal model. Cambridge University Press, New York
Shapiro M (1994) The "Globalization" of judicial review. In: Friedman LM, Scheiber HN (eds) Legal culture and the legal profession. Westview Press, Boulder, pp 19–135
Shapiro M (1999) The success of judicial review. In: Constituional dialogues in comparative perspective. McMillan Press, Houndsmills, pp 193–219
Simmons BA, Danner A (2010) Credible commitments and the international criminal court. Int Organ 64(2):225–256
Smithey SI, Ishiyama J (2002) Judicial activism in post-communist politics. Law Soc Rev 36(4):719–42
Slaughter AM (2000) Judicial globalization. Va J Int Law 40(1):1103–1124
Slaughter AM (2003) A global community of courts. Harvard Int Law J 44:191–219
Smith M (2008) Political institutions and lesbian and gay rights in the United States and Canada. Routledge, New York
Songer DR (2008) The transformation of the supreme court of Canada. University of Toronto Press, Toronto
Thatcher M, Sweet AS (2002) Theory and practice of delegation to non-majoritarian institutions. W Eur Polit 25(1):1–22
Tsutsui K, Whtlinger C, Lim A (2012) International human rights law and social movements: states' resistance and civil society's insistence. Ann Rev Law Soc Sci 8:367–396
Vatter A (2009) Lijphart expanded: three dimensions of democracy in advanced OECD countries? Eur Polit Sci Rev 1(1):125–154
Vibert F (2007) The rise of the unelected: democracy and the new separation of powers. Cambridge University Press, Cambridge
Whittington KE (2008) Constitutionalism. In: Whittington KE, Kelemen RD, Caldeira GA (eds) The Oxford handbook of law and politics. Oxford University Press, Oxford, pp 281–99

Chapter 4
Measuring the Opacity of the 'Veil of Ignorance' in Constitutions: Theory, Method, and Some Results

Louis M. Imbeau and Steve Jacob

1 Introduction

As we noted in the introduction to this volume, constitutions are sets of rules that constrain the choices of policy makers. But they are also discourses that reveal the motivations that drove their drafters. Traditionally, constitutional analysis has adopted the first perspective where constitutions are viewed as contracts that define the rules of the game. Their analysis consists in describing these rules and their evolution (e.g., Congleton 2011), explaining the content of constitutions (Voigt 2011), and measuring the impact of rules on institutional and policy outcomes (e.g., Congleton and Swedenborg 2006; Persson and Tabellini 2003). The Veil of Ignorance Project (VOIP) adopts the second perspective. It looks at constitutions as discourses to infer the motivations of constitution drafters from the content of the very text they contributed to write (Imbeau 2009). In particular, the project aims at measuring the extent to which constitution drafters worked under uncertainty.

But this distinction between the contractual and the discursive approaches is not to be overstretched as both provide ample opportunities for cross-fertilization. For example, one of the connections between Congleton's research and ours is the fine-grained nature of constitutional bargaining and the resultant power relationships that a minute reading reveals.

This chapter introduces to the theory and method of the VOIP project and presents some preliminary results. We proceed in three steps. First, we expose the theoretical foundations of the project based on Buchanan's interaction approach.

We are indebted to several persons who commented previous versions of this paper: Roger Congleton, Emma Galli, Randall Holcombe, Alan Lockard, Agnes Strauss, George Tridimas, Frédéric Varone, and Stefan Voigt. We assume responsibility for any remaining shortcoming.

L.M. Imbeau (✉) · S. Jacob
Département de Science Politique, Université Laval, Québec, Canada
e-mail: louis.imbeau@pol.ulaval.ca

S. Jacob
e-mail: steve.jacob@pol.ulaval.ca

L.M. Imbeau and S. Jacob (eds.), *Behind a Veil of Ignorance?*,
Studies in Public Choice 32, DOI 10.1007/978-3-319-14953-0_4

Second, we describe the content analysis method that we used to compare the discursive content of 16 constitutions. Third, we submit some of our empirical results to validity tests before concluding.

2 Social Interactions, Power Relations, and Uncertainty: A Theoretical Perspective

Summary: In this section, we argue that constitutions are the outcome of social interactions and that these interactions are best conceptualized as power relations.

Constitutional economics makes «a categorical distinction [...] in the ultimate behavioral object of analytical attention» (Buchanan 2008: 281): choices made *within* constraints and the choice *among* constraints. Ordinary economics focuses on choices made within constraints; constitutional economics focuses on choices among constraints. This choice of constraints should be viewed, according to Buchanan, as an *exchange*. He wrote:

> [I]ndividuals choose to impose constraints or limits on their own behavior primarily, even if not exclusively, as part of an *exchange* in which the restrictions of their own actions are sacrificed in return for the benefits that are anticipated from the reciprocally extended restrictions on the actions of others with whom they interact [...]. So interpreted, the individual who joins in a collective decision to impose a generally applied constitutional rule is not, at base, acting differently from observed behavior in a setting that involves giving up one desired good, apples, for another desired good, oranges (Buchanan 2008: 282, emphasis in original).

Thus for Buchanan, constitutional economics as a research program is based on a catalectic perspective, a «science of *exchange*» among individuals. This perspective is to be contrasted with the mainstream perspective of *choices* made by utility-maximizing individuals where the main object of study is the allocation of scarce resources. «The elementary and basic approach that I suggest places 'the theory of markets' and not the 'theory of resource allocation' at the center stage» (Buchanan 1964: 217, quoted in Marciano 2009: 44). But for this research program to become a *political* economy program, it must also consider two other types of interactions—coercion and persuasion—that have formed the core of political science.

Indeed, the very definition of the state proposed by the German sociologist, Max Weber, as the organization with a monopoly on the legitimate use of violence[1] shows how coercion is central to politics. Politics is «the *authoritative* allocation of values in society» (Easton 1960: 129, emphasis added). In this perspective, the choice of constraint in a society may be made through coercion. One may force others to «choose» such constraints. This is often the case, for example, when the military imposes a new constitution after a *coup d'État*.

[1] Weber wrote: «Something is "a 'state' if and insofar as its administrative staff successfully upholds a claim on the monopoly of the legitimate use of violence in the enforcement of its order" (1964: 154).

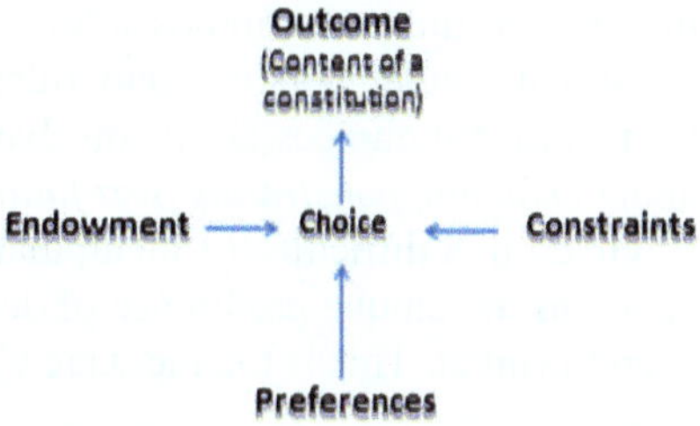

Fig. 1 Casual relations in a choice model

Moreover, the choice of a constraining rule may be the result of persuasion, the other side of politics. Let's turn to Buchanan again. He wrote:

> The very term *politics* tends to conjure up a mental image of potential conflict among those persons who are members of the politically organized community. This conflict may be interpreted to be analogous to scientific disputes, in which separate participants or groups seek to convince one another of the *truth* of their advanced propositions. […] [P]olitics may seem, by its very nature, to involve conflict between and among individuals and groups within a polity (2008: 285).

Thus, influential people may persuade constitutional drafters to include a specific constraint on the behavior of future participants to collective decisions, such as a rule giving precedence to, or outlawing, a specific religious group.

2.1 Two Models of Decision-Making

Two psychological models of decision-making are implied in Buchanan's argument about the opposition between an exchange approach and a choice approach or between a «theory of markets and a theory of resource allocation»: the choice model and the interaction model.

The *choice model* is the usual model we use in public choice analyses. It sees the outcome of the decision-making process (here, the constitutional document) as ensuing from the choices made by individuals. Typically, these choices are a function of the individual's preferences, endowment, and constraints (see Fig. 1).

Buchanan provided a list of the constraints that limit the choices an individual can make[2]: Nature, history, past choices, custom and convention, other persons, rules and laws. For all practical purposes, the first four constraints cannot be easily manipulated in the context of the specific decision-making process over an issue like the drafting and the adoption of a constitution. One can certainly not remake history to erase past choices but one can perhaps alter their impact on an ongoing decision-making process through various rhetorical and heresthetic techniques. It may be difficult, for example, to reconsider a convention based on past choices concerning the decision rule once the decision-making process has started though

[2] Here, we ordered them according to the extent to which they can be manipulated.

this is certainly not impossible.[3] The manipulation of the last two types of constraint—other persons, and rules and laws—is easier and more often done. Constitutional choices are themselves made under constraints in addition to being about *choosing constraints* over *future* decisions.

Given this difficulty of manipulating constraints and assuming utility maximization as the unique preference of decision-makers, the main explanation of choice is endowment. This is the message Charles Beard conveyed. Here is how he put it:

> Suppose [...] that substantially all of the merchants, money lenders, security holders, manufacturers, shippers, capitalists, and financiers and their professional associates are to be found on one side in support of the Constitution and that substantially all or the major portion of the opposition came from the non-slaveholding farmers and the debtors—would it not be pretty conclusively demonstrated that our fundamental law was not the product of an abstraction known as 'the whole people,' but of a group of economic interests which must have expected beneficial results from its adoption? (Beard 2004 [1913]: 17)

More recently, the work by McGuire and Ohsfeldt proceeded from the same choice perspective. In their analysis of the ratification of the American constitution, they assumed that a delegate's utility of voting on a constitutional proposal is a function of his personal interests and ideology as well as of his constituents' interests and ideology. They showed that, at the ratifying stage, the support for the proposed constitution was significantly related to the interests and ideology of the delegates but, at the drafting stage, the *constituent*s' interests are a better predictor of a delegate's choice than his own interests (McGuire and Ohsfeldt 1989; McGuire 1988). Stable preferences may be a good predictor of choice.

But the choice model reaches its limit when it fails to explain the outcome, i.e., the content of constitutions. Then, the *interaction model* proves to be useful. Indeed, as noted by Scheinkman, «[m]odels of social interaction seem particularly adapted to solving a pervasive problem in the social sciences, namely, the observation of large differences in outcomes in the absence of commensurate differences in fundamentals» (Scheinkman 2008: 1). William Riker provided a nice example of the effect of social interactions on the content of the American constitution. He told this fascinating story of how the constitutional provision for the Electoral College in the election of the president was created and adopted in the Federal Convention of 1787. He showed in particular how the *interaction* between Gouverneur Morris and his fellow delegates completely changed an early vote of 8-2 in favor of a provision for the national legislature to elect the president to a final vote of 9-2 in favor of an election by an electoral college. A choice model

[3] The Canadian constitutional experience of the 1970s and 1980s witnessed such reconsideration. In 1971, the Victoria Charter proposed a set of amendments to the Canadian constitution defining, among others, a new amending formula. The Charter was dropped because one provincial premier rejected it. The convention was that such constitutional decisions required unanimity. However, the 1981 agreement was adopted with the support of only nine of the ten provinces. The Supreme Court later ruled that this agreement though unconventional was not illegal [(1981) 1 S.C.R. 753]. In 1992, the Charlottetown Accord including a new set of constitutional amendments was dropped after a failed referendum even though no mention is made to a referendum in the amending formula adopted in 1981. These two changes in constitutional conventions were made while the decision-making process was in progress.

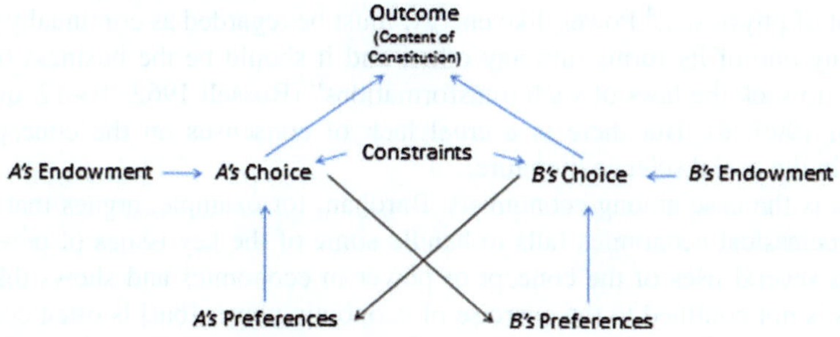

Fig. 2 Causal relations in an interaction model

with stable preferences would be unable to account for this switch. But an interaction model could. Indeed, for Riker, Morris achieved this change through «heresthetics or the dynamic manipulation of the conditions of choice» (Riker 1984: 1).

In an interaction model, there are several individuals making the choice of entering or not into an interaction on the basis of the others' choice. Adopting the interaction approach means endogenizing preferences. Contrary to the choice model where preferences are stable, an interaction model allows for changing preferences as each participant to the decision-making process can alter another's incentive structure, i.e., his evaluation of the expected costs and benefits of a proposal. Thus, preferences may change depending on the structure of interactions. In this context, a decision-maker may use his or her resources to influence another's choice so as to help produce the desired outcome. From this viewpoint, the content of a constitution is the result of the social interactions among the drafters (see Fig. 2).

An individual's endowment allows him or her to enter into interaction with another individual. In Buchanan's *exchange* perspective, one individual exchanges his vote for another's vote: «I will support a constraint over my future actions if you do the same». This is the usual vote trading or logrolling behavior. One uses one's endowment (one's vote) to make an exchange with another constitution-maker. But other resources can be put to use in this context. One may use *coercion* or *persuasion* to reach the same goal. Thus, facing uncertainty as to one's future position in society, one could trade a constraint over one's own future actions for a constraint over another's future actions; or one could *force* another, or one could *persuade* another, to support the adoption of such a constraint depending on the resource that one is endowed with. Let us see how exchange, coercion, and persuasion can be conceived as three forms of power relations.

2.2 *Power and Constitutional Choice: A Conceptual Framework*

As the famous philosopher Bertrand Russell noted, "the fundamental concept in social science is Power, in the same sense in which Energy is the fundamental concept of physics....[4] Power, like energy, must be regarded as continually passing from any one of its forms into any other, and it should be the business of social science to seek the laws of such transformations" (Russell 1962: 10–12, quoted in Gordon 1999: 8). But there is a cruel lack of consensus on the conception of power in the social science literature.

This is the case among economists. Bardhan, for example, argues that «orthodox neoclassical economics fails to handle some of the key issues of power». He reviews several uses of the concept of power in economics and shows that «economics is not confined to the exercise of economic power [but] is often concerned with [...] other forms of power, particularly political and ideological» (Bardhan 1991: 265). As Randall Bartlett, another economist, noted: «In economics, the study of power is clearly in a 'prescientific' state» (1989: 4).[5] Apart from references to monopoly power or to bargaining power, neoclassical economics, for example, generally ignores the concept of power only to state that it is absent from markets. Power and markets would be mutually exclusive... except for Herbert Simon who argued that submission to authority is what is being purchased in labor markets. Therefore power is something that can be traded! (Simon 1957, quoted in Bartlett 1989: 6) Institutional economists have a wider, more general, conception of power. Among them, Philip Klein is quite vocal about the attitude of mainstream economists vis-à-vis the concept of power. He wrote: «while [power] might be equally distributed, it is clearly *unequally* distributed among the participants in social interaction in the real world as viewed from the perspective of *all* the social sciences. That distribution [...] is in reality the principal focus for analysis in all the social sciences except economics, where the studious avoidance of that reality has been honed, polished, and embroidered into a fine art. It remains enshrined there, rationalized as 'a simple and logical starting point' and as the 'norm' which the overwhelming thrust of standard theory almost never succeeds in moving» (Klein 1980: 873). Power conceived as coercion is assumed away. Another institutional economist, William Dugger, defines power as «the ability to tell other people what to do with some degree of certainty that they will do it. When power wielders must coerce others, power is tenuous and obvious. When coercion is unnecessary, power is secure and unnoticed» (Dugger 1980: 897). In this vision, power is not necessarily linked with coercion. It can appear in other apparels. Randall Bartlett has developed what seems to be the most elaborate theory of power in economics. He defines power as «The ability of one actor to alter the decisions made and/or welfare experienced by another actor relative to the choices

---

4 This section is based on Imbeau (2007, 2009) and Imbeau and Jacob (2011).

5 In Thomas Kuhn's *Structure of Scientific Revolutions*, 'prescience' is a period in which «different men confronting the same range of phenomena, but not usually all the same particular phenomena, describe and interpret them in different ways [...] [S]uch initial divergences should ever largely disappear [...with] the triumph of one of the pre-paradigm schools, which, because of its own characteristic beliefs and preconceptions, emphasized only some special part of the too sizable and inchoate pool of information» (Kuhn 1970: 17).

that would have been made and/or welfare that would have been experienced had the first actor not existed or acted» (Bartlett 1989: 30). With this broad definition, he identifies four forms of power: decision power (simple economic power and decision control power), event power, agenda power, and value power (1989: 41 sq). Under the assumption of bounded rationality, he argues that economic activity is an exercise of power. In summary, the visions of power presented by mainstream economics depend on theoretical assumptions (power is «assumed away»), whereas institutional economists focus on the empirical object they are observing. We are confronted here with the classical trade-off between parsimony and realism. Some argue for the strict observance of neoclassical dogmas, often falsely thinking that assumptions are statements about truth; others question the orthodoxy when they feel that mainstream assumptions block the way toward a better understanding of reality.

Political science is also in a prescientific stage when it comes to the study of power. There is no dominant paradigm of power at the moment. But the literature on power in this discipline is much more developed than in economics.[6] As Klein noted:

> «if economics customarily assumes away most of the implications of power, mainstream political science appears to begin by assuming that the distribution of power is the preeminent conditioner of how the political system operates. Power is the prime determinant of most of the decisions that lead to particular market prices. Power and wealth are mutually supportive. One is used to acquire more of the other. Together they seep through most of our attitude-forming institutions and, in the process, affect mightily what consumers want, whether and to what extent producers will produce efficiently, and for whom products will be produced. [...] It is clearly misleading to say that 'the market' determines resource allocation, since power constellations have previously conditioned the market and determined the manner in which it will present choices» (Klein 1980: 883–4).

Despite the profusion of conceptions that one finds in the political science literature on power, one can readily identify a cumulative development in the contributions of Weber (1964) [1922], Russell (1962), Dahl (1957), Bachrach and Baratz (1962; 1963), Lukes (1974), and Dowding (1991).[7] In the rest of this section, we dwell on this literature to propose a conceptual framework which will help us see how uncertainty may impact on the content of constitutions. Doing so, we will intentionally depart from the prevailing assumptions of mainstream economics in hope that our conceptualization will help build a «*political* economy» of constitution-making.

Power and rational choice Bertrand Russell defined power as «the ability to produce intended effects» (Russell 1938). This definition implies intentionality. Reaching an effect by accident is not a manifestation of power but of luck (Dowding 1996: Chap. 3). More importantly, it also implies a disposition rather than an action. Indeed, this definition of power is 'dispositional,' writes Dowding (1996: 3), in the sense that it denotes a disposition of an agent to do something.

[6] See, for example, the review presented by Haugaard (2002).

[7] For a synthesis of this literature, see (Imbeau and Couture 2010).

To have power means to have the capacity or the ability to do something. Therefore, having power does not necessarily imply exercising power. One may well have the power to do something but choose not to do it. Power may remain potential, much like water behind a hydroelectric dam. Furthermore, the *exercise* of power does not imply action. One may exercise power by remaining silent, thus suggesting one's approval; or one may prevent an issue from reaching the public agenda, thus discarding an option without any decision being taken about it. Bachrach and Baratz (1962; 1963) coined the term «nondecision» to refer to this possibility. Riker (1984) talked about heresthetics—i.e., «structuring the situation so that others accept it willingly»—to describe a mechanism through which nondecision is effective. Finally, Lukes (1974) defined a third-dimensional type of power where «*A* may exercise power over *B* [...] by influencing, shaping or determining his very wants. Indeed, is it not the supreme exercise of power to get another or others to have the desires you want them to have—that is, to secure their compliance by controlling their thoughts and desires?» (Lukes 2005: 27) Power is a capacity that does not need to be actualized for it to exist.

Power as a capacity is based on resources with which its holder is endowed. To have the power to do something implies to control the resources necessary to exercise it. As mentioned above, power does not necessarily imply force, coercion, or authority. It may also be exercised through other means. Indeed, power as a capacity is recognizable in policy processes through three main resources which may be used to produce intended effects: *force* or authority, *wealth* or things of value, and *knowledge* or information with rhetoric. These define the sources of power.

Russell's definition of power also implies a target of power, the «intended effects». The literature generally identifies two types of target: events or things, and persons. One may produce, or help produce, an effect by directly acting on things or events like casting one's vote in an election. But one may also indirectly produce, or help produce, an effect by making another act on things or events. Thus in defining power, we need to distinguish two types of power relation: instrumental power or *power to*, and social power or *power over* (Göhler 2009). Instrumental power is the capacity of an agent to produce, or to help produce, an outcome by acting on events or things. Social power is the capacity of an agent deliberately to change the incentive structure of another agent so as to produce, or to help produce, an outcome (Dowding 1991: 48). In Fig. 2, social power corresponds to the arrow linking *B*'s choices to *A*'s preferences (or *A*'s choices to *B*'s preferences). *B* (*A*) has the ability to modify *A*'s (*B*'s) preferences, thus making *A* (*B*) choose what would make the outcome closer to what *B* (*A*) prefers. Instrumental power rather corresponds to the arrow linking *A* and *B* to the outcome. Thus through their choices—their vote, for example—*A* and *B* have the ability to help produce a desired outcome.

To modify *A*'s incentive structure, *B* must exercise instrumental power by using his resources. For example, *B* might use his authority or force to threaten *A* of a punishment, or *B* might offer *A* a reward in exchange for the desired behavior, or *B* might suggest arguments that could modify *A*'s beliefs about his costs and benefits. This is why we say that social power implies instrumental power. But the

Table 1 The forms of power relations

	Forms of power relations		
	Political	Economic	Preceptorial
Power resource	Force/authority	Wealth/things of value	Knowledge/information with rhetoric
Method	Threat/coercion	Exchange	Persuasion
Impact of social power on target's incentive structure	Costs	Benefits	Beliefs about costs or benefits

reverse is not true. *A* may exercise instrumental power without exercising social power. For example, in order to coerce a fast driver to slow down on the expressway (social power), a police officer needs to have the capacity to give the recalcitrant driver a fine and ultimately to put him in prison (instrumental power). But consider this other example. I may have the power to contribute to elect the prime minister through my vote (instrumental power) while having absolutely no capacity to make others do so (social power), if, for example, I am physically impaired to the point that contacting other people is almost impossible; I have (arguably very limited) instrumental power but no social power. Social power implies instrumental power.

Turning back to the interaction model of Fig. 2, we see that the source of *B*'s (*A*'s) choices is *B*'s (*A*'s) endowment. In terms of power relations, *B* (*A*) uses the power resources with which he/she is endowed either to help bring about a desired outcome or to make *A* (*B*) help bring it about. To be sure, to each resource corresponds a specific method and a main effect on the incentive structure of the target of social power (see Table 1). One may use the force or the authority one is endowed with to make another do what he would not do otherwise (or to prevent him from doing what he would otherwise) by increasing his costs through coercion or the threat of punishment. This is political power. Tribunals exercise political power when they threaten delinquents with fines or prison, thus increasing the cost of the unwanted behavior. Dictators do the same. But power may also be economic when a holder of wealth, or of something of value, makes another do what he would not do otherwise by offering a valued compensation in exchange for the wanted behavior. A minister of Finance, for example, makes wealthy people give up the use of part of their wealth by issuing government obligations, thus acting on the investor's benefits. If the interest rate offered is high enough, the investor transfers part of her wealth to the government, something she would not do otherwise. Finally, power may be preceptorial when it is based on knowledge through persuasion. A clergyperson may use her knowledge to persuade a disciple that his benefit-to-cost ratio would be more favorable if he performed an action he would not otherwise—like detonating a bomb on the market place—or if he did not perform an action that he would otherwise—like having sex outside marriage. In these three cases, the process is the same. A power resource is used by an agent to change the incentive structure of the target agent through a specific method.

Table 2 Types of social power relations

		Resource used by the influenced agent (*A*)		
		Force	Wealth	Knowledge
Resource used by the Influencing Agent (*B*)	Force	1 $B_F \rightarrow A_F$	2 $B_F \rightarrow A_W$	3 $B_F \rightarrow A_K$
	Wealth	4 $B_W \rightarrow A_F$	5 $B_W \rightarrow A_W$	6 $B_W \rightarrow A_K$
	Knowledge	7 $B_K \rightarrow A_F$	8 $B_K \rightarrow A_W$	9 $B_K \rightarrow A_K$

Social interactions therefore could be conceptualized to have nine forms, according to the resource used by the influencing agent (the one who exercises power) and the resources the influenced agent would be expected to use if he were to comply (cf. Table 2). Thus *B*, the minister of Finance, may use his authority, for example, to make *A*, the taxpayer, pay a tax. This is a type 2 interaction. Likewise, when the minister of Finance makes the investor buy government bonds by offering a sufficiently high interest rate, we have a type 5 interaction[8]; or when an agent hides information from his principal to make the principal make a decision serving the interest of the agent (a principal-agent relation), we have a type 7 interaction; or when an entrepreneur bribes a politician to obtain a favorable decision, we have a type 4 interaction; etc.

Another source of choice in the interaction model of Fig. 2 is *preferences*. *B*'s choices are dictated by his preferences, i.e., his utility function. A power approach would lead us to assume that there are at least three arguments in an agent's utility function: Agents want to maximize their authority, their wealth, and their knowledge *relative to others*. More accurately, they want to maximize the return they can get from the combination of their authority, wealth, and knowledge. Indeed, when they act over events or things—or when they exercise some form of instrumental power—agents essentially act over the distribution of power resources: **F** (the distribution of force or authority), **W** (the distribution of wealth or things of value), and **K** (the distribution of knowledge or of information and rhetoric). More precisely, the distribution of a power resource tells us who has more or less authority, wealth, or knowledge relative to others. For example, when a taxpayer pays his tax, he changes the distribution of wealth as he ends up having less and the government having more. Therefore, it is reasonable to consider that the outcomes that *A* and *B* ultimately look for are their respective positions on the distribution of authority, wealth, and knowledge. Considering the drafting of a constitution, for

[8] Of course, investors may also exercise power over the minister of Finance and make him offer higher interest rates in exchange for their wealth, something he would not do otherwise. It is not always easy to determine who exercises power over whom in this example. When a government has the political capacity not to borrow money, i.e., when it can increase taxes or decrease expenditures without fearing an electoral backlash, then it may be in a position to exercise power over investors. But the more a government indulges in deficit financing the more vulnerable it becomes to investors and to their demands until it has no other alternative but to comply or to default. I thank Alan Lockard for bringing this point to my attention.

Table 3 Types of instrumental power relations

		Distribution of power relations		
		Force	Wealth	Knowledge
Resource used by the agent exercising instrumental power (B)	Force	1 $B_F \rightarrow F$	2 $B_F \rightarrow W$	3 $B_F \rightarrow K$
	Wealth	4 $B_W \rightarrow F$	5 $B_W \rightarrow W$	6 $B_W \rightarrow K$
	Knowledge	7 $B_K \rightarrow F$	8 $B_K \rightarrow W$	9 $B_K \rightarrow K$

example, drafters and adopters want to include provisions that will optimize their future relative positions in those three distributions. Thus, we can conceptualize nine types of instrumental power by crossing the targeted distribution of power with the power resource. According to the power resource an agent uses and the distribution of these resources upon which she wants to impact, one may identify nine types of instrumental power (cf. Table 3).[9]

2.3 Power Relations Behind the «Veil of Ignorance»

Buchanan and Tullock argued that decision-makers choose differently when they are uncertain about their future position—when they stand behind a veil of ignorance—as compared to when they are relatively certain. The informational characteristics of the decision-making context makes them follow their own preferences under relative certainty but to move toward the preference of the majority—or the median preference—under uncertainty. As the theory has it, decision-making under uncertainty is typical of constitutional decision-making. Because constitution choices last longer, the uncertainty of decision-makers is more prevalent than in in-period choices. Hence, decision-makers tend to serve the preferences of the median voter as her future situation might later be closer to his than it now is.

However, in in-period choices, the veil of ignorance is lifted. The time horizon is shorter and the majority requirement for changing rules is less stringent, thus making it easier for one whose position will have deteriorated to change rules in the future. Therefore, when the decision-maker is relatively certain about his future position, she chooses according to her own preferences. Now, it is more difficult to gather a winning coalition under a more demanding constitutional decision rule when everybody follow their own preferences than when each tend to move toward the median position. Therefore, constitutions contain choices mainly corresponding to areas of uncertainty for constitution drafters as choices corresponding to areas of certainty fail to reach the required majority and thus are postponed to the in-period process.

[9] For examples of each of the nine types of instrumental power, see (Imbeau and Couture 2010: 58–59).

In a power perspective, the preferences of agents are evaluated in terms of their power position in society. They use their power to maintain or improve their position, somewhat like the entrepreneur uses his wealth to produce more wealth (or to avoid losing too much). Therefore, uncertainty refers to the future power position of an agent: Will she be higher or lower in the future distribution of power? If she is uncertain about her future position, she will choose according to the median preference. If her co-deciders make the same evaluation concerning their own future position, the decision-making body will more easily arrive at a decision. Under relative certainty, the opposite will prevail. Constitution drafters will follow their own private interest and no constitutional decision will be made, the issue being postponed to the in-period process.

Now, it is quite obvious that constitution drafters occupy the higher part of the three main power distributions in society. They have more authority, more wealth, and more knowledge than the median individual in each of these distributions. Unless they are uncertain about their future position, they will work hard to protect or to improve their position. But if they think that the distribution of power is volatile and that they might drop toward the median position, then they will be careful to adopt rules that would protect them in the future.

This volatility of power positions is not equal from one distribution to the next. We can safely say that volatility is higher in the distribution of political power, especially in democratic regimes where majorities often shift with electoral results. When this occurs, a whole class of decision-makers changes position on the distribution of political power, some leaving, others entering government circles. Thus, constitutional drafters are quite uncertain about their future political position. But they are less uncertain about their economic power position. Without being absolutely certain, they expect to keep their economic position in the future and even to bequeath their wealth to their children. The distribution of wealth is much more stable than the distribution of authority but relatively less stable than the distribution of knowledge. Indeed, those who are considered as knowing—clergy persons in some societies, policy experts in others, etc.—occupy a preceptorial-power position that is quite stable. It takes a long time for a society to change the criteria it uses to determine what is true and what is good. Consequently, there is less uncertainty in preceptorial power than in economic power and less in economic power than in political power.

Our power theory of uncertainty in constitution-making is summarized in the following causal diagram:

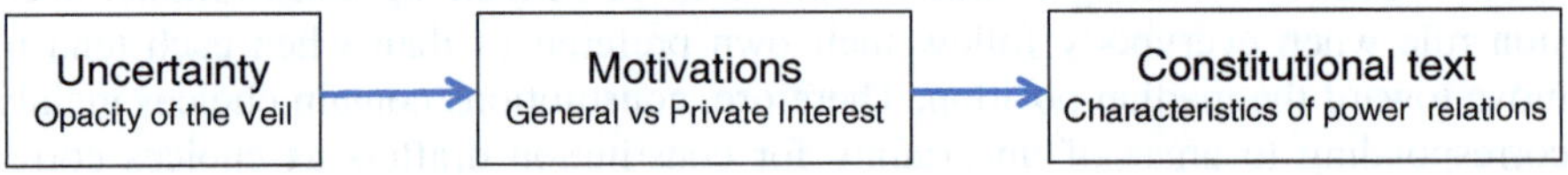

The more opaque the veil of ignorance is in a constitution-making process, the more drafters will attend to the general interest, and the more constitutional documents resulting from this process will be concerned with (1) political power rather than economic or preceptorial power—because it is easier to reach a collective decision when most decision-makers attend to the general interest than when they attend to their own private interest, (2) social rather than instrumental power relations—because uncertain drafters will be more concerned with power over persons than over events or things—, and (3) negative (denying capacities) rather than positive (assigning capacities) power relations. It is expected that the motivations of drafters will crystallise into the constitutional text and that, by analyzing the actual content of a constitution, we can trace the effects of these motivations. Then, through an abductive reasoning,[10] we can infer, from the content of the text, the motivations of constitutional drafters and therefore the degree of their uncertainty. Thus, by measuring the extent to which a constitutional text insists relatively more on political (or social, or negative) power relations, we also measure the opacity of the veil of ignorance or the degree of uncertainty that prevailed when the constitutional text was being drafted.

Such is the objective we have set to ourselves in this project. We want to assess the validity of three definitional propositions related to the three dimensions of power relations we have identified:

Because uncertainty prevails in a constitution-making process, the following should be true:

1. There are more concerns for political power than for economic or preceptorial power in a constitution.
2. There are more concerns for social power than instrumental power in a constitution.
3. There are more concerns for negative than positive power relations in a constitution.

These propositions are «definitional» in the sense that, in the context where many constitutions are being compared on these dimensions, the variation in the intensity of concerns for each of these dimensions can be considered as an operational definition of the opacity of the veil of ignorance or the prevalence of uncertainty in a given constitution-making process.

3 Research Design

We follow the procedure designed by Imbeau (2009) and by Imbeau and Jacob (2011). We consider constitutional documents not as sets of rules but as discourses about power relations in society through which drafters reveal their preferences. If they attend to the general interest, they will refer more often to *political* power relations, i.e., to relations of authority, as compared to *economic* (exchange) and *preceptorial* (persuasion) power relations; they will also refer more often to social power than to instrumental power, and to negative than to positive power relations. Sixteen national constitutions were «content analyzed».

[10] Abduction, a term first introduced by the American philosopher Charles Peirce, is a form of logical reasoning that goes from the data to an explanation that accounts for the data. Deduction derives a consequence from a cause. Abduction reverses the process and derives a cause from a consequence. When the cause is unobservable, like the opacity of the veil of uncertainty in a decision-making process, an abductive reasoning allows one to infer the cause on the basis of the consequence. For a discussion of Peirce's contribution in the context of economic institutionalism, see (Mirowski 1987); for an application to constitutional decision-making, see (Imbeau 2009).

3.1 Content Analysis Procedure

Content analysis is a data generating technique involving two steps: *unitizing* and *coding*. The first step of the analysis consists in extracting meaningful contents from the constitutional document. The «walk-talk» perspective adopted here considers a constitutional document as a *discourse* rather than as a contract or a legal document. This means that we are not interested in the legal or contractual implications of the document but in its literal content. Following the conceptual framework provided above, we are looking for «power relations» defined as:

> The description of the relationship between an *agent* and a *capacity* such that: (1) an agent has the capacity to do something (or is prevented from doing something), or (2) an agent has the capacity to make another agent do something or to prevent another agent from doing something (or is denied such capacity).

Therefore, in terms of the literal content of a constitutional document, we were looking for this particular discursive structure:

An explicitly identified agent (individual or collective)	**Has the capacity to do something or is denied the capacity to do something (instrumental power or social power)**

Each time we found this type of discursive structure, we had a «*power relation*» and we created a unit of analysis.

The second step in the content analysis procedure is the coding of the units of analysis on various dimensions (variables). Each unit of analysis was coded on three variables: source, type, and direction.

*V1-**Source** of the power relation*:
Which resource would the influencing «**Agent**» use to perform the action he has the capacity to perform or to make another perform an action: Authority, wealth, or knowledge?
*V2-**Type** of the power relation (instrumental vs social power)*:
Could this action add (or remove) a possibility of choice to (from) the choice set of another explicitly identified agent? Yes (social power) or No (instrumental power).
*V3-**Direction** of the power relation*:
Positive (the «Agent» has the capacity to do something) or Negative (the «Agent» is denied the capacity to do something).

More details are provided in the codebook reproduced in an annex below.

Two senior undergraduate students in political science were trained to do the unitizing and the coding of excerpts from three constitutional texts, the constitutions of Canada, Belgium, and Cameroon. The training consisted in two steps. First, after they had read a first version of the codebook, the coders were assigned a common set of 30 paragraphs drawn from one constitution and were asked to unitize them independently of each other. Then, they would compare their unitizing decisions and discuss each of the discrepancies trying to formulate general rules that would solve them. When we felt that the level of agreement was satisfactory, we did a second attempt with a new set of paragraphs, discussing the discrepancies and amending the codebook. This process was repeated until the coders reached a Krippendorff's alpha level larger than 0.80. We then proceeded to the second step and trained the coders to code each unit. We started with units commonly agreed upon in the first set of paragraphs and let the coders code them independently of each other. We then compared their coding, discussed the discrepancies, and amended the codebook. We repeated this process until we reached an K-alpha larger than 0.80.

3.2 Reliability Tests

Krippendorff (2004: 215) identifies three types of reliability in content analysis. *Stability* refers to the degree a unitizing or coding process is unchanging over time, or yields the same results on repeated trials. Instability is caused by intra-observer inconsistencies which «may be due to insecurity, carelessness, openness to distractions, difficulties in comprehending written instructions, or the tendency to relax performance standards when tired» (*Ibid.*). Measuring stability implies that coders reread and recode the same text after some time has elapsed (a test-retest process). *Reproducibility* «is the degree to which a process can be replicated by different analysts» (*Ibid.*). In other words, can different coders working in different locations with similar instruments come to the same results? Reproducibility is assessed through a test–test process. For Krippendorff, reproducibility is a stronger measure of reliability than stability. But *accuracy* is the strongest form of reliability. It measures «the degree to which a process conforms to its specification and yields what it is designed to yield» (*Ibid.*). Accuracy is assessed through a test-standard process in which the tested coding is compared to a coding that is taken to be correct.

We performed our reliability tests using Krippendorff's alpha statistic (K-alpha) using Hayes' SPSS macro (Hayes and Krippendorff 2007). In its simplest form, K-alpha is defined by

$$\alpha = 1 - (D_o/D_e)$$

where D_o is the observed disagreement and D_e the expected disagreement under pure chance. The statistic can be adapted for any number of coders and values and for any measurement level.[11] Krippendorff argues that the reliability tests should reach at least a value of 0.80 for a content analysis to be valid.

We tested *stability* several times at the beginning of the training process, and we consistently reached satisfactory results. *Reproducibility* was harder to reach.

[11] For an extended description with computing formulas, see (Krippendorff 2004: 221–241). Andrew Hayes provides an SPSS macro for computing a Krippendorff alpha on his Web site http://www.comm.ohio-state.edu/ahayes/. For details about the working of this macro, see (Hayes and Krippendorff 2007).

Table 4 Inter-coder reliability tests (k-alpha)

Date of test	Unitizing	Coding		
		*V*1	*V*2	*V*3
June 2011	0.96	0.72	0.83	1
June 2011	0.96	0.72	0.89	1
July 2011	0.91	0.91	0.94	1
July 2011	0.94	0.96	0.91	1
July 2011	0.98	0.78	0.66	0.79
July 2011	0.96	0.91	0.72	1
July 2011	0.98	0.81	0.74	1
September 2011	0.92	0.77	0.85	1
August 2011	0.98	0.81	0.79	1
October 2011	0.98	1	0.9	1
November 2011	0.61	0.63	0.86	1
December 2011	0.89	0.91	0.77	1
Mean	0.92	0.83	0.82	0.98
Standard deviation	0.099	0.106	0.083	0.058

Actually, we used the training process to improve the k-alpha from its unsatisfactory value in the first attempt to the minimum level of 0.80. Once this satisfactory level was reached, we launched the actual content analysis.[12]

The actual content analysis extended over six months.[13] At regular intervals during this period, we performed reliability tests, the results of which are reported in Table 4. The unitizing and coding are reliable as the mean k-alphas vary from 0.82 to 0.98.

4 Results

4.1 Measuring the Opacity of the Veil

We performed a content analysis of the constitutions of 16 countries (see Table 5). The length in words of the constitutional texts varies from 2,643 words (Libya) to 26,917 (Greece).[14] On average, we extracted 564.6 power relations from each constitution

[12] Since we did not have a «standard», we could not perform the accuracy test. However, the supervision of the coders by the main investigator all along the training process gives an assurance that the unitizing and coding are accurate.

[13] Coders worked full time in July and August and part time from September to December 2011.

[14] One should use caution when comparing the length of constitutional texts because of the use of versions in French and in English. Texts in French usually count a higher number of words than their equivalent/translation in English. However, this has no effect on the identification of units of analysis which are «Power relations».

Table 5 Characteristics of constitutional documents

	Language	Words	Units	Density	Origin
Belgium	F	14,478	572	39.5	1831
Cameroon	F	7,814	415	53.1	1972
Canada	F	13,893	519	37.4	1867
Chad	F	10,917	541	49.6	1996
Egypt	F	12,958	603	46.5	1971
Estonia	E	11,181	530	47.4	1992
France	F	10,648	507	47.6	1958
Germany	E	26,797	1,114	41.6	1949
Greece	E	26,917	893	33.2	1974
Italy	E	10,836	488	45.0	1948
Libya	F	2,643	134	50.7	1969
Niger	F	12,848	632	49.2	2010
Switzerland	F	17,710	931	52.6	1999
Syria	F	7,533	381	50.6	1973
Tunisia	F	6,975	329	47.2	1958
USA	E	7,858	445	56.6	1787
Mean		12,625.4	564.6	46.7	
Standard deviation		6,381.8	233.8	6.0	
CV (%)		51	41	13	

Note: Words number of words. *Units* number of power relations extracted. *Density* number of units per thousand words. *Origin* year of first adoption. *Language* language of the text analyzed (*F* French; *E* English)
The text analyzed was the most recent version of the constitution in force as of July 2011. We used the official version in French when available; otherwise, we analyzed the official version in English or an official translation in English

(coefficient of variation = 41 %). This corresponds to a mean of 46.7 power relations per thousand words (density). The highest density was found in the American constitution (56.6), the lowest one in the Greek constitution (33.2). The oldest constitution is the American one, the youngest is the constitution of Niger adopted in 2010.

We can deduce several measures of the opacity of the veil of ignorance (or, equivalently, the prevalence of uncertainty in constitution-making) from the coding performed on each power relation found in the constitutional documents. Four are reported in Table 6. They refer to variables *V*1, *V*2, and *V*3, defined above, and to a combination of *V*1 and *V*2.

The first column reports the proportion of the total number of power relations that refer to authority as the main source of capacity for the agent holding power. In the Belgian constitution, for example, 84 % of the 572 power relations that we extracted refer to holders of authority (1 % refer to holders of wealth, 8 % to holders of knowledge; for 7 % of the power relations, it was not possible to make a precise decision on this issue. Note that these last results are not reported in the table). On average, 75 % of power relations refer to authority as the source

Table 6 Measures of the opacity of the veil of ignorance (Ratio Freq./N)

	Source of power: authority (*V*1)	Type of power: social (*V*2)	Direction: negative (*V*3)	Authority and social *V*1*V*2	N
Belgium	0.84	0.46	0.04	0.42	572
Cameroon	0.76	0.51	0.01	0.40	415
Canada	0.73	0.52	0.01	0.37	519
Chad	0.74	0.45	0.04	0.36	541
Egypt	0.75	0.5	0.05	0.41	603
Estonia	0.81	0.48	0.05	0.42	530
France	0.76	0.55	0.03	0.44	507
Germany	0.79	0.51	0.03	0.43	1,114
Greece	0.78	0.45	0.05	0.38	893
Italy	0.73	0.5	0.04	0.37	488
Libya	0.74	0.35	0.02	0.31	134
Niger	0.68	0.46	0.06	0.33	632
Switzerland	0.62	0.37	0.02	0.26	931
Syria	0.73	0.46	0.02	0.34	381
Tunisia	0.71	0.48	0.03	0.35	329
USA	0.85	0.51	0.1	0.43	445
Mean	0.751	0.473	0.038	0.376	564.6
Standard deviation	0.055	0.051	0.022	0.049	241.43
CV (%)	7.4	10.7	57.7	12.9	42.8

of power. This result confirms Buchanan's and Tullock's intuition. Because they are more uncertain of their future *political* position, drafters tend to agree more often on contents that relate to political power rather than economic or preceptorial power. The cross-country variation is quite modest with a coefficient of variation of 7 %. The constitution that manifests the highest degree of uncertainty is the American constitution at 0.85. According to our assumptions, the drafters of the American constitution manifested more uncertainty than any other group of drafters in the sample. The lowest value is Switzerland's at 0.62.

The second and third columns report the proportions of social and negative relations, respectively. As was argued above, social power relations (i.e., the capacity to act over another person) and negative power relation (i.e., the capacity to *prevent* someone from performing an action) denote a higher level of uncertainty than instrumental or positive power relations. The average proportion of cases of social relation is 0.47 suggesting that the discourse in constitutional texts is divided more or less equally between social and instrumental power relations. France has the highest score on this variable (0.55) and Switzerland the lowest (0.37). The average proportion of negative power relation is very low at 0.04. That means that almost all the power relations that were extracted denoted a *positive* direction. This means that constitutional texts tend to assign (positive power relation) rather than restrain (negative power relation) powers. Even though these proportion are low, there still is an important variation (CV = 58 %). The USA has the highest score which denotes more uncertainty, Cameroon and Canada the lowest.

Figure 3 shows the scatterplot of Source-Authority by Type-Social with four quadrants defined by the variable means. The diagram identifies one group of countries where, according to the two variables, the level of uncertainty was high (the north-east quadrant): USA, Estonia, Germany, Cameroon, and France. The southwest quadrant shows the countries where uncertainty was the lowest: Switzerland, Libya, Chad, Syria, and Niger. The other countries occupy a middle range position on one or the other variables.

To translate the clusters of Fig. 3 into a continuous variable, we computed the ratio of the frequency of references to authority *and* to social power over the total number of power relations (fourth column of Table 6). This variable might be interpreted as a stronger version of our measure of the prevalence of uncertainty because it takes into consideration the two dimensions already mentioned. On average, 36 % of the power relations extracted from constitutional documents refer to authority *and* to social power. The variation is relatively modest with a coefficient of variation equal to 13 %. France, together with the USA, Germany, and Belgium exhibit the highest scores and Switzerland the lowest.

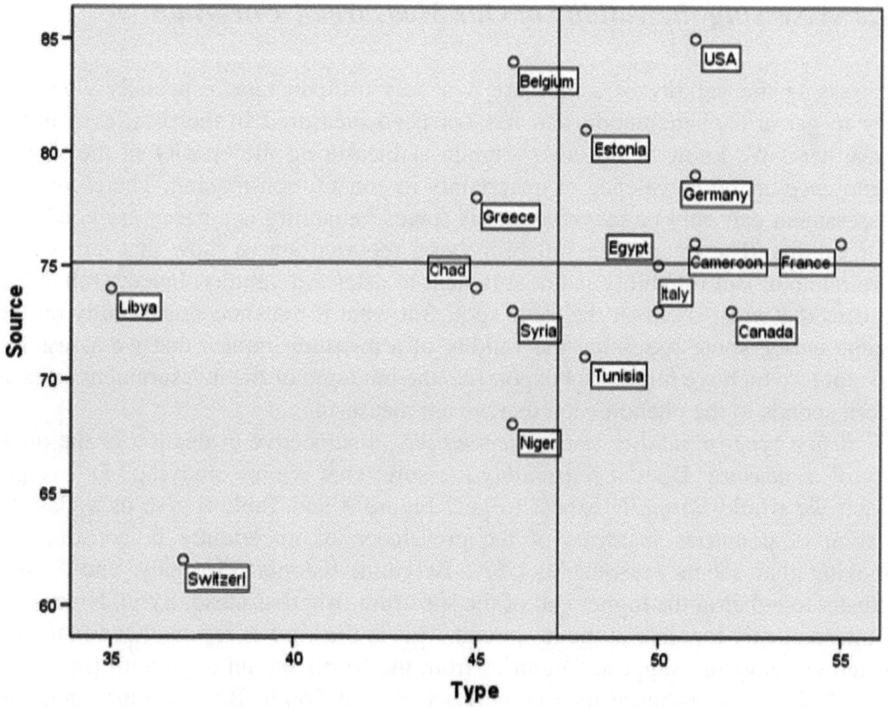

Fig. 3 Scatterplot of source-authority * type-social

Table 7 Correlation matrix

		Type: social	Direction: negative	Authority and Social
Source: authority	Pearson correlation	0.426	0.466	0.842
	Sig. (bilateral)	0.100	0.069	0.000
	N	16	16	16
Type: social	Pearson correlation		0.177	0.793
	Sig. (bilateral)		0.513	0.000
	N		16	16
Direction: negative	Pearson correlation			0.359
	Sig. (bilateral)			0.172
	N			16

The correlations between these variables are reported in Table 7. They suggest that the combined variable Authority-Social is a summary of the variation in the two variables included in it. The weaker correlations between Direction-Negative and the other variables suggest that this variable maybe captures a different phenomenon. We will just ignore it.

4.2 Assessing the Validity of Our Measure of Uncertainty

Assessing the validity of a measure is a very difficult task, especially when we try to get at a phenomenon that has not been measured in the past, as it is the case here. We know of no other attempt at measuring the opacity of the veil of ignorance or the prevalence of uncertainty in constitution-making. Therefore, any assessment can only be tentative at this stage. Reliability is a necessary condition for validity. The inter-coder reliability tests reported above show that our results are reliable. But reliability is not sufficient to establish validity. Indeed, reliability means that most shots hit the same spot. But what if the shots consistently hit the same *wrong* spot? Assessing the validity of a measure implies that we assess the extent to which we hit the right spot, i.e., the outcome of the measurement process corresponds to the phenomenon that we are measuring.

A first type of validity test is *face validity*, a subjective evaluation of the quality of a measure: Does it *reasonably* measure what we are studying? Do we get what we would *normally* expect to get? Figure 3 and Table 6 give us a classification of countries in terms of the prevalence of uncertainty in constitution-making that seems reasonable. USA, Belgium, Estonia, Germany, and France cluster together at the higher end of the spectrum, whereas Chad, Syria, Niger, and Tunisia cluster together at the lower end. This is the kind of results that a first educated guess would suggest. Countries from the North should align with Buchanan and Tullock's view more than countries from the South. But one case seems to be oddly located in this regard. Switzerland has the lowest score on *V1V2* (0.26) at 2.37 standard deviations under the mean. According to the educated guess just mentioned, Switzerland should get a score much closer to that of Germany, for example. Our measure fails a face validity test.

This odd result for Switzerland reminds one of the position of Switzerland on Borrelli and Royed's index of strength of government (1995: Table 4). In their paper, these authors tested the hypothesis linking government strength to change in fiscal deficit for 16 OECD countries over the 1959–1990 period. To perform this test, Borrelli and Royed had constructed an index of 'strength of government.' According to this index, Switzerland had the lowest score in government strength whereas it was one of the three countries which had never had a fiscal deficit in that period (the other two countries were, according to Borrelli and Royed's figures, Norway and Finland). Borrelli and Royed noted «the extremely 'weak' value registered by Switzerland, which might strike some readers as undeserved [...] Arguably, these numbers are an artifact of Switzerland's traditionally 'consociationalist' politics [...] rather than symptoms of inherent 'weakness'» (Borrelli and Royed 1995: 245). On the face of it, the score for Switzerland was invalid. But Borrelli and Royed correctly chose not to adjust their index arbitrarily to make Switzerland appear 'stronger.' They ran regressions with and without Switzerland and found that their results were robust.

This strategy applied by Borrelli and Royed corresponds to a validity test called *construct-validity*. Here, we ask the question: How does the measure relate to another measure with which it should be theoretically related? In the case of uncertainty in constitution-making, we argued above that one source of uncertainty for constitution drafters is the possibility not to be in government anymore when comes the time to make decisions under the rules set by the constitution they are drafting. And we suggested that this uncertainty was higher in democratic settings. Therefore, uncertainty should be higher in democratic systems. Another source of uncertainty is the historical depth of a polity: The longer the history of living together, the *lower* the uncertainty. Using data from the Polity IV Project (Marshall et al. 2010), we explored these two hypotheses by regressing our measure of uncertainty (*V1V2*) on the variables 'Polity' and 'Persist.' The Polity variable ranges from +10 (very democratic regime) to −10 (very autocratic regime). The Persist variable is the number of years the regime has persisted without a recorded change in values on any of the six Polity component variables. The values of the two variables are reported in Table 9. The regression results are reported in Table 8.

The first two regression models show that the level of democracy ('Polity') is positively related to uncertainty. More democratic countries show higher uncertainty in constitution-making. This result is not significant in the first model, but it is in the second one where the 'Persist' variable is introduced. In this model, the coefficients of the two variables are significant and have the appropriate sign. The R-square is relatively important at 0.35. This convincingly supports the contention that our measure is construct-valid.

The other four regression models are variants of the first two that show the robustness of the 'Polity' variable and that confirm the sign of the 'Persist'

Table 8 Regression results, dependent variable: uncertainty (*V*1*V*2) (std. error in parentheses)

	1	2	If Switzerland = Germany		Switzerland excluded	
			3	4	5	6
Constant	0.368*** (0.014)	0.382*** (0.014)	0.372*** (0.010)	0.378*** (0.011)	0.372*** (0.010)	0.373*** (0.012)
Polity	0.002 (0.002)	0.004* (0.002)	0.004* (0.001)	0.004** (0.001)	0.003* (0.001)	0.004* (0.002)
Persist		−0.001* (0.0002)		−0.0002 (0.0002)		−0.000006 (0.0002)
$R2$	0.10	0.35	0.37	0.43	0.36	0.36
N	16	16	16	16	15	15

*** $p < 0.001$; **$p < 0.01$; *$p < 0.05$

Table 9 Level of democracy (*Polity*) and regime persistence (*Persist*)

	Polity	Persist
Belgium	8	3
Cameroon	−4	19
Canada	10	88
Chad	−2	15
Egypt	−3	6
Estonia	9	11
France	9	25
Germany	10	20
Greece	10	25
Italy	10	63
Libya	−7	12
Niger	3	1
Switzerland	10	162
Syria	−7	10
Tunisia	−4	9
USA	10	139
Mean	3.9	38.0
Standard deviation	6.79	48.03
CV (%)	175	126

variable. In models 3 and 4, we arbitrarily adjusted the score of Switzerland on *V*1*V*2 to make it equal to that of Germany. Note that, per Table 9, Germany has a similar score on 'Polity' but a very different one on 'Persist.' The coefficient for 'Polity' is now significant in the bivariate model (model 3), and 'Persist' has a negative, though insignificant, coefficient in model 4. The *R*-squares are higher than in the first two models but of the same magnitude. In models 5 and 6, we simply dropped Switzerland from the sample and got similar figures. The differences that we note in models 3–6 do not justify a special treatment for Switzerland.

The conclusion to draw from these tests is that our measure of uncertainty passes the test of construct-validity. There is no reason to be unhappy with Switzerland's score. Quite the opposite! Like it was constructed, our measure of uncertainty not only confirms the hypothesis of higher uncertainty under democracy but it reveals the importance of historical depth. A longer history of living together prompts constitution drafters to be more confident in the future and to agree more easily on issues that involve economic or preceptorial powers.

5 Conclusion

This chapter presents the Veil of Ignorance Project. It views constitutional decisions as the outcome of social interactions among drafters as proposed by James Buchanan. In order to develop a *political* economic approach to constitutional design under uncertainty, it proposes a conceptual framework based on power relations. We assume that drafters want to maintain or to improve their political, economic, and preceptorial power position in society through specific constitutional contents. As they are more uncertain about their future political power position as opposed to their future economic or preceptorial power position, we infer that the level of uncertainty in the constitution-making process is higher when the content of a constitution refers more often to political power, to social as opposed to instrumental power, and to restraining rather than granting powers. Adopting a discursive approach to analyzing constitutions, we proposed a research design based on content analysis procedures. We show that there is a substantial variation in the level of uncertainty among 16 national constitutions and that this variation is explained by the level of democracy and the length of time since the last important constitutional change.

Decision-making under uncertainty is certainly an important issue when it comes to understanding why specific constitutional decisions are made. This project presents the first systematic empirical exploration of this issue. The results presented here suggest that a discursive approach to constitutional analysis may be fruitful as they highlight how a content analysis coupled with a theory of power relations can help understand the playing of uncertainty in constitutional design.

Annex: Codebook of the Veil of Ignorance Project (VOIP)

Summary of unitizing definitions and rules

Definitions:

1. **Unit of analysis**: a power relation
   Power relation:
      An **agent**
      Has the **capacity to do** (or is denied this capacity)
2. **Agent** = individual or collective
   - Explicitly identified agent
   Or
   - General expression (everyone, none, etc.)
   Examples: - one or several delegates = 1 agent
      - one delegate or several delegates = 2 agents
      - everyone = 1 agent

3. **Capacity**:
   - Verb of action
   - Verb form / verb expression / substantive directly transposable into a verb of action
      N.B. If the substantive is the complement of a verb of action, then only one capacity is extracted (Ex : The Queen declares by proclamation; The President sends a request; the president presides over the debates of the house; the house may refuse the ratification;) but there are 2 actions in: the house may refuse to ratify («may refuse» and «may ratify»).
   - Passive form if directly transposable into active form with verb of action

Rules:

1. A unit of analysis is created when a discursive structure of the type: "Agent / Capacity to do something (or is denied the capacity to do something)" is found. Only the «Agents» and the «Capacities» *explicitly* identified in a clause are considered for a unit to be extracted.

2. A separate unit is created for each combination of «Agent» and «Capacity» found in a clause.

3. In case of doubt, abstain! If, after a reasonable time of thinking, there is still doubt about the existence of a specific power relation, do not unitize it and pass on to the next segment of text.

4. Examples of verbs of action: give, nominate, appoint, vote, declare, do, authorise, impose, receive, supervise, adopt, represent.

5. «Want» and «desire» are not verbs of action.

To help identify the resource used by the influencing agent (**V1**), here is a non-exhaustive list of verbs that may most often be associated with each power resource:

Authority / Force	Wealth / Things of value	Knowledge / Information & rhetoric
Consent	Pay	Advise
Authorize	Buy	Address
Request	Spend	Counsel
Exercise	Sell	Express opinion
Appoint	Subsidize	Teach
Perform duties	Borrow	Instruct (= teach)
Adopt a law	Loan	Give speech
Limit	Exchange	Give advice
Legislate	Trade	Publish
Preside	Give / grant money	Write
Decide	Etc.	Communicate information
Demand		Inform
Vote		Study
Enact		Investigate
Sign a petition		Declare (except «declare war»)
Agree		Affirm
Assent		Practice religion
Concur		Join in worship
Regulate		Judge
Make treaty		Estimate
Recognize		Evaluate
Ensure		Think fit
Refer matters		Etc.
Give instructions		
Give orders		
Preserve, protect institutions, territory, etc.		
Declare war		
Enforce		
Choose policy		
Claim right		
Etc.		
If the resource is not clear and if the verb of action cannot be associated with one of the verbs given above, **code 8**. For example: 'respect the law', 'respect the constitution', 'swear', 'pledge fidelity', etc.		
Verbs that are not considered as verbs of action: Own Have Be Enjoy Want Desire In general, verbs that denote a quality		

Summary of coding rules
***V1**- The **source** of the power relation: Which resource would the influencing «**Agent**» use to perform the action he has the capacity to perform or to make another perform an action?*
1- Authority/Force
2- Wealth/Things of value
3- Knowledge/Information and rhetoric
8- Indeterminate (when the information contained in the text is not sufficient to make a precise coding)
N.B. If the answer is 1 and/or 2, code 2
1 and/or 3, code 3
2 and/or 3, code the most important one, otherwise, code 8.
Consider only the action, not the identity of the agent, when coding a unit on V1.
***V2**- The **type** of the power relation: Could this action add or remove a possibility of choice in the choice set of another agent explicitly identified?*
1- Yes (Social power)
2- No (Instrumental power)
8- Indeterminate (when the information contained in the text is not sufficient to make a precise coding)
***V3**- **Direction** of the power relation:*
*If instrumental power (**V2** is coded 2)*
1- Positive (the «Agent» has the capacity to do something)
2- Negative (the «Agent» is denied the capacity to do something)
8- Indeterminate (when the information contained in the text is not sufficient to make a precise coding)
*If social power (**V2** is coded 1):*
1- Positive (the «Agent» has the capacity to add or to remove a possibility of choice in the choice set of another agent
2- Negative (the «Agent» is denied the capacity to add or to remove a possibility of choice in the choice set of another agent
8- Indeterminate (when the information contained in the text is not sufficient to make a precise coding)

References

Bachrach P, Baratz MS (1962) Two faces of power. Am Polit Sci Rev 56(4):947–952

Bachrach P, Baratz MS (1963) Decisions and nondecisions: an analytical framework. Am Polit Sci Rev 57(3):632–642

Bardhan P (1991) On the concept of power in economics. Econ Politics 3(3):265–277

Bartlett R (1989) Economics and power: an inquiry into human relations and markets. Cambridge University Press, Cambridge

Beard CA (2004 [1913]) An economic interpretation of the constitution of the United States. Dover Publications Inc, Mineola

Borrelli SA, Royed TJ (1995) Government "strength" and budget deficits in advanced democracies. Eur J Polit Res 28:225–260

Buchanan JM (1964) What should economists do? South Econ J 30(3):213–222
Buchanan JM (2008) Constitutional political economy. In: Rowley CK, Schneider FG (eds) Readings in public choice and constitutional political economy. Springer, New York, pp 281–294
Congleton RD (2011) Perfecting parliament: constitutional reform, liberalism, and the rise of western democracy. Cambridge University Press, Cambridge
Congleton RD, Swedenborg B (eds) (2006) Democratic constitutional design and public policy: analysis and evidence. MIT Press, Cambridge
Dahl RA (1957) The concept of power. Behav Sci 2(3):201–215
Dowding KM (1991) Rational choice and political power. Edward Elgar, Aldershot
Dowding KM (1996) Power. Open University Press, Buckingham
Dugger WM (1980). Power: an institutional framework of analysis. J Econ Issues (Association for Evolutionary Economics) 14(4):897
Easton D (1960) The political system. Alfred A. Knopf, New York
Göhler G (2009) Power to and power over. In: Clegg SR, Haugaard M (eds) The Sage handbook of power. Sage, Los Angeles, pp 27–39
Gordon S (1999) Controlling the state: constitutionalism from ancient Athens to today. Harvard University Press, Cambridge
Haugaard M (ed) (2002) Power: a reader. Manchester University Press, Manchester
Hayes AF, Krippendorff K (2007) Answering the call for a standard reliability measure for coding data. Commun Methods Measures 1(1):77–89
Imbeau LM (2007) Leviathan or Geryon? Safeguards against power abuse in democratic societies. In: Marciano A, Josselin J-M (eds) Democracy, freedom, and coercion: a law and economics approach. Edward Elgar, Cheltenham, pp 171–191
Imbeau LM (2009) Testing the «veil of ignorance» hypothesis in constitutional choice: a «walk-talk» approach. J Public Financ Public Choice 26(1):3–21
Imbeau LM, Couture J (2010) Pouvoir et politiques publiques. In: Paquin S, Bernier L, Lachapelle G (eds) L'analyse des politiques publiques. Presses de l'Université de Montréal, Montréal, pp 37–72
Imbeau LM, Jacob S (2011) Is the "veil of ignorance" in constitutional choice a myth? An empirical exploration informed by a theory of power. In: Marciano A (ed) Constitutional mythologies. Springer, Dordrecht
Klein PA (1980) Confronting power in economics: a pragmatic evaluation. J Econ Issues (Association for Evolutionary Economics) 14(4):871–896
Krippendorff K (2004) Content analysis: an introduction to its methodology. CA, Sage Publications, Thousand Oaks
Kuhn TS (1970) The structure of scientific revolutions. Int Encycl Unified Sci 2(2):1–210
Lukes S (1974) Power: a radical view. Macmillan, London
Lukes S (2005) Power: a radical view. Palgrave, Houndmills
Marciano A (2009) Buchanan's constitutional political economy: exchange vs. choice in economics and in politics. Const Polit Econ 20(1):42–56
Marshall MG, Jaggers K et al (2010) Polity IV project: political regime characteristics and transitions, 1800–2010, center for systemic peace
McGuire RA (1988) Constitution making: a rational choice model of the federal convention of 1787. Am J Polit Sci 32(2):483–522
McGuire RA, Ohsfeldt RL (1989) Self-interest, agency theory, and political voting behavior: the ratification of the United States Constitution. Am Econ Rev 79(1):219–234
Mirowski P (1987) The philosophical bases of institutionalist economics. J Econ Issues (Association for Evolutionary Economics) 21(3):1001–1038
Persson T, Tabellini G (2003) The economic effects of constitutions. The MIT Press, Cambridge, Massachusetts
Riker WH (1984) The heresthetics of constitution-making: the presidency in 1787, with comments on determinism and rational choice. Am Polit Sci Rev 78(1):1–16

Russell B (1962 [1938]) Power: a new social analysis, Allen & Unwin, London
Scheinkman JA (2008) Social interactions (theory). In: Durlauf SN, Blume LE (eds) The new palgrave dictionary of economics online. Palgrave Macmillan, UK
Simon H (1957) Models of man, social and rational. Wiley, New York
Voigt S (2011) Positive constitutional economicsII—a survey of recent developments. Public Choice 146:205–256
Weber M (1964 [1922]) The theory of social and economic organization, Oxford University Press, New York

Part II
Case Studies

Chapter 5
Uncertainty and the General Interest in the American Constitution: Testing the "Veil of Ignorance" Hypothesis in Constitutional Choice

Cristine de Clercy

Our Constitution is in actual operation;
everything appears to promise that it will last;
but nothing in this world is certain but death and taxes.
Benjamin Franklin, 1789

1 Introduction

Uncertainty permeates politics, and it shapes outcomes in important ways. Despite this central role, it is often viewed by social scientists as an unsolvable mystery, or else relegated to the analytical margin by being treated simply as an "error term" in quantitative models (Cioffi-Revilla 1998: xiii). Political economy was the first field to recognize the significance of uncertainty, and several early works established the theoretical foundations for exploring the role of uncertainty within a variety of political contexts. Among these works lies Buchanan and Tullock's (1962) study of *The Calculus of Consent* which focused attention on the idea that constitutional choices are made under conditions of uncertainty. This inevitably and predictably affects the outcome of efforts to draft constitutions, they argued, because it is uncertainty about the future that leads constitutional architects to establish rules serving the general interest, rather than their own self-interest.

This insight suggests constitutional laws are different from other sorts of law, owing to the "veil of ignorance" imposed by uncertainty. In the 51 years since the publication of Buchanan and Tullock's treatment, analysts have explored this proposition albeit to a limited extent (see for examples Mueller 2003: 641–642; McGuire 1988). In new research, Louis Imbeau and Steve Jacob probe the role of uncertainty in constitutional design by focusing on two broad questions: which

C. de Clercy (✉)
Department of Political Science, The University of Western Ontario, London, Canada
e-mail: c.declercy@uwo.ca

L.M. Imbeau and S. Jacob (eds.), *Behind a Veil of Ignorance?*,
Studies in Public Choice 32, DOI 10.1007/978-3-319-14953-0_5

national constitutions belong to the constitutional level of decision-making and which do not; and what explains the variation (Imbeau 2009a; Imbeau and Jacob 2011, 2015)?

This chapter follows their approach and investigates the role of uncertainty with respect to the creation of the United States Constitution. This chapter complements the others in this collection owing to its use of a common positive approach and identical methodological strategy. So, it helps us within a comparative context to pursue answers to Imbeau and Jacob's two questions. At the same time, the American case is unique in a few interesting respects. First, *The Calculus of Consent* clearly is marked by the origins of its authors. Buchanan and Tullock were born and educated in the USA, and taught at American universities (McFadden 2013; Tullock 2013). In the introduction, they credit the body of work by American academic luminaries Kenneth Arrow, Duncan Black, Robert A. Dahl, Charles E. Lindblom and Anthony Downs for its "direct relevance to both the methodology and the subject matter under consideration in this book" (1962, 8). Their analysis presents an abstracted model of political organization, yet their understanding was shaped by the particular influence of American political economy.

Second, although much of the content of the *Calculus of Consent* discusses political institutions and dynamics at the abstract, theoretical level there are persistent references to the early American constitutional context. For example, in the second chapter, Buchanan and Tullock consider what sort of individuals would inhabit their model society. They answer, perhaps facetiously, that "A nation of small freeholders, perhaps roughly similar to the United States of 1787", would fit their model well (14). Also, chapter three considers "Politics and the Economic Nexus", and it starts with two quotes. In the first, Gunning Bedford of Delaware warns the founding constitutional convention of 1787: "I do not, gentleman, trust you". The second quote is from Thomas Jefferson, and it holds that "free government is founded in jealously and not in confidence" (Buchanan and Tullock, 17). So, this chapter represents a unique test of Buchanan and Tullock's thesis precisely because the US Constitution serves as one key referent for their model.

Examining the "veil of ignorance" hypothesis with respect to the US Constitution is interesting in a third way. As Robert McGuire notes, several early analysts suggested self-interested behaviour played a large role in constitutional construction (McGuire 1988: 485). Then, esteemed historian Charles A. Beard published *An Economic Interpretation of the Constitution* in 1913, synthesizing some of these views and arguing the second founding reflected the effort of an economic elite seeking to preserve its property and interests. Beard's thesis was the predominant view until the 1950s, when new interpretations challenged it (1988: 485). Buchanan and Tullock address the Beard thesis early on, ostensibly to preclude the possibility of a serious misinterpretation of their work (1962: 27). They distinguish their "individualist-economic" approach from Beard's "class approach", dismissing the latter as essentially Marxist (1962: 26). So along with its comparative utility, this chapter contributes to a long standing debate focused directly on the role of economic self-interest within the US Constitution. To sum up, this chapter stands out among its companions in this collection because in overt and subtle ways *The Calculus of Consent* is a distinctly American text.

Relying on Imbeau and Jacob's theoretical approach, core propositions and coding framework, this examination tests whether support for their central hypotheses exists by systematically extracting the power relations embedded in the American constitution as discourse, and communicating empirical findings concerning their presence and direction. The next section introduces the case by reviewing the founding of the American colonies and their move to declare independence from Great Britain. The context of the first constitution is discussed. Then, key events leading to the 1787 constitutional convention in Philadelphia are surveyed, along with a brief description of the ratification process. Finally, the position and interests of the Framers and the ratifying delegates are noted. Then, Sect. 3 reviews the main assumptions supporting this study and summarizes the results of the content analysis of the constitutional document. The results of this analysis support Imbeau and Jacob's main hypothesis: the US Constitution clearly reflects the general interest more than the drafters' private interests. So, Buchanan and Tullock's propositions are confirmed in the American case: uncertainty is an important guarantor of the general interest. These results are discussed, then, in light of the overarching hypotheses in the final part of this chapter.

2 Historical Context of the Drafting and Adoption of the US Constitution

As suggested above, explaining the formation of the United States Constitution has been a controversial subject among historians and political scientists (McGuire 1988: 485). Analysts have employed a variety of perspectives and focused on several discrete factors and pressures towards explaining the document's scope, provisions and success (e.g. Beard 1941; Riker 1984; McGuire 1988; Alexander 1990; Ceaser 2011). What is common among most treatments, however, is agreement that the 1787 founding occurred in a context marked by deep uncertainty both domestically and internationally. David J. Siemers reminds us that a necessary step in understanding the dynamics of the founding is to "recapture the uncertainty and fear that so animated action and advocacy during this time" (Siemers 2002: 1).

The USA began as thirteen separate British colonies located along the Atlantic seacoast, and all of these exercised a considerable level of self government. Until the 1760s, the British loosely ruled the colonies and dealt with each colony individually as the need arose (Katz 2006: 298). However, Britain developed a distinct colonial policy and began treating the American colonies as a group rather than as separate governments. As well, at this time, the British government was seeking new revenue sources, and it reasoned that its North American colonies were paying relatively little in taxation while receiving many expensive benefits, such as Britain's help with defending the colonies during the French and Indian Wars of 1754–1763. So, in the 1760s, the British government sought to impose new, but modest, taxes on the colonists such as the *Sugar Act* of 1764, which affected trade and commerce generally in the colonies. As well, these new revenue measures particularly affected businesspeople located in New England and the South (Lowi et al. 2006: 39–40).

Before 1763, the colonies paid duties on trade to London, and the colonists considered these payments as measures to regulate commerce rather than as taxation measures. However, new taxes such as the *Sugar Act* outraged the inhabitants of the thirteen colonies, who argued that as English citizens they could be taxed only by their elected representatives and not directly by the British Parliament (Tannahill 2008: 37). In part, this view reflected the substantial level of self-rule the colonies enjoyed. Each of the original thirteen colonies had legislatures with at least one house elected by the colonists (Katz 2007: 3).[1] Connecticut and Rhode Island had governors chosen in the colony and the ability to legislate free of royal veto. For the other colonies, their great distance from Britain meant any legislation sent overseas for approval could take many months before it was approved or vetoed. A larger portion of the populace was enfranchised in the colonies than in Britain at the time, and the class system in the New World was marked by an absence of upper nobility alongside the presence of much upward mobility. These factors, along with the youth and rapid growth of the colonies, were important elements in the American challenge to British rule that was initiated with the iconic slogan "no taxation without representation".

Northern merchants and southern planters organized opposition to the new taxes, and other groups such as shopkeepers, farmers and labourers were pressed to join this movement. Tensions rose and a violent confrontation between British soldiers and the colonists on the night of 5 March 1770 produced the Boston Massacre. The troops opened fire, killing five and wounding eight people in front of a Boston customs house. This event fuelled anti-British sentiment in the colonies, and some radical leaders such as Samuel Adams advocated for an end to British rule (Lowi et al. 2006: 40–41).

Three years later, a set of events occurred that produced widespread support for colonial self-rule. In 1773, Samuel Adams and his followers dumped tea owned by the East India Company into Boston Harbour. The point of this act was to signal the colonies' displeasure with the new tea monopoly that the British had given the East India Company. Radicals hoped the Boston Tea Party would cause the British government to react with harsh reprisals, which it did (Jensen 1966: 48–49). These repressive measures helped to broaden public support for independence in the colonies, and in 1774, the First Continental Congress was convened. This assembly represented all the colonies and called for a total boycott of British goods. On 2 July 1776, the Congress voted to "dissolve the connection" with Great Britain (McCullough 2005: 135).

[1] Katz notes, as in England, the colonial electorate at this time was limited to men of substance which generally meant men who owned property. In the American colonies, however, at least 25 % and probably closer to 50 % of adult males could vote, while it is estimated only about 10 % of adult men in Britain could vote.

The *Declaration of Independence* was created in 1776 and adopted by the Second Continental Congress the same year. This document's purpose was to articulate common grievances and to identify a set of principles with which to bind the colonies together. Also, it famously asserted that certain rights, including life, liberty and the pursuit of happiness, could not be abridged by governments. The document declared

> these United States are, and of Right ought to be FREE AND INDEPENDENT STATES; that they are Absolved from all Allegiance to the British Crown, and that all political connection between them and the State of Great Britain is and ought to be totally dissolved, and that as Free and Independent States, they have full Power to levy War, conclude Peace, Contract Alliances, Establish Commerce, and to do all other Act and Things which Independent States may of right do (Government of the United States 2012c).

As a result of these events, a wave of émigrés left the colonies. Many of these people were elites who lost economic and political privileges as a result of the American Revolution; others simply were loyal to the British crown or suspicious of the post-revolutionary experiments with radical forms of government (Lowi et al. 2006: 44). Known as the United Empire Loyalists in Canada, and Tories in the former southern colonies, some forty thousand people emigrated to the northern British settlements that later became Canada (Bourinot 1901: 13).

In the wake of declaring independence from Britain, the new republican colonies then set about creating an overarching governing structure. The United States' first written constitution, the *Articles of Confederation and Perpetual Union,* was adopted in 1777. Concerned to ensure the states retained more power than the central government, this first constitution provided for a largely powerless Congress. The central government had no authority to deal with internal affairs, and its powers were largely confined to areas of common external interest, such as diplomacy, war and common defence. As each state retained its sovereignty, power and independence, this arrangement properly was a confederation, rather than a federation. It was sufficient to direct the War of Independence, but it was unable to meet the challenges of the post-war period. In time, this constitution's problems and limitations were realized, and this set the stage for the second founding of the republic.

There were four particularly pressing problems with the original constitution. First, trade among the states was difficult. Congress could not prevent one state from discriminating against another state through protectionist legislation. As well, each state issued its own currency. Second, some of the states suffered political and economic instability. Members of the elite classes worried that property and economic development were vulnerable to such instability, and also that personal liberty was endangered. These two sorts of problems contributed to a significant level of domestic uncertainty.

Two additional problems with the original constitution reflected international concerns. Britain and Spain maintained interests in North America and so the USA could not discount future military threats on its soil. American leaders were unsure that the first constitution's defence provisions were adequate to the challenge of mounting a colonial defence against foreign invasion. (Indeed, tensions between the colonists and Britain continued to be considerable after the War of Independence ended in 1783.)

Another problem was located in the attitude of foreign governments to the new USA during its progress towards independence. Many foreign governments were suspicious of its weak confederal government, and so the USA encountered difficulty in securing loans and enforcing treaties (Katz 2006: 299). Foreign scepticism concerning the durability of the United States' constitution was further exacerbated by the sentiment that social, political and economic conditions in the new world generally were difficult soil in which to sow prosperity. James W. Ceaser points out that many leading European historians of the time believed the new world inherently was prone to degeneration, and so the events of the 1780s were considered to herald a decline in the quality of the government rather than an improvement (Ceaser 2011: 70). The "degeneration thesis" contributed to foreign uncertainty about whether the American experiment would end well.

In addition to uncertainty emanating from the first constitution's context and weaknesses, there was uncertainty extant in the environment preceding the Philadelphia convention. Economic times were difficult, extraordinary inflation had begun as paper money flooded into the country, and there was a sense of general malaise. The difficult economic conditions bankrupted many small farmers, and so helped to spur Shay's Rebellion in 1786–1787, which fed fears among the wealthy that anarchy soon might come to pass (King 2012: 34).

The environment of economic insecurity was documented extensively in the newspapers of the era. In his careful study of news media coverage of the constitutional convention, John K. Alexander confirms that the media generally presented "a bleak view of conditions in America" in the months preceding the Philadelphia assembly. He notes that

> Well before Congress authorized the convention, writings bemoaning the hard times confronting American had become a staple press offering. The economic news published in February [of 1787] seemed bleak. A southerner voiced common complaints when he depicted the times as gloomy and lamented that the South's commerce stood on a precarious footing. Northward, things seemed just as bad. A New Yorker grumbled that commercial affairs remained in an embarrassing situation. Shipbuilding has ceased in New York, and most sailors could not get berths. When they did, it was on foreign vessels.... Both accounts, which circulated widely after Congress authorized the convention, reflected the serious complaints about the economy regularly seen in print during the postwar economic downturn (Alexander 1990: 17).

2.1 Philadelphia

In May 1787, delegates from twelve of the thirteen states met in Philadelphia. Twelve states were represented: Connecticut; Delaware; Georgia; Maryland; Massachusetts; New Hampshire; New Jersey; New York; North Carolina; Pennsylvania; South Carolina; and Virginia. Suspicious of the meeting, the leadership of Rhode Island did not send delegates to the convention. In total, 74 delegates were named, 55 attended sessions and 36 delegates signed the final document.

Originally, the meeting was called to try to propose amendments towards remedying some of the apparent flaws in the first constitution. Quickly, however, the effort became one of creating a new constitution to support a new national governmental structure. There were several issues that challenged the delegates' efforts, such as how to ensure small and large states were fairly represented, how to reconcile the interests of the southern states where slavery existed with the northern-free states, and how to reconcile those favouring strong states' rights with the proponents of a more powerful centralized government. The solution to all of these conflicts ultimately was the invention of modern federalism, an entirely new governmental system that was neither unitary nor confederal.

The new model closely reflected the original confederal arrangement in that the power to rule was delegated from the states to the central government, and all powers that were not specifically assigned to the central government were retained by the states. At the same time, a key innovation was the protection of the central government's powers within a constitution that could not be changed without the consent of central representative institutions. The new constitution created a federal system where powers were divided among the states and the central government, and each was sovereign within its own sphere of jurisdiction. As well, to ensure the national government's capacity was effectively limited to prevent it from exceeding its authority, the Framers of the American constitution created three separate and distinct branches of government, divided power between the executive (the President) and the legislature and, within Congress, between the House of Representatives and the Senate (Katz 2006: 299–300).

The separation of powers and the decentralized basis of the new constitution were created expressly to guard against the possibility of unjust rule by a group in power. James Madison, more than any other individual, gave this constitution its basic structure and he summarized its core philosophy in this paragraph:

> It may be a reflection on human nature, that such devices should be necessary to control the abuses of government. But what is government itself, but the greatest of all reflections of human nature? If men were angels, no government would be necessary. If angels were to govern men, neither external nor internal controls on government would be necessary. In framing a government which is to be administered by men over men, the great difficulty lies in this: you must first enable the government to control the governed; and in the next place oblige it to control itself. A dependence on the people is, no doubt, the primary control on the government; but experience has taught mankind the necessity of auxiliary cautions (Dawson 1966: 360).

The final vote on the draft document took place on 25 September 1787. Privately assessing the constitution's chances for ratification, Alexander Hamilton wrote

> The new Constitution has in favor of its success these circumstances: A very great weight of influence of the persons who framed it, particularly in the universal popularity of General Washington. The good-will of the commercial interest throughout the States, which will give all its efforts to the establishment of a government capable of regulating, protecting, and extending the commerce of the Union. The good-will of most men of property in the several States, who wish a government of the Union able to protect them against domestic violence, and the depredations which the democratic spirit is apt to make on property, and who are besides anxious for the respectability of the nation.

> The hopes of the creditors of the United States, that a general government possessing the means of doing it, will pay the debt of the Union. A strong belief in the people at large of the insufficiency of the present Confederation to preserve the existence of the Union, and of the necessity of the Union to their safety and prosperity; of course, a strong desire of a change, and a predisposition to receive well the propositions of the convention.
>
> Against its success is to be put the dissent of two of three important men in the convention, who will think their characters pledged to defeat the plan; the influence of many *inconsiderable* men in possession of considerable offices under the State governments, who will fear a diminution of their consequence, power, and emolument, by the establishment of the general government, and who can hope for nothing there; the influence of some *considerable* men in office, possessed of talents and popularity, who, partly from the same motives, and partly from a desire of *playing a part* in a convulsion for their own aggrandizement, will oppose the quiet adoption of the new government (some considerable men out of office, from motives of ambition, may be disposed to act the same part). Add to these causes the disinclination of the people to taxes, and of course to a strong government; the opposition of all men much in debt, who will not wish to see a government established, one object of which is to restrain the means of cheating creditors; the democratical jealousy of the people, which may be alarmed at the appearance of institutions that may seem calculated to place the power of the community in few hands, and to raise a few individuals to stations of great pre-eminence; and the influence of some foreign powers, who, from different motives, will not wish to see an energetic government established throughout the States (Hamilton 1904, emphasis in original).

Hamilton concluded in view of the divisions over the document, it was difficult to form any judgment as to whether the new constitution would be ratified in the state houses.

2.2 *Ratification*

Indeed, the campaign to ratify the new constitution in each of the thirteen states was marked by a fierce debate between two main sides. The Federalists supported the constitution and preferred a strong national government, while the Anti-Federalists opposed the document and preferred a more decentralized system of government. In New York, the new constitution was besieged in the press by a series of essays signed "Cato". Beginning in October 1787, a series of anonymous pamphlets signed "From the Federal Farmer to the Republican" focused on some potential flaws in the document and worked to mobilize sentiment against ratification (Bennett 1978: xxxv). The *Letters from the Federal Farmer to the Republican* were part of an effort to secure amendments to the new constitution. Alexander Hamilton and James Madison, in response, were the main contributors to a series of essays which became known as the *Federalist Papers.* Ultimately, Madison came around in support of a series of amendments to the constitution in part because these would defuse the Anti-Federalists' objections (Government of the United States of America 2012b).

Pennsylvania was the first state to call a ratifying convention, and four of the smaller states (Delaware, New Jersey, Georgia and Connecticut) promptly ratified the constitution. In other states, the margin of victory was very slim. As indicated

Table 1 Ratification dates and vote totals

State	Ratification date	Vote: yes	Vote: no
Delaware	December 7, 1787	Unanimous	
Pennsylvania	December 12, 1787	46	23
New Jersey	December 18, 1787	Unanimous	
Georgia	January 2, 1788	Unanimous	
Connecticut	January 9, 1788	128	40
Massachusetts	February 6, 1788	187	168
Maryland	April 26, 1788	63	11
South Carolina	May 23, 1788	149	73
New Hampshire	June 21, 1788	57	47
Virginia	June 25, 1788	89	79
New York	July 26, 1788	30	27
North Carolina	November 21, 1789	195	77
Rhode Island	May 29, 1790	34	32

Source Padover (1969: 38)

in Table 1, Virginia favoured ratification by a margin of ten votes, while in New York, the constitution squeezed through by a mere three votes. By 21 June 1788, when New Hampshire ratified the document, the new constitution had the support of the required nine states and so it went into effect. Padover (1969: 37) notes that opposition was so great in North Carolina and Rhode Island that the document was not ratified until the federal government was already set up.

Overall, the Federalist vision won the debate, and the constitution enacted in 1789 created a stable governmental system that has endured for more than 200 years. The new model of federalism shaped in Philadelphia sought to create a powerful national government while at the same time preserving the liberty of the states (Elazar 1988: 128–129). The American experiment was of interest to many people in other countries then and later, and the federal principle of divided power was imitated in many other nations. To underscore the main theme of the above discussion, the new constitution was created in a context of significant socio-economic uncertainty. And once the draft document was finalized and then disseminated across the colonies for consideration, for a long time, it was not at all clear that its supporters outnumbered its opponents.

2.3 The Drafters and the Adopters: Motivation and Interests

The success of the second founding owed in no small part to the effort and capacity of the Framers. Among the assembled delegates to Philadelphia were some of the best minds of the time. George Washington, for example, served as the president of the convention. Its deliberations were informed by Benjamin Franklin,

Alexander Hamilton and James Madison. Among the delegates were men with wide experience in business and government. Half of them were lawyers or government officials trained in law. Some were governors, and more than two-thirds had served in the Continental Congress. Many were scholars; half were college graduates. The average age was 42 years. The oldest delegate at 81 years was Benjamin Franklin while the youngest, at 27 years, was Jonathan Dayton. Their viewpoints ranged from the "tough conservatism" of Alexander Hamilton who favoured aristocratic government to James Wilson who championed democracy. Above all, most of them shared "the great eighteenth century belief in reason and regard for the individual" (Padover 1969: 16).

Many analysts have argued that the constitutional document was a truly significant achievement that created an efficient system of government founded upon grand overarching principles such as justice and tolerance. As Saul Padover notes, "The aim of the delegates was the construction of a political framework that would both protect property against revolutionary expropriation and secure liberty from a potentially tyrannical government. What they wanted, in other words, was a government that would have power, but not exercise it capriciously or cruelly (1969: 15–16)". Similarly, writing about John Jay's perspective on the constitution, Andrew C. Lenner suggests

> Jay clearly believed that the Constitution of the United States was more than a collection of individual wills expressed in positive law. It was more than a device for securing individual rights against the authority of a central government. It was more than a pact to be dissolved at the discretion of the contracting parties. For Jay the Constitution was an embodiment of moral and philosophical principles that had long been esteemed and revered- of laws in existence long before 1787... The Constitution, in short, was grounded upon universal, self-evident propositions – the principles of natural law, and the law of nations – and could only be understood in light of those propositions (2001: 4).

Interestingly, at the same time, there is no shortage of accounts arguing the architects of the Constitution were motivated by concealed goals and riven with self-interest. Rhode Island's leaders refused to send delegates in part because they suspected the Philadelphia convention was a conspiracy to overthrow the established government. Patrick Henry refused to attend the convention because he "smelt a rat". He correctly suspected that Madison's goal was to subvert the authority of the state legislatures and build a powerful central government (Government of the United States of America 2012b). Although several of the convention's memberships were towering figures, others were less impressive. James Wilson would, later in life, be forced to flee his home to avoid prosecution for indebtedness, and a fair number of the delegates (including Benjamin Franklin) personally held securities in the public debt of the government. Several of the delegates were then or later engaged in land speculation schemes, some of them quite impressive in terms of their total valuation (Beard 1941: 150–151). As mentioned briefly in the introduction to this chapter, Charles Beard's thesis proposes that support for the constitution on the part of the delegates to Philadelphia may be explained by referring to the economic advantage they expected from their actions (Beard 1941). Beard's thesis has been debated and studied since he first proposed it, and examining whether the content of the constitution reflects the general interest, as per the "veil of ignorance" thesis, or the Framers' private interest is the task of the next section.

3 The Constitution's Content from a Power Relation Framework Perspective

To test the "veil of ignorance" hypothesis with respect to the US Constitution, this study follows Imbeau's "walk-talk" perspective which considers a constitutional document as a discourse, rather than a contract or legal document (Imbeau 2009a, b; Imbeau and Jacob 2015). So, the focus is on the text's literal content. Accessing the original text document from the National Archives' collection, the US Constitution has seven main articles and twenty-four sections in total (Government of the United States 2012a). It contains 4,609 words, excluding its title and including the names of the original signatories. In addition to this, the Constitution has been amended 27 times; the first ten amendments are known as the Bill of Rights. Including the amendments, there are 7,858 words in the constitution. The document was unitized and coded according to the procedure outlined in Louis M. Imbeau and Steve Jacob's codebook for the "Veil of Ignorance Project" by two research assistants under the supervision of these authors in the summer of 2011 (Imbeau and Jacob 2015).

The unit of analysis is the "power relation", which grants, or denies, capacity to an agent. The textual analysis identified and coded the source, type and direction of the power relation. Three specific *sources* of power then were coded: authority; knowledge and wealth. Each of these resources is associated with a method: authority with threat and coercion; wealth with exchange; and knowledge with persuasion (Imbeau and Jacob 2015: 63). As well, two *types* of power are distinguished: instrumental power or "power to"; and social power or "power over" (Imbeau 2009a: 7). Finally, the *direction* of the power relation was examined and coded positive if the agent had the capacity to do something, and negative if the agent was denied such capacity. In all cases, units were coded as indeterminate if there was not enough information in the text to assign a precise coding (Imbeau and Jacob 2015).

The results of this analysis of the content of the US Constitution revealed 445 power relations. This is to say there are 445 cases where a clear relationship exists between two agents, or between an agent and an object. As Table 2 suggests, 85.4 % of these relations, or 380 in total, are rooted in Authority as the source of power.

The text identifies a variety of agents and ascribes capacities to each. Many of these agents are predictable entities. The congress and the president, for example, are granted a variety of powers and capacities as one expects. As well, other collective agents such as the states, or the people of the USA, are empowered in

Table 2 Source of power

		Score	Percentage	Percentage valid	Cumulative percentage
Valid	Authority	380	85.4	85.4	85.4
	Wealth	9	2.0	2.0	87.4
	Knowledge	27	6.1	6.1	93.5
	Indeterminate	29	6.5	6.5	100.0
	Total	445	100.0	100.0	

specific ways. Interestingly, the US constitution recognizes the militia as an agent and grants it several capacities, such as the ability to execute the laws of the union, suppress insurrection and repel invasions (Article 1, s.8). Most of the agents in the constitution are formal groups or office-holders, such as conventions of delegates or the vice-president. Only rarely are private individuals recognized and empowered in the document. Probably reflecting trenchant shipping problems that preceded the constitutional convention, vessels (ships) are granted certain capacities within the constitution such as the ability to enter and clear state jurisdiction (Article 1, s.9).

Given the longstanding debate over the role of economic self-interest in constitutional creation as discussed above, it is somewhat surprising that a mere nine instances of all the revealed power relations, or two per cent of the total, concern those where wealth is a source of power. Of this small group, several specified measures address the ability of institutions such as Congress to assume debt, or repay it as per Article 1, s.8. So, very few of the power relations revealed concerned wealth as a source of power or empowered private actors.

Examining the sorts of constitutional capacities located within the document, it is clear that there is a fairly even division between sections that allocate capacity to act over events or things (instrumental power), and those sections allocating capacity to act over other agents (social power). This finding suggests the Framers paid fairly equal attention to empowering agents to act on things and events, as well as people, as per Table 3.

In view of these clear positive capacities, one may well then ask what sorts of capacities, if any, does the text take from these agents? In other words, what sorts of actions or behaviours are agents restricted from accomplishing? The content analysis reveals there are surprisingly few restrictions in the American constitution. One sort of restriction occurs in Article 1, s.6 which prevents

Table 3 Power relations in the American constitution by type

	Frequency	Percentage
Social power	226	50.8
Instrumental power	219	49.2
Total	445	100

sitting senators and representatives from being appointed to any civil office, and reciprocally restricts anyone holding an office from sitting in the Congress. Other restrictions such as those contained in Article 1, s.10 forbid the subnational governments from a class of actions contradictory to the general purpose of union, such as entering into treaties, coining money, keeping troops during peacetime, engaging in war or passing laws impairing contractual obligations. Another set of restrictions occur in Amendments 24 and 26. These serve mainly to ensure governments cannot deny citizens' right to vote on grounds such as failing to pay taxes or being older than 18 years of age. As Table 4 suggests, most of the capacities articulated in the constitution, in sum, are positive ones while only about ten per cent of all the power relations are negative, or restrictive, ones.

Tables 5, 6 and 7 present cross-tabulations of the frequency distributions of the key variables. The patterns here, however, are largely predictable owing in part to the large portion of all the scores accounted for by the "Authority" and "Positive" variables. This is to say that owing to the large scores recorded in the "Authority" and "Positive" cells, and the crosstabs reveal few unexpected relationships among the variables.

Table 4 Power relations in the American constitution by direction

	Frequency	Percentage
Positive	402	90.3
Negative	43	9.7
Total	445	100

Table 5 Power relations in the American constitution by source and type (frequency distributions)

Source of power	Type of power	
	Social	Instrumental
Authority	192	188
Wealth	4	5
Knowledge	20	7
Indeterminate	10	19
Total	226	219

Table 6 Power relations in the American constitution by source and direction (frequency distributions)

Source of power	Direction	
	Positive	Negative
Authority	341	39
Wealth	7	2
Knowledge	26	1
Indeterminate	28	1
Total	402	43

4 Discussion

So, in light of the empirical results reported above, does the US Constitution accord with the "veil of ignorance" model? Imbeau and Jacobs' (2011: 10) first hypothesis proposes that because "there is less uncertainty in preceptoral power than in economic power and less in economic power than in political power", it follows that constitutional documents should be more concerned with political power than economic or preceptoral power. The US constitution clearly is concerned with political authority, as Table 2 suggests. Most of the power relations extracted here are based upon "Authority", or political power. So, the first hypothesis is supported. The Framers seemed to labour under a deeply "opaque veil of uncertainty", as Imbeau and Jacob wrote in their chapter.

In contrast, Imbeau and Jacob's second main hypothesis—that by adopting the preference of the less privileged individual in the distribution of power, constitutional drafters tend to limit power rather than ascribe it—is not supported here (Imbeau and Jacob 2011: 10). As Table 4 depicts, over 90 % of the 445 power relations identified in the US constitution were positive ones, or statements that grant power rather than restrain it. Interestingly, the results reported here align with some of the other findings reported in this volume. For example, concerning the German constitution's discourse, Agnes Strauss reports in this volume that a mere 31 relations of the 1,081 in total were negative ones, or 1.9 %. These results challenge Imbeau and Jacob's position that constitutional drafters labouring under deep uncertainty will be more concerned with denying capacities than with ascribing them.

Finally, Imbeau posits that the more opaque is the veil of ignorance in a constitution-making process, the more constitutional drafters will be concerned to allocate power over persons, rather than power over events or things. In contrast, this study finds, as per Table 3, that the power relations in the American constitution are fairly evenly allocated among the instrumental and social power categories. This finding suggests the Framers were as concerned with the capacity of agents

Table 7 Power relations in the American constitution by direction, source and type (frequency distributions)

Direction	Source of power	Type of power	
		Social	Instrumental
Positive	Authority	169	172
	Wealth	4	3
	Knowledge	20	6
	Indeterminate	9	19
	Total	202	200
Negative	Authority	23	16
	Wealth	0	2
	Knowledge	0	1
	Indeterminate	1	0
	Total	24	19

to act on things and events, as they were with the capacity of agents to act over other people. So, these results suggest the Framers of the US Constitution were moderately uncertain, rather than extremely uncertain.

5 Conclusion

In considering the results of this test of the veil of ignorance thesis, it is worth pondering the deep uncertainty that pervaded the second founding. Troublesome events preceded, coincided with and followed the 1787 constitutional convention, such as revolution, war, massive inflation, economic malaise, fraught international relations, the radicalization of politics and the Loyalist outmigration. One expects such ongoing and widespread uncertainty must have deeply influenced the Framers' calculus, as Burden observes, because the environment inevitably affects agents:

> Although in theory an actor could be uncertain about its own behavior or about something external such as an event or condition, being unsure about the latter usually heightens uncertainty in the former. Not knowing what the world will be like when a decision is made, what the consequences of the decision will be, or perhaps even what alternatives will be available at the time all induces uncertainty about one's own intentions (Burden 2003: 9).

As well, it is helpful to appreciate that to secure their goals and preserve liberty while ensuring unity, the Framers created an entirely new system of government. And, as the words of Benjamin Franklin located at the beginning of this chapter suggest, the success of the new system remained in questions for several years after the second founding. So, the American case surely constitutes a "best case" scenario so far as aiming to probe the constitution-making process under conditions of deep and extensive uncertainty.

This analysis has been located within Imbeau and Jacob's social contract approach which seeks to explore James Buchanan and Gordon Tullock's proposition that uncertainty about the future guides constitutional architects to labour on behalf of the general interest, rather than to serve their self-interest. The results of this study of embedded power relations within the US Constitution support the core hypothesis: the American constitution reflects the general interest more than the constitution drafters' private interests. Uncertainty clearly appears to be an important guarantor of the general interest, and these findings interestingly are in line with Madison's 1787 observation: "[it is] my profound & solemn conviction, derived from my intimate opportunity of observing and appreciating the views of the Convention, collectively and individually, that there never was an assembly of men, charged with a great & arduous trust, who were more pure in their motives…" (Madison 1966: 19). Along with the others in this volume, the US case makes a new and substantial contribution to the constitutional political economy literature generally, and particularly those studies focusing on how uncertainty shapes social choice.

References

Alexander JK (1990) The selling of the constitutional convention: a history of news coverage. Madison House, Madison
Beard CA (1941) Economic Interpretation of the constitution of the United States. The Free Press, New York
Bennett WH (ed) (1978) Letters from the federal farmer to the Republican. The University of Alabama Press, Tuscaloosa
Bourinot JG (1901) A manual of the constitutional history of Canada. Copp, Clark Company, Toronto
Buchanan J, Tullock G (1962) The calculus of consent: logical foundations of constitutional democracy. University of Michigan Press, Ann Arbor
Burden BC (2003) Everything but death and taxes. In: Burden BC (ed) Uncertainty in American politics. Cambridge University Press, New York, pp 3–23
Ceaser JW (2011) Designing a polity: America's constitution in theory and practice. Rowman and Littlefield, Lanham
Cioffi-Revilla C (1998) Politics and uncertainty: theory, models and applications. Cambridge University Press, New York
Dawson HB (1966) The federalist. Charles Scribner's Sons, New York
Elazar DJ (1988) The American constitutional tradition. University of Nebraska Press, Lincoln
Government of the United States of America (2012a) The U.S. National Archives and Records Administration. The charters of freedom: constitution of the United States. Accessed online at http://www.archives.gov/exhibits/charters/constitution_transcript.html
Government of the United States of America (2012b) The U.S. National Archives and Records Administration. A more perfect union: the creation of the U.S. Constitution. Accessed online at http://www.archives.gov/exhibits/charters/constitution_history.html
Government of the United States of America (2012c) The U.S. National Archives and Records Administration. Declaration of independence. Accessed online at http://www.archives.gov/exhibits/charters/declaration_transcript.html
Hamilton A (1904) Impressions as to the new constitution. In: Lodge HC (ed) The works of Alexander Hamilton, vol 1. Liberty Fund Publications, Indianapolis. Accessed at http://oll.libertyfund.org/?option=comtaticxt&staticfile=show.php%3Ftitle=1378&chapter=64200&layout=html&Itemid=27
Imbeau LM (2009a) Testing the "veil of ignorance" hypothesis in constitutional choice: a "walk-talk" approach. J Public Choice Public Finan XXVI(1):3–21
Imbeau LM (ed) (2009b) Do they walk like they talk? Speech and action in policy processes. Springer, New York
Imbeau LM, Jacob S (2011) Is the "veil of ignorance" in constitutional choice a myth? An empirical exploration informed by a theory of power. In: Marciano A (ed) Constitutional mythologies: new perspectives on controlling the state. Studies in Public Choice 23. Springer, Berlin
Imbeau LM, Jacob S (2012) Codebook of the veil of ignorance project. Unpublished, accessed at http://www.fss.ulaval.ca/cms_recherche/upload/veil_ignorance/fichiers/codebook__jan_2012.pdf
Imbeau LM, Jacob S (2015) Measuring the opacity of the 'veil of ignorance' in constitutions: theory, method and some results. In: Imbeau LM, Jacob S (eds) Behind a veil of ignorance? Power and uncertainty in constitutional design. Springer, New York
Jensen M (1966) The articles of confederation. The University of Madison Press, Madison
Katz E (2006) United States of America. In: Akhtar M, Ronald LW, Douglas MB (eds) Distribution of powers and responsibilities in federal countries. McGill-Queen's University Press, Montreal
Katz RS (2007) Political institutions in the United States. Oxford University Press, New York
King A (2012) The founding fathers v. the People. Harvard University Press, Cambridge
Lenner AC (2001) The federal principle in American Politics 1790–1833. Rowman and Littlefield/Madison House, Lanham

Lowi T, Ginsberg B, Shepsle KA (2006) American government, 9th edn. WL Norton, New York
Madison J (1966) Notes of debates in the federal convention of 1787. Ohio University Press, Athens
McCullough D (2005) 1776. Simon & Schuster, New York
McFadden RD, Buchanan JM (2013) Economic scholar and nobel laureate, dies at 93. The New York Times, online edition. January 9th. At http://www.nytimes.com/2013/01/10/business/economy/james-m-buchanan-economic-scholar-dies-at-93.html?pagewanted=all&_r=0
McGuire RA (1988) Constitution making: a rational choice model of the federal convention of 1787. Am J Polit Sci 32(2):483–522
Mueller DC (2003) Public Choice III. Cambridge University Press, New York
Padover SK (1969) The living U.S. constitution. Meridian, New York
Riker W (1984) The heresthetics of constitution-making: the presidency in 1787, with comments on determinism and rational choice. Am Polit Sci Rev 78:1–16
Siemers DJ (2002) Ratifying the republic: antifederalists and federalists in constitutional time. Stanford University Press, Stanford
Tannahill N (2008) American government: policy and politics, 9th edn. Pearson Longman, New York
Tullock G (2013) Gordon Tullock: biographical sketch. George Mason University, School of Law home page. Available at http://www.law.gmu.edu/faculty/directory/emeritus/tullock_gordon

Chapter 6
Constitution-making Process Under Uncertainty: The Case of Canada

Louis M. Imbeau and Thomas C. Eboutou

1 Introduction

The Canadian Constitution was drafted and adopted at the end of the «rising tide of modern constitutionalism, 1776–1849» (Dippel 2013), a context of rich constitutional creativity in Europe and in the Americas. As Roger Congleton noted, "two political revolutions occurred gradually in northern Europe during the nineteenth and early twentieth centuries. First, political authority shifted from kings to parliaments. Second, parliaments became more broadly grounded in popular suffrage» (Congleton 2011: ix). The unification of the British North America colonies into the Dominion of Canada in 1867 participated in this movement. It marked the beginning of a process of increasing autonomy of Canada vis-à-vis the British monarch and the constitutionalization of the parliamentary institutions that still govern this country.

This constitutional effervescence stemmed from the uncertainties that characterized this epoch. Uncertainties concerning the outcome of a process of industrialization that seemed to be shaking the traditional social order; uncertainties about the viability of the political institutions that were emerging; uncertainties for the élites vis-à-vis their future position in this new political order. It comes to no surprise that the drafters of the new Canadian Constitution, as member of the local elite, expressed their uncertainties in the constitutional text itself.

In this chapter, we undertake to implement the Veil of Ignorance Project framework and procedure on the Canadian Constitution. However, for the whole exercise to further our knowledge of the making process of the Canadian Constitution, we need to bring together actual historical events as they are narrated by historians and the reconstituted story we got from analyzing power relations extracted

L.M. Imbeau (✉)
Université Laval, Quebec City, Canada
e-mail: Louis.Imbeau@pol.ulaval.ca

T.C. Eboutou
Université de Montréal, Montreal, Canada
e-mail: eboutouthomas.ancien@gmail.com

L.M. Imbeau and S. Jacob (eds.), *Behind a Veil of Ignorance?*,
Studies in Public Choice 32, DOI 10.1007/978-3-319-14953-0_6

from the constitutional texts. Accordingly, the structure of this chapter is as follows. In the first section, we cover the historical context of the drafting and adoption of the Canadian Constitution. In the second section, we analyze the Canadian Constitution in terms of power relations. A discussion section and a conclusion follow.

2 Historical Context of the Drafting and Adoption of the Canadian Constitution

The Canadian Constitution is an amalgamation of 41 texts: acts of the British Parliament until 1982 when Canada ceased to be formally under Britain's tutelage for modifying its constitution and acts of the federal parliament from 1982 on.[1] The current chapter would not suffice to present the story of the making of all these texts. In this section, we will therefore focus our attention on the British North America Act (BNAA) of 1867, later renamed the Constitution Act of 1867, which can be viewed as the output of the primal constitutional deal of the Canadian society. It established the Dominion of Canada that would evolve to become the Canada we know today, and it contained the base rules and principles that still dictate the functioning of Canadian institutions. Following a discussion on the making of the BNAA of 1867, we will discuss its evolution till the twenty-first century.

2.1 The Making of the British North America Act of 1867

2.1.1 The Context that Led to the Drafting and the Adoption of British North America Act of 1867

It is a particular economic and political context that brought up the issue of the making of the BNAA of 1867. The British North America colonies[2] up to the union had built their economy on foreign trade (McInnis and Horn 1982: 302). A series of changes in policy from their main trading partners, first the adoption of free trade by Britain in 1846 and later the denunciation of the Reciprocity Treaty in 1854 and the adoption of protectionist policy by the USA, encouraged the colonies seriously to consider the formation of a trade union among themselves (Francis et al. 2009: 487). A step toward that ambition was the building of physical links, notably railways, between the colonies and such task required that they put their resources together.

[1] A list is provided in Table 4.

[2] These colonies were the Province of Canada (Upper and Lower Canada, later renamed Ontario and Quebec), New Brunswick, Nova Scotia, Prince Edward Island, and Newfoundland.

The political context too provided a fertile ground to the idea of a union of British North America colonies. To begin with, there were security challenges faced by the colonies. First, there was the fear of an American annexation because of the British support, even though unofficial, of the south during the civil war (Waite 1997: 315). Second, the challenges posed by Fenians' military activities along the borders with the USA[3]: In April 1866, the Fenians attacked a customs house in New Brunswick and on June 2, 1866, they defeated the Canadian militia at Ridgeway (Francis et al. 2009: 489). These security challenges along with a decision of Britain to limit its military expenditures and establishments in its North America colonies suggested to the colonies the formation of a union to provide for their own defense.

In addition to the above-mentioned issues, there was the political situation in the Province of Canada. The assembly of the Province of Canada was fragmented by a religious/linguistic cleavage between catholic mostly French-speaking and protestant English-speaking populations. When the two original colonies (Upper Canada and Lower Canada) had been united into one province in 1840, the English-speaking population concentrated in Upper Canada was smaller than the French-speaking one concentrated in Lower Canada. By giving the two communities equal status in the assembly, it was hoped that, with the economic domination of English merchants and increased immigration from the British Isles, the French-speaking community would be assimilated within a couple of generations, as suggested by Lord Durham in his 1839 Report. By the mid-1850s, the English-speaking population of the Province of Canada had already surpassed in number the French-speaking population. English-speaking members of the assembly mostly thought that a new federal arrangement would be advantageous to them. French-speaking members were divided, but a majority of them thought that a federal structure would protect the future of their community by giving it its own institutions.

The assembly of the province was also highly fragmented in terms of its political families and that made it difficult for any of the two main parties of the province, the Reform and the Conservative party, to form a strong and stable coalition to run the government. Between 1861 and 1864, the Province of Canada had two elections and four different governments (Waite 1997: 316). An opportunity to the end this instability cycle appeared when Georges Brown, the Reform leader, unexpectedly accepted to enter MacDonald's Conservative cabinet under the condition that some of his demands be put among the priorities of the future coalition cabinet. Among other things, Brown wanted the coalition government to work on the transformation of the province from a legislative union to a federation of its two entities Canada West and Canada East because he perceived, like many of his contemporaries, that the provincial political difficulties had deep roots in the antagonism between the French-speaking community majorly peopling Canada East and

[3] Founded in 1857 by Irish settlers in the USA, the *Fenian Brotherhood* was a secret movement aimed at helping free Ireland from British rule. It was active both in Ireland and in North America in the second part of the nineteenth century.

the English-speaking essentially established in Canada West (Waite 1997: 314). Brown's proposition was accepted and even expanded: Some politicians, notably Alexander Galt, thought that the participation of Canada West and Canada East in a larger federation of all British North America colonies would be more advantageous and the coalition cabinet resolved to work further the idea of a union of British North America colonies.

2.1.2 The Drafting and the Adoption of the British North America Act

The BNAA which gave birth to the union of the British North America colonies was shaped by political leaders of the colonies, the Fathers of Confederation as they would later be called, during three constitutional conferences.

The first conference was held in September 1864 in Charlottetown, Prince Edward Island. Four British North America colonies participated: Nova Scotia and Prince Edward Island sent 6 delegates each, New Brunswick and Canada 5 and 8 delegates, respectively. The conference was originally intended to be a discussion about a Maritimes union (Nova Scotia, Prince Edward Island, and New Brunswick), but that topic was supplanted by discussions about the Canadian idea of a larger union of all the British North American colonies. The delegates at the Charlottetown Conference were quite convinced by the Canadian project (McInnis and Horn 1982: 347); however, nothing firm and concrete was really decided.

The second constitutional conference held in Quebec from October 10 to 27, 1864, was more determining in the drafting of the British North America Act. Indeed, the delegates at the Quebec Conference came up with a document of 72 resolutions known as the Seventy-two resolutions or the Quebec resolutions which is considered as the first real draft of the BNAA. Actually, the Canadian delegation came to the conference with a text it had elaborated in the interval of the two conferences (Francis et al. 2009: 479). Thus, the Quebec Conference was in fact a debate over that Canadian text.

Newfoundland who did not participate in the previous conference sent 2 observers at the Quebec Conference. In addition to those present in Charlottetown, Canada sent 4 more delegates—all the members of the provincial cabinet were sent—New Brunswick and Prince Edward Island sent, respectively, 3 and one more delegates. Nova Scotia resent the same delegation as in Charlottetown. In all the cases, members of the delegations were chosen from and by the legislative assembly of their respective province. Thus, all the delegates at the Quebec Conference were active politicians; however, before entering politics, most of them were journalists and the rest were either lawyers or businessmen.

Just like in Charlottetown, the Canadian delegation was particularly active during the conference: The recording secretary (Hewitt Bernard, senior civil servant of the Province of Canada) and the Chairman of the Conference (Sir Étienne-Paschal Taché, prime minister of the Province of Canada until his death in 1865) were Canadians; the Canadians were charged with setting up each day's agenda, and most of the resolutions were initiated by Canadian delegates (Whitelaw 1967: 10–11).

John A. Macdonald, the attorney general of the Province of Canada, who would later become the first prime minister of the union, is notable in that he initiated most of the resolutions.

As far as the debate is concerned, the most contentious points had to do with the distribution of Senate seats among provinces, the selection mechanism of senators and the financial or fiscal relations between the federal government and the provinces (Whitelaw 1967: 16–25; Francis et al. 2009: 479).

On the issue of the distribution of Senate seats among provinces, «the most heated and prolonged controversy» in the words of the historian Whitelaw (1967: 17), the principle of regional equality, was preferred to that of provincial equality advocated by delegates from small provinces. It was agreed that each of the three regions Ontario, Quebec (previously Canada West and Canada East, respectively), and the Maritimes would have 24 seats (New Brunswick and Nova Scotia 10 seats each, Prince Edward Island 4 seats).

With regard to the selection mechanism of senators, delegates from small provinces had the sentiment that the Canadian proposal, life appointment by the central government, would lead to appointments made on partisan bases (McInnis and Horn 1982: 348). The conference delegates finally agreed that the first senators would be chosen from existing legislative councils and appointed by their respective provincial government. The application of the principle of life appointment by the central government was not abandoned but was deferred.

A last important source of discordance at the Quebec Conference concerned the federal-provincial relations notably the financial or fiscal relations. The Canadian delegates, notably John A. Macdonald, favored a strong central government and the fiscal arrangement they proposed was consistent with that position. The central government was given important obligations (notably the administration of national defense, the completion of railways linking the colonies and the taking on of a portion of provincial debts), and this required that it controlled the main sources of revenues. Alexander Galt, a delegate from Canada who would later become the first minister of Finance of the federation, proposed that the provinces transfer some of their wealth to the federal government (their bank balances and their public properties) and that the federal government be given the right to collect indirect taxes notably custom and excises duties (which were among the most important source of revenues for the provinces) (Whitelaw 1967: 21). Under that scheme, the federal government would pay annual subsidies to the provinces according to the size of their population to compensate for their loss of revenues.

As one could imagine, the Galt's scheme was long discussed and not easily accepted by the Maritimes delegates. A new agreement was reached as some concessions were made. Under the new arrangement, it was proposed that New Brunswick retained its power to levy export duties on its most important export (timber) and received a special subsidy of 63,000 dollars annually for the next 10 years after the union to compensate the expenses it had already incurred before the union in building railways linking it to other provinces (Whitelaw 1967: 22). It was also proposed that Nova Scotia kept the power to levy duties on some of her minerals (coal notably) and that Newfoundland be paid an annual subsidy of

150,000 dollars for an undetermined period for surrendering its land and mineral rights (Whitelaw 1967: 22). At the end of the conference, when all the contentious points had been resolved, the final text, the Quebec resolutions, was signed by all the delegates.

The third and the last conference in the drafting process of the BNAA were held in December 1866. Delegates met in London to draft the text that would be introduced to the British Parliament for enactment. Newfoundland and Prince Edward Island did not take part in that conference, for their respective legislature had rejected the Quebec resolutions. Nova Scotia and New Brunswick participation was secured only after they had been assured by Canadians that the agreement settled in Quebec on the completion of railways linking the provinces would be included in the final text. Ultimately, 19 delegates attended: 7 from Canada, 6 from Nova Scotia, and 6 from New Brunswick.

Despite the wish of the Maritimes delegates (especially those from Nova Scotia) to see the powers of the central government reduced, the text that would finally be presented to the British officials departed little from the Quebec resolutions (McInnis and Horn 1982: 354). The term federation was changed to confederation, the annual subsidy to be received by the provinces was increased, and a provision was added making the right to establish separate schools applicable in all the provinces of the future union. After the integration of the aforementioned changes, a new text was produced, sometimes called the London resolutions, which would serve as the basis of the bill to be introduced to the British Parliament. The preparation of the bill itself was handed to professional draftsmen (assigned by the British government) under the supervision of a committee of delegates. The British Parliament ratified the bill without any amendments.

2.1.3 The Adoption of the British North America Act

The BNAA was adopted in two sequences. Its first draft, the Quebec resolutions, was adopted by the provincial assemblies and later the final version was adopted by the British Parliament.

At the end of the Quebec Conference, the delegates resolved to submit the Quebec resolutions (the draft constitution) to their respective provincial legislature for approval. Finally, Canada, Nova Scotia, and New Brunswick accepted the Quebec resolutions, while Prince Edward Island and Newfoundland rejected them. In all the cases, the state of the public opinion played an important role in the adoption process.

In Canada West where there was a relative popular support for the union and the Quebec resolutions, the political debate among the members of the Canadian assembly from Canada West centered more on the adoption procedure than on the terms of the Quebec resolutions (McInnis and Horn 1982: 351–354; Francis et al. 2009: 482). In Canada East, the opinion was much more divided: Across those who supported the text, there were those who argued that the text did not guarantee the Francophone rights and distinctiveness and that the union that it would bring about would increase the tax burden of the citizens (Francis et al. 2009: 483). The vote results in the provincial assembly reflected well the state of the opinion prevailing in each section of the province. While 54 of the 62 members of the Canadian assembly from Canada West voted in favor of the Quebec resolutions, only 37 of the 62 members from Canada East voted for the text (McInnis and Horn 1982: 351).

In Nova Scotia and in New Brunswick, the public opinion was just like in Canada East, generally reticent and even, to some extent, averse to the project of a union of British North America colonies. In Nova Scotia, despite the growing popular opposition to the union, the prime minister, Charles Tupper, assured the passage of the Quebec resolutions through the provincial assembly only thanks to his party strong legislative majority. In New Brunswick, the incumbent party who favored the union and the Quebec resolutions was defeated in the 1865 election to the benefit of parties who opposed the union. However, the state of the public opinion would dramatically evolve notably due to the Fenians threat (Francis et al. 2009: 484). Their 1866 raid in New Brunswick alarmed the opinion and played in favour of the union. As the popular support to the union grew stronger, the pro-union party was brought back to power in the 1866 election; that change allowed for an easy passage of the Quebec resolutions through the provincial legislature.

Once the assemblies of Canada, Nova Scotia, and New Brunswick had adopted the Quebec resolutions, it then required Britain's approval. The Father of Confederation with the Quebec resolutions expressed an aspiration to more autonomy in the conduct of domestic affairs, but did not mean the total end of Britain's tutelage. As a consequence, for the Quebec resolutions to take effect, it still needed to be enacted by the British Parliament. Britain's approval was not hard to get. Indeed, Britain supported the project of a union of its North America colonies because she wanted to get rid of the costs of administrating and defending them (Francis et al. 2009: 487). The bill on the union of British North America colonies was lightly debated, and its passage was swift in both houses of the British Parliament.

2.2 *The Evolution of the BNA 1867 till the Twenty-First Century*

After the adoption of the BNAA on March 29, 1867, there would be several acts that added to or modified the rules agreed upon previously. Here, we briefly discuss the amendments to the BNAA of 1867 that have not been repealed. In 1871, the British parliament passed a constitutional amendment that allowed the creation or the admission of new provinces in Canada. In 1886, a constitutional amendment gave to the federal Parliament the power to allow representation in the federal Parliament of territories belonging to Canada. The constitutional amendment of 1907 added to the rules concerning the payment of subsidies by the federal state to the provinces. The constitutional amendment of 1915 increased the total number of seats in the federal Senate to allow for representation of the newly admitted western provinces—Manitoba, Saskatchewan, Alberta, and British Columbia. The text provided that the western provinces would be represented by 24 senators. The constitutional amendment of 1930 transferred from the federal government to the western provinces, the ownership rights on natural resources on their territory. The constitutional amendment of 1940 transferred the responsibility over unemployment insurance to the federal parliament. After the referendum of July 1948, Newfoundland finally agreed to enter into union with Canada and the Newfoundland Act of 1949 set forth the provisions for the official admission of Newfoundland into the confederation of Canada. The amendment of 1960 set the retirement age for superior court judges at 75 year old. The amendment of 1964 gave to the Parliament of Canada competencies over old age pensions. The act of 1965 extended the mandatory retirement age of 75 to Senators, thus replacing the principle of life appointment that had prevailed thus far. The amendment of 1974 reviewed the rules concerning the representation of provinces in the federal House of Commons. In 1975, two amendments were adopted: The first made arrangements for the representation of the Yukon Territory and the Northwest Territories in the federal House of Commons, while the second was concerned with their representation in the federal Senate.

The changes mentioned thus far were of a small scale compared to those brought by the Constitution Act and the Canada Act of 1982 (Lederman 1984: 339). Before these legislations, there was no formal amendment procedure of the Canadian Constitution; all the amendments to the BNAA mentioned previously were done following customary rules and passed by the British Parliament. The Constitution Act of 1982 would remedy to that situation by fully transferring the constituent power to the Canadian Parliament and by laying out formal rules for amending the Constitution. Furthermore, the Constitution Act of 1982 provided to the citizens of Canada a set of rights judicially enforceable (the Charter of rights and freedom) and also reviewed important elements of provincial-federal relations. For example, it provided the foundation for an equalization system and it reviewed the division of power between the two levels of government over the natural resources. Finally, the Constitution act and the Canada act clarified the definition of the Constitution of Canada which, following the adoption of the two legislations, would be understood as an amalgamation of the texts explicitly listed in the Constitution act.

The context that called for these important constitutional reforms was marked by a crisis of the Canadian federalism (Imbeau 1990; Imbeau and Laforest 1991; Laforest 1995; Stein 1984): The sovereigntist government of Quebec threatened to withdraw the province from the federation. In May 1980, the Quebec government convoked its people to a referendum on the sovereignty-association option (the recovering of Quebec's political sovereignty but the maintaining of particular economic relations with Canada). A way to save the federation, in the view of federal authorities, was to profoundly review the constitutional rules agreed upon previously (Stein 1984: 125; Lederman 1984: 347). The federal government then initiated a project of constitutional reform that would meet certain resistances especially from Quebec on the question of the amending formula and on the issue of linguistics rights. In the end, the project was adopted first by the Canadian Parliament and nine provincial governments, and later by the British parliament, without the consent of Quebec whose national assembly unanimously rejected it.

The «renewed» Constitution of 1982 would continue to evolve. Some notable changes after 1982 concerned the Representation Act of 1985 which reviewed the distribution of seats in the parliament, the Constitution amendment of 1987 which gave Quebec the power to organize school boards according to linguistic criteria, the New Brunswick Act of 1993 which put English and French on an equal footing in the province of New Brunswick, and the Constitution Act of 1999 which allowed the representation of the territory of Nunavut in the federal Senate.

Now that we have a good idea of how the Canadian Constitution came to birth and evolved, we can analyze it in terms of power relations.

3 Power Relations in Canadian Constitution

3.1 Statistical Results from the Content Analysis and Measure of Uncertainty

Using the content analysis method devised by Imbeau (2009) and Imbeau and Jacob (2011) and presented in Chap. 4 of this book (Imbeau and Jacob 2015), we extracted 519 power relations from the Canadian Constitution as it now stands. Table 1 presents the statistical results. From these results, we derived measures of the uncertainty faced by the drafters.

The first measure to which we turn our attention is related to the source of power relations. Of the 519 power relations from the Canadian Constitution, 378 are political power relations, 71 are preceptoral and 22 are economic. Political

Table 1 Power relations from the Canadian Constitution according to source, the type, and the direction of power

		Number of power relations	Proportion
Resource of power	Authority	378	0.73
	Wealth	22	0.04
	Knowledge	71	0.14
	Indeterminate	48	0.09
	Total	519	1.00
Type of power relation	Social	272	0.52
	Instrumental	247	0.48
	Total	519	1.00
Direction of power	Positive	513	0.99
	Negative	6	0.01
	Total	519	1.00

power relations refer to discursive structures implying that a given agent would use force or his/her position of authority to perform an act or to influence another person. As the theory predicted, most power relations found in the Canadian Constitution relate to that kind of power. Preceptoral power relates to the use of knowledge as the power resource. These instances are recognizable in the constitutional text by verbal expressions such as «express», «desire», «advise», «instruct», «declare», «petition», and «speak». We found only 71 of them (14 %). Finally, economic power refers to wealth or things of value as a power resource. We found very few of those (22 or 4 %). They refer to expressions such as «use of land», «ownership», «salary», «payment», «pension», «debt», «subsidy», and «standard of living». Those results show that, for the great majority of power relations, force or authority is the influencing agent's resource of power. Wealth and knowledge as power resources are only referred to marginally. According to the theory presented in Chap. 4 above, the important proportion of political power relations, 0.73, suggests a high level of uncertainty at the time of the drafting and adoption.

When power relations are classified according to their type, we obtain 272 social power relations versus 247 instrumental power relations. In other terms, we have as many situations where an agent is given capacity over another (other) agent(s) as situations where an agent is given capacity over events or things. For example, when the constitution says: «It shall be lawful for the Queen [...] to declare by Proclamation [...] that the provinces of Canada, Nova Scotia, and New Brunswick shall form and be One Dominion under the Name of Canada; and on and after that Day those Three Provinces shall form and be One Dominion under that Name accordingly» (art. 3), we have an instance of social power: The Queen has the capacity «to add or remove a possibility of choice in the choice set» of these provinces.[4] But when the constitution declares: «a Senator shall, subject to the provisions of this Act, hold his place in the Senate for life», we have a case of instrumental power since by holding his place for life, a Senator does not add or remove a possibility of choice to the choice set of any other *explicitly identified* agent. Our theory holds that under uncertainty, drafters will more often try to limit the capacities of agents to act over other agents (social power) than to act over events or things (instrumental power). The proportion of social power relations, our second measure of uncertainty, is 0.52 and also suggests a high level of uncertainty but not as assertively as the first measure.

Turning to the direction of power relations, we found that the Canadian Constitution unequivocally tends to ascribe power (positive) rather than to restrain it (negative). There are 513 positive power relations and only 6 cases of negative power relations. The low proportion of negative power relations, 0.01, suggests that the drafters did not work under uncertainty, an interpretation radically opposed to those we got thus far. As it is suggested in Chap. 3 above, this third measure of uncertainty proves not to be useful as there is no variability. Therefore, we will not consider it anymore.

---

[4] See the codebook in Chap. 4 of this volume.

Table 2 Resource of power by type of power relation (%)

		Type of power relation		Total
		Social	Instrumental	
Resource of power	Authority	37.4	35.5	72.8
	Wealth	2.9	1.3	4.2
	Knowledge	9.2	4.4	13.7
	Undecided	2.9	6.4	9.2
Total		52.4	47.6	100.0
(*N*)		(272)	(247)	(519)

The last measure of uncertainty devised in Chap. 4 combines two dimensions instead of one like the first three: the source of power (Authority) and the type of power (Social). More formally, it is the proportion of power relations that are both political and social, i.e., have authority as source of power and refer to the power of an agent over another agent. In the Canadian case, that proportion is 0.37 attesting some level of uncertainty at the time of the drafting of the constitution (see Table 2).

The analysis of the Canadian Constitution in terms of power relations can go beyond the measures of uncertainty presented above. In the following sections, we outline the agents involved in the power relations and changes in the level of uncertainty over time.

4 Which Agents Are Identified in the Constitution?

The Canadian Constitution explicitly identifies a large number of agents, the most frequently mentioned being provincial legislatures (77 occurrences), the governor-general (63 occurrences), the parliament (56 occurrences), the Senate or senators (51 occurrences), lieutenant governors (40 occurrences), the House of Commons (36 occurrences), and the queen (24 occurrences). Table 3 shows the categories of influencing agents evoked in the power relations extracted from the text. A total of 52.9 % (23.3 + 27.9 + 1.5 + 0.2) of agents belong to the federal level compared to 36.1 % belonging to the provincial level, testifying to both the federal nature of the system created by the constitution and the higher importance given to the federal level of government. We should mention that there is no mention of agents pertaining to the local level. As the saying goes, in Canada, municipalities are the creations of the provinces. The judicial agents are also almost completely absent as influencing agents in the Canadian Constitution, while the executive and the legislative branches of government are represented equally (42.8 and 43.7 %, respectively). It is not clear why it is so. It may be because uncertainty has never been important concerning the role of judges and tribunals. Hence, drafters preferring to rely on the regular (as opposed to the constitutional) decision-making process to define the role of the judiciary, they chose not to consider it in the constitution. This attitude is compatible with the culture of common law dominating

Table 3 Categories of agents identified in the constitution by power resources and by types of power relation (%)

		Resource of power				Type of power		Total
		Authority	Wealth	Knowledge	Undecided	Social	Instrumental	
Category of agents	Fed. executive	17.5	1.0	4.0	0.8	14.3	9.1	23.3
	Fed. legislative	22.5	1.5	1.3	2.5	11.2	16.8	27.9
	Fed. juduciary	1.0	0	0.6	0	1.2	0.4	1.5
	Fed. other	0	0	0	0.2	0	0.2	0.2
	Prov. executive	14.1	1.3	2.5	1.5	12.3	7.1	19.5
	Prov. legislative	11.8	0.2	1.7	2.1	8.5	7.3	15.8
	Prov. judiciary	0	0	0.2	0	0	0.2	0.2
	Prov. other	0.6	0	0	0	0.4	0.2	0.6
	Civil society	4.2	0.2	3.3	2.1	4.0	5.8	9.8
	Other	1.2	0	0	0	0.6	0.6	1.2
Total		72.8	4.2	13.7	9.2	52.4	47.6	100.0
(*N*)		(378)	(22)	(71)	(48)	(272)	(247)	(519)

British traditions. The power resource of the influencing agents belonging to the executive and the legislative branches is predominantly related to authority, another sign that uncertainty was playing. However, things are not as clear with regard to the type of power relations. Though this still indicates the prevalence of uncertainty, social power is only slightly more important than instrumental power, particularly for agents from the executive.

5 Evolution of the Constitution Over Time

The constitutional text analyzed so far is the consolidated text that is now in force. That means that it includes all the amendments that were made over time, adding new clauses and repealing others. From 1867 to 2001, 41 constitutional texts were adopted.[5] They are listed in Table 4. A look at their characteristics may give us a bird's-eye view of the evolution of uncertainty in constitution making over these

[5] Maton (2011) identifies 41 texts, two of which do not include power relations as per our codebook: The Constitution Act of 1965 which counts only two clauses, and the Constitution Act of 1975 (No. 1) which counts only three clauses. These two texts were excluded from our analyses.

Table 4 Analysis of the 39 texts forming the Canadian Constitution and in which we unitized power relations as per our codebook[a]

Text title	Year	Authority	Social	Authority * Social	*N*
Constitution Act, 1967	1867	0.72	0.62	0.46	370
Manitoba Act, 1870	1870	0.78	0.53	0.42	90
Rupert's Land and North-Western Territory Order	1870	0.68	0.49	0.26	69
British Columbia Terms of Union	1871	0.74	0.74	0.47	19
Constitution Act, 1871	1871	0.92	0.81	0.73	26
Prince Edward Island Terms of Union	1873	0.82	0.86	0.73	22
Parliament of Canada Act, 1875	1875	0.75	0.63	0.33	9
Adjacent Territories Order	1880	0.73	0.36	0.08	12
Constitution Act, 1886	1886	0.83	0.58	0.42	12
Canada (Ontario Boundary) Act, 1889	1889	0.85	0.46	0.31	13
Canadian Speaker (Appointment Deputy) Act	1895	0.82	0.82	0.64	11
Alberta Act	1905	0.76	0.75	0.51	63
Saskatchewan Act	1905	0.77	0.67	0.46	61
Constitution Act, 1907	1907	0.42	0.83	0.25	12
Constitution Act, 1915	1915	0.92	0.31	0.23	26
Constitution Act, 1930	1930	0.88	0.77	0.65	26
Statute of Westminster, 1931	1931	0.95	0.48	0.43	44
Constitution Act, 1940	1940	0.73	0.64	0.36	11
British North America Act, 1943 (repealed)	1943	0.73	0.64	0.36	11
British North America Act, 1946 (repealed)	1946	0.80	0.47	0.27	15
Newfoundland Act, 1949	1949	0.63	0.58	0.42	19
British North America Act (No. 2), 1949 (repealed)	1949	0.77	0.62	0.38	13
British North America Act, 1951 (repealed)	1951	0.77	0.62	0.38	13
British North America Act, 1951 (repealed)	1952	0.78	0.56	0.33	9
Constitution Act, 1960	1960	0.67	0.67	0.33	15
Constitution Act, 1964	1964	0.77	0.62	0.38	13
Constitution Act, 1974	1974	1.00	0	0	2
Constitution Act, 1975 (No. 2)	1975	0.67	0.67	0.33	6
Constitution Act, 1982	1982	0.64	0.43	0.25	151
Constitution Amendment, 1983	1983	0.69	0.77	0.50	26
Constitution Act, 1985 (Representation)	1985	0.71	0.57	0.29	7

(continued)

Table 4 (continued)

Text title	Year	Authority	Social	Authority * Social	N
Constitution Amendment, 1987 (Newfoundland Act)	1987	0.80	0.60	0.47	15
Constitution Amendment, 1993 (New Brunswick Act)	1993	0.82	0.65	0.53	17
Constitution Amendment, 1993 (Prince Edward Island)	1993	0.86	0.57	0.50	14
Constitution Amendment, 1997 (Newfoundland Act)	1997	0.84	0.55	0.47	38
Constitution Amendment, 1997 (Quebec)	1997	0.91	0.36	0.36	11
Constitution Act, 1998 (Newfoundland Act)	1998	0.81	0.50	0.38	16
Constitution Act, 1999 (Nunavut)	1999	0.67			3
Constitution Amendment, 2001 (Newfoundland and Labrador)	2001	0.85	0.38	0.31	13
Overall uncertainty measures vand (*N*)		0.75	0.59	0.41	(1,323)

aAs per the Constitution Act of 1982 and Maton (2011)

134 years. Before looking at uncertainty measures, let us note that there is a wide variation in the length of the documents analyzed as given by the number of power relations unitized in each text. For example, the Constitution Act of 1974 in its version in French is three pages long and counts 978 words. It contains only two power relations. This is to be compared with the 1867 Act which is 21 pages long and counts 9,490 words for a total of 370 power relations. The reader should keep these differences in mind while looking at the evolution of our measures of uncertainty. Our treating each text as a single entity may bias the conclusion since longer texts are given the same weight as shorter ones.

Overall, we found 1323 power relations in the 39 constitutional texts with the following levels of uncertainty: 0.75 for «Authority», 0.59 for «Social», and 0.41 for «Authority * Social». These results are quite comparable to those for the consolidated text as reported above. Despite some differences, they have the same magnitude.

Though there is a strong similarity between the consolidated constitution and the whole set of 39 constitutional texts, we see an important variation from one text to the next. Table 5 provides descriptive statistics. The means for each of the three measures of uncertainty is very close to the overall measures.

Table 5 Descriptive statistics of three measures of uncertainty in 39 constitutional texts

	N	Minimum	Maximum	Mean	Standard deviation
Authority	39	0.42	1.00	0.776	0.1047
Social	39	0	0.86	0.569	0.1905
VIV2	39	0	0.73	0.384	0.1613
N	39	2	370	33.9	62.01

Table 6 Regression analyses (OLS) on three measures of uncertainty

	Authority		Social		Authority * Social	
	B	Std. error	B	Std. error	B	Std. error
Constant	0.771***	0.041	0.695***	0.079	0.445***	0.064
Real growth	−0.864**	0.361	0.030	0.700	−1.013*	0.563
Crisis	0.078	0.049	−0.019	0.095	0.026	0.076
History	0.0003	0.0004	−0.002*	0.001	−0.001	0.001
R_2	0.220		0.121		0.129	
N	34		34		34	

*** $p < 0.01$; ** $p < 0.05$; * $p < 0.10$

However, the variation in «Authority» is somewhat lower than the variation in «Authority * Social»: coefficients of variation of 13 and 42 %, respectively. «Social power» exhibits a coefficient of variation equal to 30 %.

What explains this variation in uncertainty? To answer this question, we ran several regression analyses (OLS) with two sources of uncertainty as predictors: economic growth (the higher the real GDP growth, the lower the uncertainty) and social crises (the occurrence of a war or of the depression increases uncertainty). We also included a variable «History», the number of years since 1867, to account for any additional effect of a time-related trend.[6] Results are displayed in Table 6.[7]

This model only explains a very small proportion of the variance in the dependent variables, from 22 % («Authority») to 12 % («Social»). We certainly need to develop more our theoretical thinking to provide a better explanation of the observed variance. However, we can see from Table 6 that some of our hypotheses are supported by the data. For one, economic growth negatively affects «Authority» and «Authority * Social». Uncertainty is significantly higher when growth is smaller or negative. Uncertainty is also higher in times of social crisis for these two measures but not significantly (though the coefficient is almost significant for «Authority»). GDP Growth has no effect on «Social», our second measure of uncertainty, but «History» does. Power relations related to social power (as opposed to instrumental power) are less frequent as we move over time which would suggest that uncertainty is lower the further we get away from the founding date.

[6] Data for GDP growth in constant dollars were drawn from three sources. 1870–1926 from Urquhart 1993; 1927–1930 from Altman 1992; 1931–1946 from CANSIM 380-0040; 1949–1960 from CANSIM 379-0013; 1961–2001 from www.usherbrooke.perspective. "Social crisis" is a dummy variable for years of war (1914–1918 and 1939–1945) and for years of depression (1929–1933).

[7] To test the robustness of our results, we estimated several additional models, one supplementing missing data for GDP Growth in 1867 and 1870 with their US equivalent, others dropping cases with small number of observations (N < 4 and N < 10). Results were strongly consistent.

6 Discussion

We took two different pictures of the Canadian Constitution. First, we looked at the consolidated version of the constitution as it now stands. This view is useful to allow cross-national comparisons, as was done in Chap. 4 by Imbeau and Jacob, where it was shown that the Canadian Constitution exhibits a level of uncertainty similar to that of Italy on both the «Authority» and the «Authority * Social» measures. These two countries stand at the ninth position out of 16 countries. Imbeau and Jacob also shown that these two measures are highly correlated (Pearson's $r = 0.84$).[8] As far as the «Social» measure of uncertainty is concerned, Canada fared quite high at the second rank after France. This suggests that we may be measuring two different dimensions of uncertainty which we might be able to identify more precisely with the time-related analysis.

Indeed, the second picture we considered in this paper was that picture involving 39 texts forming the Canadian Constitution. By analyzing each constitutional text separately, we got an evolutionary view going from 1867 to 2001 which allowed us a cross-time comparison. Here, our analysis seems to lead to the same conclusion as that by Imbeau and Jacob. Indeed, our regression analyses are consistent with the idea that we are measuring two dimensions of uncertainty, one that seems to be related with economic uncertainty as the coefficient for real GDP growth is negative and significant with «Authority» and «Authority * Social» but not with «Social», another that seems to be related to what we might call *political* uncertainty as the coefficient for «History»—or what Imbeau and Jacob called «persistence», i.e., length of time since the birth of a country—is negative and significant for «Social» but not for the other two measures. This last result can be interpreted as an indication that constitution drafters seem to be less uncertain of their future as they are more experienced in living together. This suggests a deeper, more structural form of uncertainty, compared to the first one which seems to be more related to the conjuncture.

7 Conclusion

The historical account of the making of the Canadian Constitution shows that there were numerous sources of uncertainty for the drafters. These were both political (v.g., the threats coming from the American neighbor, and the conflictual relationship between English- and French-speaking elites in the province of Canada) and economic (v.g., the gradual withdrawal of Britain's economic support coupled with protectionist policies on the part of the USA, and the need for the costly construction of railroads necessary for the development of trade). These

---

[8] The correlation between "Authority" and "Social" was 0.43 and between "Social" and "Autority * Social" it was 0.73.

uncertainties motivated the «Confederation Fathers» to overcome their differences and to agree on compromises that made the adoption of the constitution possible. In the absence of such uncertainties, we may conjecture that the 1867 creation of the Canadian federation would have been postponed or altogether abandoned.

This historical narrative is consistent with the content analysis of the consolidated text as well as of 39 constitutional documents that the Canadian Constitution comprises. Our analysis revealed that the proportion of power relations related to authority was much higher than those related to wealth or knowledge, thus denoting the expression of the uncertainty faced by the drafters. We arrived at a similar conclusion concerning social, as opposed to instrumental, power relations. The longitudinal analysis covering the period going from 1867 to 2001 showed that the variation in one form of uncertainty was related to economic growth, whereas the other was related to the passage of time, a proxy for the experience of living together. In brief, the narrative and the analytical approaches confirmed Buchanan's and Tullock's proposition: The drafters of the constitution were highly motivated by the uncertainty they faced.

References

Buchanan JM, Tullock G (1962) The calculus of consent: logical foundations of constitutional democracy. The University of Michigan Press, Ann Arbor

Congleton RD (2011) Perfecting parliament: constitutional reform, liberalism, and the rise of western democracy. Cambridge University Press, Cambridge

Dippel H (ed) (2013) Constitutions of the world from the late 18th century to the middle of the 19th century. Retrieved 4 June 2013 from http://www.modern-constitutions.de/nbu.php?page_id=cf2bf1a9ce737906a2cc483486798452

Francis DR, Jones R, Smith DB (2009) Origins. Canadian history to confederation. Nelson Education, Toronto

Hood P (1982) The Canada Act 1982. Int Comp Law Q 31(4):845–848

Lederman WR (1984) Canadian constitutional amending procedures: 1867–1982. Am J Comp Law 32(2):339–359

Imbeau LM (1990) Voting games and constitutional decision: the 1981 constitutional negotiation in Canada. J Commonwealth Comp Politics 28(1):90–105

Imbeau LM (2009) Testing the 'veil of ignorance' hypothesis in constitutional choice: a 'walk-talk' approach. J Pub Choice Pub Finance 26(1):3–21

Imbeau LM, Jacob S (2011) Is the 'veil of ignorance' in constitutional choice a myth? An empirical exploration informed by a theory of power. In: Marciano A (dir.) Constitutional mythologies: new perspectives on controlling the state. Springer, New York, pp 53–69

Imbeau LM, Jacob S (2015) Measuring the opacity of the 'veil of ignorance' in constitutions: theory, method and some results. In: Imbeau LM, Jacob S (eds) Behind a veil of ignorance? power and uncertainty in constitutional design. Springer, New York

Imbeau LM, Laforest G (1991) Quebec's distinct society and the sense of nationhood in Canada. Quebec Stud 13:13–26

Laforest G (1995) Trudeau and the end of a Canadian dream. McGill Queen's University Press, Montréal

Maton WF (2011) Canadian constitutional documents: a legal history. Retrieved 21 Mar 2013 from http://www.solon.org/Constitutions/Canada/English

McInnis E, Horn M (1982) Canada. A political and social history. Holt Rinehart and Winston of Canada, Toronto

Stein MB (1984) Canadian constitutional reform, 1927–1982: a comparative case analysis over time. Publius J Federalism 14(1):121–139

Waite P (1997) Between three oceans: challenge of a continental destiny. In: Brown C (dir.) The illustrated history of Canada. Key Porter Books, Toronto

Whitelaw WM (1967) The Quebec conference. The Canadian Historical Association Booklet No 20, Ottawa

Chapter 7
Uncertainty and Cleavages at Stakes: Do the Belgian Constitutions of 1831 and 1993 Stabilize Political Power?

Nathalie Schiffino and Steve Jacob

1 Introduction

In our modern States, Constitutions underlie political power and its institutional settings. Two different texts lay the foundation of the Constitutional history of Belgium: the Constitution of 1831 and that of 1993. Each arose during a period of historical change. In 1831, in the shadow of decolonization from the Netherlands, the Constitution created a unitary State. In 1993, in a context of the Europeanization of politics, the Constitution declared a federal State. Over the years, the Belgian polity has undergone dramatic changes. What is puzzling about Belgium is that the constitution-making process has consistently remained in a State of uncertainty. In spite of path dependency and lesson-drawing, constitutional lawmakers, it seems, have not been able to avoid drafting decisions under a veil of ignorance.

In reality, from the nineteenth to the twenty-first century, the Belgian State overcame several deep cleavages. To guarantee the viability of the State as it now exists, political elites opted for deep Constitutional changes. The in-depth revisions of the Constitutions aimed at adapting the institutional settings to the evolution of the cleavages and their impact on society. Assuming this was a rather rational choice made by the decision-makers involved, we conjecture they manage both the political and the constitutional processes.

Yet, as we shall see in this chapter, uncertainty was at work at the time of drafting and adopting both Constitutions, in 1831 and in 1993. Moreover, from the nineteenth to the twentieth century, conditions of uncertainty under which constitutional choices were made remain unchanged. To put in a nutshell, at different times,

N. Schiffino (✉)
Université Catholique de Louvain, Louvain-la-Neuve, Belgium
e-mail: nathalie.schiffino@uclouvain.be

S. Jacob
Département de Science Politique, Université Laval, Québec, Canada
e-mail: steve.jacob@pol.ulaval.ca

L.M. Imbeau and S. Jacob (eds.), *Behind a Veil of Ignorance?*,
Studies in Public Choice 32, DOI 10.1007/978-3-319-14953-0_7

the veil of ignorance hung similarly before the drafters' eyes. Indeed, we posit that cleavages and the necessity for consociationalism (to overcome cleavages) partly explain this veil of ignorance at different stages of Belgian history. Thus, we put forward a tension between the rationality (albeit limited or bounded) of the drafters and the uncertainty of the context in which their decisions were embedded.

Section 2 focuses on the historical overview surrounding the Constitution in 1831. It explains the emergence of both cleavages and consociationalism. In Sect 3, we investigate the content of the Constitution of 1831 and that of 1993. This approach aims to explain how different texts share similar characteristics when drafted and adopted under uncertainty. In Sect 4, we discuss the results of the content analysis of the two Constitutions. Three main sets of explanatory factors will be highlighted: foreign surveillance in 1831 and EU membership in 1993, cleavages and consociationalism, and unframed devolution. In doing so, the Belgian case study gives a hand into theorizing the veil of ignorance, the general purpose of this book.

2 Historical Context of the Drafting and Adoption of the Constitutions

2.1 What Issues and Historical Events Led to the Drafting and Adoption of the 1831 Constitution?

In 1831, a national revolution triggered constitutional work. Domestic political issues cannot be disentangled from international turmoil at a time when civil wars were spreading throughout Europe. Among these wars, "Les Trois Glorieuses" or "La Révolution de Juillet" in France, the revolutionary movements in Germany and Italy, and the November uprising in Poland illustrate the mobilizations and upheavals that began to sprout across Europe in 1830. The Belgian and Greek revolutions were both leading toward independence, from the Netherlands and the Ottoman Empire, respectively. As such, they were each required to draft and adopt a Constitution for these new States.

The general historical context for the drafting and adoption of the Constitution cannot ignore domestic economic and social issues. During the nineteenth century, Belgium developed industry (notably the sectors of textiles and coal mines), railways (Cockerill), river traffic, and harbors. The first decade of Belgian independence was characterized by a difficult economic conjuncture (Witte et al. 2005: 125–143), and the nascent State was obliged to consolidate its financial and monetary policies. Moreover, social claims accompanied industrial developments in spite of the fact that social classes, especially the working class, were not yet organized for a class struggle (Mabille 1992: 96). At this moment in time, religion persisted as the main domestic social issue. As early as 1830, Liberals (traditionally secular) and Catholics formed two dominant pillars, each corresponding to a political family (political parties were created until 1846 and 1884), with its own advocacy groups, its own press, etc.

Divergent visions emerged regarding the role of the State and the Church to organize education, charity, and the supervision of citizens in general. To secure the independence of the State, and to favor its stability, these political families put their philosophical differences aside. The period from 1830 through 1839 became known as the so-called unionist period. Catholics and Liberals agreed to remain united, rather than at odds, on this important domestic issue. This acquiescence was a necessary condition in order for the Belgian State to be recognized by the Great Powers (France, the United Kingdom, Germany, and Russia). In 1830, they could not know where this cleavage would lead them in the future. This uncertainty is taken into account when we analyze the drafting and adoption of the Constitution.

Besides, in 1830, conflict over linguistic or cultural cleavage was not yet obvious. It was the French-speaking elite who participated in the revolution, gained the independence for the State, and engaged in drafting and adopting the Constitution. Further, it was the French language that distinguished Belgian citizens from their Dutch-speaking colonizers. French was also the language commonly spoken by the elites, should they live in the North or in the South of the country. However, it is important to point out that local idioms were already present. Observers were already expressing uncertainty as how to tackle the Flemish and "Picard" dialects.

To summarize the global sources of uncertainty at the time of the drafting and adoption of the Constitution, we point to several notable elements. First, on an international scale, the need to maintain a stable Europe mortgages Belgium's future (Witte et al. 2005: 74–80). Were it to be considered as a divided and unstable brand-new country, its independence would be compromised. Rather, domestic issues were managed and decided upon by Liberals and Catholics through negotiation. Their goal was to anesthetize the potentially conflict-inducing effects of cleavages. The main Constitutional choices, such as opting for a parliamentarian monarchy as a regime, were made largely based on international constraints in order to limit uncertainty.

2.2 *Who Were the Drafters and the Adopters? Why Did They Get Involved in the Process? Did They Have Divergent Interests?*

The drafters of the Constitution in 1830 can be separated into two groups (Mabille 1992: 104–108). On October 6, 1830, the new government asked a Commission to draw up a first draft of the country's constitution. The 12-members Commission, composed mostly of jurists, worked on the draft from October 12 to 16, 1830. We consider this Commission a first group of drafters.

At the same time, the government prepared the election of the so-called National Congress. It was a unicameral parliament created with a sole objective: to discuss the first draft prepared by the commission, to amend the proposal, if necessary, and finally to put it to a vote. On November 3, 1830, 46,099 Belgians voted for the 200-person National Congress. Among the voters, 38,429 had paid the poll tax. A further 7,670 voters possessed a degree that qualified them to vote. The 200 congressmen, elected that day, constituted a second group of drafters and adopters of the Constitution. Their profile was mixed up diversity and homogeneity. From a geographical perspective, they represented heterogeneous ridings (e.g., rural and urban). The provinces where they were elected covered the whole spectrum of possible demographic configurations. But in terms of social class, all 200 were part of the Belgian elite. They formed a homogeneous group of decision-makers, all French-speakers, although they differentiated themselves into either the Catholic or Liberal block.

It is highly relevant questioning the motivations of the drafters and adopters of the Constitution of 1831. These lawmakers wanted to ensure rights, power, and autonomy for the pillars they belonged to. At the same time, they did not know how the Belgian State and Belgian society were to evolve along the lines of existing cleavages. Considering Rokkan's writings on liberation struggles (Rokkan 1970), and Lijphart's analysis of consociationalism (Lijphart 1999), we know that three main cleavages delineate crucial pillars in Belgium: religious, economic, and linguistic. In 1831, the religious cleavage fundamentally divided the Catholics and Liberals. Along the economic cleavage, the working class and the *bourgeoisie* opposed one another, most notably from the mid-1830 onward. The linguistic cleavage divided the French-speakers and the Dutch-speakers especially since 1840.

There are many illustrations of the motivations of the Congressmen in the midst of the prevailing uncertainty. We can have a greater understanding as to what motivated the drafters and the adopters of the Constitution in 1831 based on discourse among their contemporaries and investigations by historians. For instance, the Archbishop de Méan wrote a letter to congressmen on December 13, 1830, calling for the Catholic Church's recognition in the Constitution. The clergy declared that depriving Catholics the freedom of religion, education, and organization could trigger crises within the new State.

The objective interests of the adopters of the Constitution can be inferred from their position in the structure of political, economic, and preceptorial power (Imbeau 2009; Imbeau and Jacob 2011). They share different ideologies that they want to protect and preserve. Equilibrium was to be found between secular and non-secular structures. The adopters belonged to a mono-linguistic elite, but they knew those who spoke the prominent dialects formed a social and cultural patchwork that had to be carefully handled. They formed part of the nobility or the upper middle class and, as such, their economic and knowledge resources were patent. But the first years of the 1830s were marked by monetary and financial crises while the working class cried for reforms, notably education for the underprivileged. From an individual point of view, these elements highlight potential sources of uncertainty. We can find some *souvenirs* of the congressmen that illustrate these sources. Several *mémoires* dating from this period still provide valuable piece of information, including for example works by Louis de Lichtervelde, Theodore Juste, and Jacques van den Heuvel.

2.3 *How Did the Drafting and Adoption Processes Actually Evolve? What, When, Where, How?*

The National Congress met for the first time on November 10, 1830, in the "Palais des Etats Généraux" in Brussels, the newly proclaimed capital of the nascent country. Of the 200 members, 152 were present. Louis De Potter, the eldest member of the government, formally installed the Congress, with his official speech evoking the terms freedom, equality, and constitutional rights. From his *souvenirs*, it seems that there was not a general consensus on what to say at that moment. The National Congress was meant to be an ad hoc forum; its primary function was to vote on the Constitution while the government managed social and economic programs. Both were considered to be temporary organs, with the government intended to be in place until February 1831 and Parliament until September 1831. This exemplifies that decision-makers were uncertain about the period of time during which they could exert power. They were uncertain whose prerogative it would be to make future decisions and in which sense that would happen.

In the days following November 10, 1830, the congressmen gathered again and voted on the main features of the State: They confirmed the already-declared independence, they opted for a Constitution and representative monarchy, and they excluded any chance of the Netherlands providing a ruling King.

Weeks later, on December 4, 1830, Congressmen began to debate the project of the Constitution as such. From the project prepared by the commission, mentioned above, they preserved 108 articles in their original form. They modified articles relating to the composition of the future Parliament. They elected to install a bicameral parliament composed of directly elected members. They also changed articles relating to the relationship between the State and the Church, guaranteeing freedom of religion and freedom of education. Their debates were influenced by positions such as the one formulated by the Archbishop in December 1830. On February 7, 1831, they ended their debate and adopted the Constitution.

Throughout this process, those participating in the National Congress, as well as their contemporaries and many historians, considered them as a real authority exerting real political power in the sense of the "Veil of Ignorance Project" (VOIP). Debate and negotiation prevailed. The Constitution of 1831 was changed only twice in the years that followed. In 1893, plural suffrage and proportional representation were put into place. In 1921, the political elite enacted universal suffrage for the people. It was not until 1970, and the preparation of the Constitution to determine a federal State in 1993, that new constitutional changes were adopted in Belgium. This timeline highlights the importance of considering, in the rest of our chapter, these two moments of constitutional history in Belgium: 1831 and 1993. The latter will be investigated in the sections two and three as a mirror effect of the Constitution of 1831.

3 Description of the Content of the Constitution in Terms of a Power Relation Framework

3.1 Description of the Constitutional Text

The Constitution of 1831 is composed of 4,982 words and 209 power relations. This Constitution is one of the shortest among the texts studied by the VOIP. The density of the power relations in the text is 41.95. By comparison, the Constitution of 1993 counts 14,478 words, marginally longer than the average Constitution scrutinized by the VOIP. The density of the Constitution of 1993 is 39.50. It is striking to note that this figure is lower than the mean power relations (per thousand words) in other case studies investigated by the VOIP (cf. Imbeau and Jacob 2015). What is more, noting the number of power relations (572), we see this is well above average, and far more than twice the number of power relations in the Constitution of 1831.

In 1831, the Belgian Constitution was structured in eight main categories. Considering the importance of territorial demarcations, especially following a revolution, the first title concerns territory, highlighting the importance of this feature within the State's recognition. The first article is also crucial because it frames the unitary character of the political regime. The first sentence of the Constitution, article 1, states: "Belgium is divided into provinces." One of the major revisions in the Constitution of 1993 is the reformulation of article 1. From 1993 until the present day, this first article has proclaimed: "Belgian is a federal State composed of regions and communities." The provinces remain, but they are presented later in the text, in article 5, which designates the provinces to the Walloon and Flemish regions.

In 1831 and 1993, the second title of the Constitution pertains to Belgian citizens and their rights. In 1831, and after, the Belgian Constitution was held up as a model for its promotion of (individual) freedom in a partly authoritarian Europe (Mabille 1992: 116). In 1993, the principles of equality, freedom, habeas corpus, the abolishment of the death penalty, and other conditions of citizenship remain unchanged.

The third title in both the 1831 and the 1993 Constitutions pertains to political authorities. It is the largest section of the Constitution, regardless of the period. This title begins with the declaration that all power comes from the Nation. This power follows directly from the legislature, which denotes the importance of the parliamentary character of the regime, developed before either the executive or the judiciary branch. In the Constitution of 1993, the adjective "federal" is added to the descriptions of both the legislative and the executive. An additional chapter concerns regions and communities. The judiciary is detailed within the articles into the different courts and their respective competences.

The fourth title in the Constitution of 1831 and the fifth title in the Constitution of 1993 are about finance and taxation. In the 1993 edition, a title has also been added about international relations. It lists the competent powers in matters of international treaties.

The following title (fifth in 1831 and sixth in 1993) relates to public forces: the army and the police (civic guards, mentioned in 1831, no longer exist in such a form). These articles concern the coercive, yet legitimate (because constitutionally guaranteed), power of these authorities.

The last titles in 1831 and in 1993 are about peculiar measures (the flag, laws to be adopted to fulfill the task in 1831, etc.) and last but not least, rules outlining the revision of the Constitution. A rigid procedure, corresponding to Lijphart's model of consociationalism (1999), was put in place requiring the presence of half of elected members and a majority in the vote in each linguistic group, plus two-third votes in both Chambers, are required to approve a revision to the Constitution.

3.2 *Statistical Results from the Content Analysis*

As mentioned, the number of power relations vastly increased in the Constitution between 1831 and 1993: from 209 to 572. This is linked to the creation and multiplication of competent authorities within the federal State. Belgium changed from a unitary frame with centralized legislative, executive, and judiciary powers to a federal structure in which the federal State shares competencies with legislative and executive organizations in three regions and three communities that do not always overlap. As a result, these new structures increased the number of power relations between these authorities and the judiciary (Table 1).

In 1831 and 1993, around 85 % of these power relations pertain to authority, i.e., political power as such (86.6 % in 1831 and 84.3 % in 1993). The second type of power appears to be knowledge, with approximately 8 % (7.7 % in 1831 and 8.2 % in 1993). The statistical distance of the economic power (just 1.9 % in 1831 and 1 % in 1993) from the political and preceptorial powers could be explained by several factors mentioned below.

In 1831, Parliament was composed of elites, as previously said. They did not worry about their future wealth and were not behind a veil, as defined in the VOIP, regarding their socioeconomic future. Even if the economy needed to be consolidated at a time of crisis, elites were the privileged, the business owners, and participated in industrial developments. In 1993, wealth issues were handled by the corporatist system settled in Belgium after the Second World War. While elites revised the Constitution at the "political Parliament," they did not have to

Table 1 Type of power per source of power in the Belgian Constitution of 1831 (proportions)

	Social power	Instrumental power	Total (N)
Authority	0.38	0.48	0.87 (181)
Wealth	0.00	0.02	0.02 (4)
Knowledge	0.02	0.05	0.08 (16)
Indeterminate	0.01	0.03	0.04 (8)
Total (N)	0.42 (87)	0.58 (122)	1.00 (209)

Table 2 Type of power per source of power in the Belgian Constitution of 1993 (proportions)

	Social power	Instrumental power	Indeterminate	Total (N)
Authority	0.42	0.42	0.00	0.84 (482)
Wealth	0.01	0.01	0.00	0.01 (6)
Knowledge	0.03	0.05	0.00	0.08 (47)
Indeterminate	0.00	0.06	0.00	0.06 (37)
Total (N)	0.46 (263)	0.54 (308)	0.002 (1)	1 (572)

worry about socioeconomic issues because these were dealt with in the so-called social Parliament instituted by the Social Pact of 1944. Moreover, these lawmakers belonged to the upper class, their incomes and education standing well above the average Belgian (Table 2).

It is highly interesting that figures denote similar trends in the nineteenth and twentieth centuries, except for the number of power relations, as such. The Constitutions of 1831 and 1993, though settling different patterns of regimes (unitary at first, followed by a federal system), keep similar statistical features in terms of power and, potentially, the opacity of the veil of ignorance.

3.3 What Agents Are Identified in the Constitution?

The legislative branch is a major agent in the Constitution of 1831, mentioned as "legislative power," or, more often, "the Chambers," "the Chamber of the Representatives," "the Senate," as well as by the terms "president," and even "members." The legislative branch is present in both collective and individual dynamics. For instance, the Constitution identifies ten members of a chamber as a relevant group to ask for the secrecy of parliamentarian debates. It also specifies conditions under which a member of the Parliament cannot exert his mandate.

The same dual logic, collective and individual, is applied to a second category of agents: "Belgians" constituting the "Belgian Nation." "Citizens" are mentioned as the one who pay the poll tax and who elect the Representatives. Sometimes it refers to all of them, as a collective group, for example regarding the fundamental right of association, and at others it refers to each of them, such as the individual right of depositing a petition signed by several others.

After the legislative branch, the next major agent appears to be the King. He is always mentioned with his prerogatives: the Constitution announces his capacities within the State. However, one article (article 64) stipulates the capacities of the King depend on a Minister, a member of the executive, who endorses the responsibility of the King's capacities.

Other agents related to the State are as follows: "the civil servants," "the Courts," and "the Judge" (again with a collective or individual label), the "Courts of Auditors" and, more scarcely, "the Minister." Apart from the centralized State, two agents are mentioned several times in the Constitution in 1831: "Provinces" and "Communes" (i.e., municipalities).

Interestingly, "the priest" also appears to be an agent in the Belgian Constitution. He is free to write to his superiors and publish his acts without State intervention or intrusion, as any interference on the part of the State could hamper the freedom of the Church.

Also, significantly, "foreign armies" appear in three units of analysis. At the time of independence, the foreign armies were forbidden by the Constitution to work for the Belgian State, to cross its borders and to occupy its territory without permission. The Constitution assertively handles the uncertainty raised by foreign States over the future of Belgium.

Comparatively, the Constitution in 1993 always favors the legislative branch as the major agent, applying the same dynamics as before. The legislative branch henceforth corresponds to several agents: the federal level and those of the other jurisdictions (i.e., federated entities). Further, the executive branch is much more present than in the original Constitution, both at the federal and federated levels. The "federal government" is individually distinguished from its members: ministers and secretaries of State. The King, as per tradition, remains a clearly identified agent. There are also new terms introduced: "regions" and "communities." They form an intermediary level between the federal State on one hand and "provinces" and "communes" on the other hand. "Courts," "judges," and "priests" remain agents within the Constitution, but the judiciary is described more in terms of its different courts. Thus, there is a dramatic increase in the number of political agents exerting authority identified in the Constitution. Power is more fragmented and dispersed among them.

Moreover, "Belgians" still appear to be "each one" and "electors." They are divided along gender lines: "women" and "men" are both mentioned. "Children" are also identified as agents in the Belgian Constitution.

Another important change is that armies are not the sole foreign agent that is mentioned. "Institutions of international public law" and citizens of a member State of the "European Union" are also presented in the text. The Constitution grants them the right to exert specific power.

3.4 What Capacities Do These Agents Have?

Generally speaking, the Belgian Constitutions in 1831 and in 1993 enhanced power through procedures, rather than granting power to some individuals over others. Statistically, the capacity to act over events or things (instrumental power) is higher than the capacity to act over other agents (social power) in both Constitutions.

What is puzzling regarding the VOIP hypothesis is that political power is primarily concerned with events or things, but not persons. Instrumental power dominates (58 % in 1831 and 54 % in 1993) over social power. How can we explain such a reversal in regard to the second hypothesis of the VOIP theoretical framework? We conjecture that cleavages and consociationalism provide explanations to this puzzling situation.

As demonstrated by the theory on consociationalism, in a deeply divided society such as Belgium, a group (actually a majority) cannot explicitly dominate another one: "consociational democracy violates the principle of majority rule" (Lijphart 1969: 214). In formal rules, especially Constitutions, that dictate the fundamentals of the polity, neither the majority nor the minority should appear as prevalent agents. To avoid such trends, persons or groups are not mentioned in the Constitution. Power relations are structured in terms of activities that are either permitted or prohibited. In a nutshell, in such a specific context, power relations are concerned with procedures rather than singling out individuals or groups. Procedures aim at reducing the risk of conflicts without identifying individuals as potential sources of these conflicts. Article 54 provides a striking illustration of this trend. It describes the so-called alarm bell procedure preventing the Flemish from adopting a law that could be harmful to the interests of the Walloons, and vice versa. However, it does so without specifically mentioning individuals.

3.5 What Capacities Does the Text Take from These Agents?

In this regard, the Belgian case study shows a second intriguing aspect that contradicts the third hypothesis of the VOIP, but which is coherent with our findings outlined previously. The vast majority of power relations (92 % in 1831 and 96 % in 1993) aims to give actors the capacity to act, rather than to prevent them from acting (these results are not reported in our tables).

In 1831, agreement between the competing groups within the nascent State implied building positive, rather than negative, power relations. Stability in domestic affairs was necessary to guarantee the viability of Belgium on the international stage. Groups cannot afford to prevent themselves from acting and thus introduce negative power exchanges. Consociationalism prevails, based on compromise, on negotiations leading to agreement (Lijphart 1969). The Constitution thus balances the capacities of the agents to conduct such positive power relations.

In 1993, devolution implied that regions and communities, provinces and communes were recognized as equal to the (henceforth federal) State. The federal constitution was not written in the perspective of preventing the federated entities to act, but rather to enhance their autonomy. As shown in the literature, the purpose was to increase self-government, especially within the regions (Keating 1998, 2009).

However, by 1993, we notice that social power catches up with instrumental power. The statistical difference between them decreases from 42 % compared with 58 % in 1831 to 46 % in comparison with 54 % in 1993. Similarly, the proportion of instrumental power diminishes if we consider that, in the first Constitution, 48 % of power relations are political (authority) and instrumental, compared with the proportion in the 1993 Constitution, which is 42 %. The devolution process explains an increase in the capacity of one agent to make another do its bidding. The federal State recognizes the federated agents' ability to act. This is coherent with the increase in the number of agents and the fragmentation of power mentioned above.

4 Discussion

On a global scale, Belgium possesses one of the highest scores (84 %) of authority as source of power, occupying second place in the VOIP ranking following only the USA (85 %). The veil of ignorance that hangs before the congressmen is opaque. Our analysis confirms the influencing agents in the Constitution use authority as a primary resource. Two factors account for it.

First, in 1831, Belgium was under the control of foreign States. Its future was uncertain because it depended on the will of those foreign powers. Had great powers considered the Belgian State as a threat, they would have prevented its independence. In 1993, Belgium was a member of the European Union (EU), a body that keeps an eye on Belgium's political process, as it does all of its members. The EU cannot let one of its member countries allow divisions along regionalist problems go too far. Had the EU considered the Belgian devolution as a threat; it would have limited its dynamics. The international context in the nineteenth and twentieth centuries is obviously different. Decolonization and Europeanization are different political processes. Yet, both embedded Belgium in institutional constraints that influence the opacity of the veil of ignorance that hung before the drafters' eyes.

Second, in 1831, Belgium favored "agreement," to use Brennan and Buchanan's words, or "consociationalism," to employ Lijphart's terminology, in its handling of domestic divisions. This was the case in the nineteenth century and especially during the so-called unionist period. In the contemporary period, this is still the case. In 1993, consociationalism still helps Belgium in overtaking cleavages. In 1831 and in 1993, internal divisions endangered the polity and increased the uncertainty of decision-makers about their future and the future of the polity. Recent literature still shows that consociationalism remains a technique in Belgium to decide when deep conflicts threaten the stability or even the very survival of the polity, which corresponds to moments of uncertainty (Deschouwer 2006).

From a theoretical perspective, this would entail the veil of ignorance is more opaque when a Constitution is adopted under international constraints that cannot be managed by the State, and under domestic cleavages that have the potential to trigger unmanageable conflicts.

This could also attest to politicians being the main agents. In 1831 and in 1993, decision-makers opted for a representative democracy with delegates holding the decision-making power. In contrast to the Swiss case, for instance, no participatory instruments are planned for or employed. Citizens are mentioned in the texts in terms of their rights, but no direct instruments of democracy are prescribed to favor participation. From the same perspective, "private" actors are "ignored" in the texts. From a theoretical point of view, this is coherent with the scientific literature contending the prevalence of the "cartel of elites" within a consociative democracy (Lijphart 1969).

In turn, this power sharing of the elites explains the rigidity of the Constitution, one criterion mentioned by the consociationalist theory. The "cartel of elites" promoted the stability of the Constitution and of the political arrangements to limit changes for which the impacts were unknown. This is most notably the case for the Constitution of 1831 from its adoption until 1970. Our paper has contrasted two periods: the first, a period of Constitutional stability and scarce revisions taking place only in 1893 and 1921; and a second, a period of greater instability building the federal State through several Constitutional revisions in 1970, 1980, 1988, and, finally, 1993. But, even in this case, the mechanisms of rigidity were promoted (special majorities, alarm bell procedure, etc.).

In circumstances where State independence must be protected, or where devolution is a never-ending process, the veil of ignorance remains opaque. To international constraints and domestic cleavages as explanatory factors, we could add a third one related to the contemporary period: the presence of an unframed devolution process. "The steering capacity of a small group of political elites reluctant to abandon political control, the presence of institutional asymmetries, the initially dual nature of dividing competencies and the slow development of intergovernmental relations" (Swenden and Jans 2006: 877) are sources of uncertainty during any routine phase of the political process, but also at the initial moment of a Constitution's adoption.

5 Concluding Thoughts

The "Veil of Ignorance Project" to which this chapter contributes states that the higher proportion of power relations related to authority, the more opaque the veil of ignorance becomes. Actually, there was a large amount of uncertainty weighing on Belgian congressmen when they adopted both Constitutions because, more than wealth or knowledge, ultimately, their political authority was at stake. The VOIP asserts that in such circumstances, lawmakers tend to put the Constitution ahead of their own private interests. According to Brennan and Buchanan (1985: 35), uncertainty introduced in any choice among rulers or institutions serves the function of making potential agreement more, rather than less, likely.

Our statistics show that in Belgium, the dominant type of power emerges from political source, i.e., authority. At a time of building a new State (in 1831) or at a time of reforming the structures of this State through an ongoing process of federalization (in 1993), the drafters and adopters of the Constitution were uncertain about their future power position. The veil of ignorance in Belgium is opaque in this regard. The more opaque the veil at the moment of drafting and adopting the Constitution, the more the Constitution refers to authority, setting aside questions over wealth and knowledge. Therefore, our case study gives a confirmation of the first hypothesis of the VOIP (Imbeau and Jacob 2015: xx).

Our case study does not, however, confirm the second and third hypothesis of the VOIP. Both entail that uncertain constitutionalists will favor social over instrumental power relations and that the Constitution will deny capacities, rather than assign them in a context of ignorance. On the contrary, the Belgian case study illustrates a dominance of instrumental and positive power relations, both in 1831 and in 1993. We relied on two types of explanatory factors to bridge this gap. The first source of uncertainty is related to foreign constraints determining Belgium's constitutional choices: foreign surveillance in 1831 and EU membership in 1993. The second source relies on domestic features weighing on constitutional decisions: cleavages and consociationalism in 1831 as well as in 1993, and the presence of an unframed process of devolution.

This chapter helps us to understand how elites at two different periods of time managed to shape a State with two contradicting visions: unitarian in 1831 and federalist in 1993. Comparing these Constitutions draws a general picture of the Belgian drafting and adoption process. Future works are needed to investigate, more deeply, constitutional material drafted and adopted since 1993 and leading to creation of today's Belgian State.

As we have witnessed, notably in 2010–2011, Belgium has maybe reached some limits in its ability to function smoothly. The weight of the current devolution process must be taken into account to fully grasp the veil of ignorance. Obviously, the revision of the Constitution in 2011 still shows that the drafters face opacity in their ability of building a State that permanently experiences the strength of its cleavages and thus divisions. In the future, political stability will be challenged by the will and the ability of the decision-makers to conclude compromises within institutional constraints.

References

Brennan H, Buchanan JM (1985) The reason of rules. Cambridge University Press, Cambridge

Deschouwer K (2006) And the peace goes on? Consociational democracy and Belgian politics in the twenty-first century. W Eur Polit 29(5):895–911

Imbeau LM (2009) Testing the "veil of ignorance" hypothesis in constitutional choice: a "walk-talk" approach. J Publ Finance Publ Choice 26(1):3–21

Imbeau LM, Jacob S (2011) Is the "veil of ignorance" in constitutional choice a myth? An empirical exploration informed by a theory of power. In: Marciano A (ed) Constitutional mythologies. Springer, Dordrecht

Imbeau LM, Jacob S (2015) Measuring the opacity of the 'veil of ignorance' in constitutions: theory, method and some results. In: Imbeau LM, Jacob S (eds) Behind a veil of ignorance? Power and uncertainty in constitutional design. Springer, New York NY

Keating M (1998) Principes et problèmes du gouvernement asymétrique. Politique et Sociétés 17(3):93–111

Keating M (2009) Social citizenship, solidarity and welfare in regionalized and plurinational states. Citizsh Stud 13(5):501–513

Lijphart A (1969) Consociational democracy. World Polit 21(2):207–225

Lijphart A (1999) Patterns of democracy. Yale University Press, New Haven-London

Mabille X (1992) Histoire politique de la Belgique. CRISP, Bruxelles

Rokkan S (1970) Citizens, elections and parties. Universitetsforlaget, Oslo

Swenden W, Jans MT (2006) Will it stay or will it go? Federalism and the sustainability of Belgium. W Eur Polit 29(5):877–894

Witte E, Gubin E, Nadnrin J-P, Deneckere G (2005) Nouvelle Histoire de Belgique. Editions Complexe, Bruxelles

Chapter 8
Testing the "Veil of Ignorance" Hypothesis in Constitutional Choice: Evidence from the German *Grundgesetz*

Agnes Strauß

1 Introduction

Deriving evidence for the existence or the texture of a veil of ignorance[1] from the content of a constitution is a challenging task. The Veil of Ignorance Project (VOIP) proposes to extract units of investigation, called power relations, from the constitution and examine whether those units are linked to uncertainty. The method used is a coding procedure of the constitution following the codebook of the project. The basic idea is that some power relations can be linked to uncertainty, while others not. Imbeau and Jacob (2015) assume that power relations dealing with uncertainty are made behind a veil of ignorance. The more power relations deal with uncertainty, the more opaque was the veil of uncertainty at the drafting process.

Examining the content of the German constitution, the so-called *Grundgesetz*, in order to find evidence confirming the existence of a veil of uncertainty is demanding. The historical development of the constitution after World War II (WWII) and the large number of involved actors and veto players—the allied forces and the German states, the *Bundesländer*[2]—impose hurdles on the endeavour to link the content of the *Grundgesetz* to uncertainty.

[1] The veil of ignorance and the veil of uncertainty describe a similar situation; however, a distinction has to be made. Ignorance means a "lack of knowledge", uncertainty is a particular kind of missing information. While ignorance encompasses missing information on individual characteristics or the like, uncertainty creates a lack of knowledge not about individual characteristics, but more on future benefits or losses. This study will use the term veil of uncertainty as it is exactly that what the VOIP tries to measure.

[2] The abbreviation *Länder* will be used throughout the text.

A. Strauß (✉)
Institute of Law and Economics, University of Hamburg, Hamburg, Germany
e-mail: agnes.strauss@ile-graduateschool.de

L.M. Imbeau and S. Jacob (eds.), *Behind a Veil of Ignorance?*,
Studies in Public Choice 32, DOI 10.1007/978-3-319-14953-0_8

This study aims to investigate whether it is possible to find evidence for the veil of ignorance from the content of the *Grundgesetz* and whether the proposed method of the VOIP produces adequate results. After shortly describing the methodology used by Imbeau and Jacobs, it summarises the historical setting of the drafting and adoption of the *Grundgesetz*. This section will also discuss the sources of uncertainty at the time of interest, the drafter's motivations, as well as the evolution of the drafting process at the two constitutional assemblies in Germany, the Herrenchiemsee Convent and the Parliamentary Council (PC). The third section presents the analysis of the statistical findings from the coding of the *Grundgesetz* following the codebook of the VOIP. The last section discusses the findings.

2 The Methodology and Theory of the Veil of Ignorance Project

The unit of analysis of the VOIP is a power relation. Constitutions organise the distribution of power within the nation state. In the constitutional text, power is fixed in the form of power relations. A power relation defines an agent and the capacities ascribed to, or taken from, this agent. The agent may have the power over *something* or over *someone*. Power is therefore defined as the capacity to bring about a particular outcome, either by oneself or by using the capacity to make someone to bring about the outcome (Imbeau and Jacob 2015).

The VOIP proposes three interpretations of the power relations as follows:

Political power is more volatile than economic or preceptoral power. In the presence of uncertainty, constitutional drafters will base power relations mainly on authority and not on wealth or knowledge. The first proposition of the VOIP therefore reads as follows: (*P 1*) *the more authority-based power relations identified in the constitution, the thicker was the veil of uncertainty.*

Power may be either *the capacity to do something* or having the means *to make someone do something*. In the first case, it is spoken about instrumental power relations and in the second case, about social power relations. Constitutional drafters are concerned with the protection of their current power position; therefore, they implement more social power relations than instrumental power relations. The second proposition of the VOIP therefore reads as follows: (*P 2*) *the more social power relations identified in the constitutional text, the thicker was the veil of uncertainty.*

An agent may be given the capacity to do something or he may have some capacity explicitly taken away. In case he is given the capacity, he has the power to do something or to make someone do something: the power relation is positive. If the capacity is taken from the agent, he is denied the power to do something or to make someone do something: the power relation is negative. The drafters of a constitution will rather limit power than ascribe it, in case they face uncertainty. The third proposition of the VOIP is as follows: (*P 3*) *the more negative power relations found in the constitutional text, the thicker was the veil of uncertainty.*

The power relations are identified in all constitutions of the project and are coded in three variables for each power relation. The first variable *V1* captures the source of power of the power relation, which can either be authority, wealth or knowledge. The second variable *V2* records whether a power relation is social or instrumental, and the third variable *V3* captures the direction of the power relation, which is either positive or negative (Imbeau and Jacob 2015).

3 The Historical Context of the Drafting and Adoption of the German *Grundgesetz*

Unlike other constitutions, the creation of the *Grundgesetz* was not initiated by the Germans themselves. On the contrary, after the loss of WWII, the occupation powers triggered the drafting process. This created a special situation which has to be taken into consideration if one plans to evaluate the veil of uncertainty hypothesis on the basis of the *Grundgesetz*. The following section provides the reader with the historical background of the *Grundgesetz* and its drafters. It will display incentives of the involved actors and developments which influenced their expectations and choices.

The drafting and adoption process of the *Grundgesetz* is probably one of the best documented and analysed constitutional geneses worldwide, as the Germans and the Allies kept records of all actions. The reason may be found in the situation of Germany in the community of states after 1945, the occupation and the problem of creating a new political system after a complete breakdown. A huge body of the literature exists in historical and political science. The following section, dealing with the historical context of Germany from 1945 until 1949, is based on Niclauss (1998), Spevack (2001), Möllers (2009), Bommarius (2009), Frotscher and Pieroth (2010). Very important sources are the edited and published protocols of the Herrenchiemsee Constitutional Convent and the PC of the *Deutscher Bundestag* (2009). The Bundeszentrale für politische Bildung (2012) in cooperation with the Stiftung Haus der Geschichte der Bundesrepublik Deutschland (2012) Bonn offers a profound evaluation of original sources when it comes to biographies of the members of the PC and their work.

3.1 The Preparation of a German Constitution

3.1.1 German Constitutional History

A glance on German constitutional history is necessary to understand the foundations of the *Grundgesetz,* which can be traced back to Germany's early democratic movement in the nineteenth century. The *Grundgesetz* is influenced by three German constitutions dated before 1945, of which only two were democratic: the constitution of St. Pauls Church of 1849, which was never implemented, the constitution of the German Empire from 1871 and the Weimar constitution of 1919. The constitution of 1849 influenced constitutional texts in Germany with regard to the basic rights it foresaw and the bicameral legislative system (Frotscher and Pieroth 2010). The *Grundgesetz* reflects the division of competences between the Federation and the Länder developed in the Weimar constitution in 1919 (Frotscher and Pieroth 2010). It addresses specifically the weak points identified in the Weimar constitution, such as the critical position of the president, the state of emergency legislation and the non-existence of constitutional review. It is necessary to understand how the political system of the Weimar constitution was gradually transformed from a parliamentary towards an authoritative presidential system in the late years of the Weimar Republic, in order to understand the preferences of the drafters of the *Grundgesetz.* The seizure of power by the Nazis was made possible by a number of important constitutional changes which took place before 1933. The Enabling Act finally transferred the legislative power including the authority of constitutional change to the executive branch. What followed was a period of political *Gleichschaltung* and subversion of the basic rights, which finally led to the unification of all authority of the state in the person of the "Führer" and a de facto abolition of the basic rights until 1945 (Frotscher and Pieroth 2010).

3.1.2 German Sovereignty After World War II (1945–1947)

After the unconditional surrender on 8 May 1945 of all German forces, the governmental and organisational powers were submitted to the four Allies who divided Germany into four zones of occupation. The Allies installed a Control Council in Berlin to coordinate their actions, which governed Germany (Frotscher and Pieroth 2010). Thus, Germany was no longer a sovereign nation state (Spevack 2001). The occupation shaped the drafting process and the lack of sovereignty and the increased number of veto players influenced the constitutional text. In contrast to a sovereign nation state, where the constituency adopts a constitution, an occupied nation state has an additional veto player. The new constitution faces not only the ratification by the people, but also requires the consent of the occupation powers. The preferences of all veto players influence the drafting process.

The question then is as follows: To which extent does the new constitution reflect the constitution of the occupier? (Elkins et al. 2008). On the one hand, the drafters already anticipate the preferences of the veto players in the drafting, and on the other hand, the occupation power has the means to influence the process and the deliberations directly (Elster 1995). It is obvious that one major incentive of the Western Allies was the maintenance of their influence on German politics. This was realised by the Occupation Statute which did not end with the ratification of the *Grundgesetz*. It was binding for all German government besides the constitution. As the occupation powers themselves were not subject to the constitution and because their particular interests were guaranteed by the Occupation Statute, it can be assumed that the implementation of individual interest did not play a major role for them. Elkins et al. (2008) find that constitutions written under occupation do not simply replicate the constitutional tradition of the occupier. They argue that for the new constitution to be successful, it is more important that it is accepted by the constituency in order that the constitutional rules are self-enforcing (Elkins et al. 2008). Their evaluation of the Japanese case shows that directly after WWII the interest of the USA was not to export its own institutions, but to find those institutions fitting the local situation (Elkins et al. 2008). It is not too far-fetched that the USA followed this policy as well for Western Germany and that the two other occupiers France and Britain, while having different ideological positions did not oppose this goal in general. The major point that led to controversies between the Western Allies and the German drafters was the degree of federalism that should be implemented by the *Grundgesetz*.

3.1.3 The Events Preceding the Constitutional Convent at Herrenchiemsee 1948 and the Parliamentary Council 1948–1949

Directly after the war, Germany was devastated and in disorder. Many cities were completely destroyed by bombings and "the entire country was in a state of collapse" (Spevack 2001). It was internationally isolated and early plans of the Allies foresaw that it should never again become a member of the international community. On the other hand, the population suffered from the permeation of Nazi thought and the aftermath of the Holocaust. The denazification undertaken by the Allies could not capture the whole problem. The situation in post-war Germany was unstable and uncertain, among other reasons due to the negligible economic production and foreign occupation. In addition, the old forces of the Nazis still persisted to a certain degree and it was an important question for the Western Allies and the upcoming German elite of how to limit the influence of the old regime to a minimum, knowing that a complete erasure of Nazi ideology would not be possible.

At the Potsdam Conference in 1945, the Allies had decided to rebuild German self-government first on the local level and then on the level of the *Länder*. Therefore, they began to appoint mayors and district administrators (*Landräte*) and allowed the formation of political parties on district level. Those parties focussed in the beginning more on *Länder* politics, because early on, the Allies hindered national associations. In 1946, the USA had already authorised the appointed prime ministers for the *Länder* of their zone of occupation to initiate the constitutional process for the *Länder*. The other Allies followed this example (Frotscher and Pieroth 2010). The first German constitutions after WWII were the constitutions of the *Länder*. For them, the creation of the *Grundgesetz* meant a reduction of their competences. Thus, their governments focussed on the maintenance of as much independence of the *Länder* as possible in the *Grundgesetz*. In addition, some of the drafters of the *Grundgesetz* gained experience in the drafting process of a *Landesverfassung*. They most likely had valuable insight in the workings of a constitutional assembly, and they already had experience in the debates on constitutional provisions. Furthermore, the *Grundgesetz* may have been influenced by the contents of the *Landesverfassungen* more than through constitutional export from the Western Allies.

The Western Allies planned to strengthen Germany's economy, namely through the Marshall Plan and the monetary reform (Spevack 2001). In opposition to that the Soviet Union favoured an agricultural Germany shaped in a communist system. It made clear that it was not willing to give up Eastern Germany from Soviet control. The increasing tensions from the struggle for world dominance led to the break of the former wartime alliance against the Nazi Regime in Germany into two parts. The conflict between East and West evolved fast and climaxed for the first time with the Berlin Blockade in June 1948, a Soviet reaction to the monetary reform in West Germany, a reform of which the Soviet sector had been left out by the Western Allies (Spevack 2001). The Berlin Blockade and the Airlift drew the West Germans towards the Western Allies and probably increased the incentives to enter into compromises in order not to lose the protection of the Western Allies and especially the USA. Another basis for the westward orientation had already been laid down during the Nazi Regime, where the Slavic nations were denunciated by the Nazis as "communist sub-humans", an ideology which was not completely erased in Germany by the denazification.

In early 1948, the Western Allies met together with the Benelux States for the London Six Powers Conference without inviting the Soviet Union, and as a result, the Allied Control Council broke up in March 1948. The Military Governors of the Western Allies handed three documents from the London Conference to the Prime Ministers of the *Länder*, which advised the creation of a German constitution, authorised the reconsideration of the borders of the *Länder* and announced an Occupation Statute organising competences between the Allies and the Germans (Niclauss 1998). The Prime Ministers wanted to avoid the division of Germany which would result from the creation of a western state and therefore only reluctantly followed the allied instruction. They argued for a provisional constitution which left the way open for a reunification with the Soviet zone in the future. The Western Allies however made clear that the provisions of the Frankfurt documents were non-negotiable. It is obvious that the chance to take the German fate back into their hands finally led the Prime Ministers to relent in general (Niclauss 1998). However, they further insisted on the term "*Grundgesetz*" for the created construct, with a suggested translation to "Basic Constitutional Law" which satisfied the German wish for a transitional construct and the Allied wish for a stable constitution (Frotscher and Pieroth 2010). It was one of the occasions, where Allied and German interests conflicted. The fact that the Germans prevailed shows that the Western Allies were willing to give as much freedom to the drafting process as possible.

The limited time horizon available for the completion of the *Grundgesetz* had an important influence on the expectations of the drafters and adopters. Most likely, they were willing to enter into more compromises with each other, as well as with the Western Allies, while expecting a quick reunification and a new constitutional drafting process within a few years. The uncertainty about the effects of the constitutional rules on the future positions of individual drafters may have been heavily reduced, and in the case that negative effects were expected, those were thought to be limited to the time span the constitution would endure; the same holding true for the positive effects.

3.2 The Drafting Process 1948–1949

The drafting process of the *Grundgesetz* was accompanied by the Cold War which dominated world politics in 1948–49. The Soviet Union expanded its influence on the Eastern European states through the strengthening of communist parties and the implementation of socialist regimes. After the monetary reform in West Germany, the Soviet Union reacted with the Berlin Blockade. The West answered with the Berlin Airlift in June 1948, which lasted until May 1949 (Spevack 2001). The question of nuclear proliferation accelerated the East–West tensions. It is clear that Germany was only "the focal point of a struggle for influence that was being fought in comparatively more remote places, such as eastern Europe and Asia" (Spevack 2001). As such, the West Germans could not be sure how future events would affect them and their position with the Western Allies. It is possible that they perceived themselves to be chess pieces in a world game, and these observations were most likely true.

The delegates at the Herrenchiemsee Convent and the PC might have followed the provisions of the Western Allies willingly, in order to maintain their patronage and protection. As such, they were inclined to implement rules which stabilised the political system in West Germany against the influence of socialist or communist regimes. Otherwise, the Western Allies were not willing to give up Western Germany to the Soviets. Germany was a very important strategic location for their troops, especially for the USA. As well, it was assumed that the power governing Germany would have major influence in Europe, despite the precarious situation of Germany after the war (Spevack 2001). Resulting from that situation the involved actors, the German Prime Ministers and the drafters of the constitution on the one hand and the Western Allies on the other hand, had strong incentives to make each other believe that abandoning the negotiations for the constitution was a real option. However, it was quite clear that the threat of the other actors was only weakly credible. Delays of the negotiations or a blockage of them therefore was part of the actors' strategies to get as much of their position realised as possible. However, it is very likely that a definite failure of the negotiations would have been avoided by both sides.

3.2.1 The Constitutional Convent at Herrenchiemsee

The *Grundgesetz* was written in two steps. A first was the meeting of drafting committee consisting of constitutional experts at Herrenchiemsee. The second, the official drafting body, was the PC in Bonn. Each one will be discussed separately, beginning with the Herrenchiemsee Constitutional Convent.

After the Western Allies had demanded the Prime Ministers to constitute a council for the drafting of a constitution for the western zones of occupation from 1 September 1948, the Prime Ministers held a meeting of constitutional experts in the old castle on the island Herreninsel in the Chiemsee in August 1948, in order to maintain the influence of the *Länder* in the future constitution of Germany (Bauer-Kirsch 2005). The goal was to create a draft which would dominate the negotiations and would serve as the most influential document for the German constitution.

The convent was organised in plenary sessions and committees. The first committee dealt with fundamental, the second with jurisdictional and the third with organisational questions. The participation in these committees varied markedly, and minutes were not systematically taken for all meetings (Bauer-Kirsch 2005). After 2 weeks of work, the representatives of the *Länder* approved an unofficial proposal for a constitution. However, the final report was prepared by the editorial committee only afterwards. It is remarkable that the members of the Constitutional Convent did not vote again on the final report which was given to the Prime Ministers of the *Länder* (Bauer-Kirsch 2005). The final report contained a draft constitution which foresaw 149 articles and a 50 page documentation of the discussions as well as a detailed commentary, which displayed the opinion of the convent on several articles. In many fundamental questions where a final decision was not reached, the convent offered several alternative wordings. They left all negotiations on disputable articles or wordings for the PC (Bauer-Kirsch 2005).

In contrast to several other drafts of a German constitution which already existed prior to 1948, the draft of the Constitutional Convent had the advantage that it was commissioned by the Prime Ministers of the *Länder* and therefore could claim a higher grade of legitimacy, as in 1948 the parliaments of the *Länder* were the highest, directly elected authorities in Germany (Bauer-Kirsch 2005). The Prime Ministers gave the draft of the *Grundgesetz* from the Constitutional Convent at Herrenchiemsee to the PC on 31 August 1948. They emphasised that the PC was free to choose how it dealt with the draft. However, as it was the only complete draft and the delegates of the PC knew that the parliaments of the *Länder* would finally have to ratify the constitution, it was the basis for most of the debates of the PC (Bauer-Kirsch 2005). The strong influence of the Herrenchiemsee draft on the work of the PC can as well be explained by the membership of some delegates in both drafting bodies. They contributed to the sustainability of the negotiations from the Herrenchiemsee Constitutional Convent to the PC, as they brought the discussions from the Convent to the negotiations in Bonn.

3.2.2 The Members of the Constitutional Convent in Herrenchiemsee

The Prime Ministers appointed representatives for each of the 11 *Länder* qualifying for the task of writing a constitution with their expertise in constitutional law. Each of them held at least a doctoral degree and many worked in academia or occupied high positions within the judicial system of their *Land* (Markovitz 2007). Every representative was accompanied by a number of assistants, who were as well all constitutional experts from academia or the public sector.

The assistants outnumbered the representatives from the *Länder* and had strong influence on the content of the *Grundgesetz*. This resulted from the fact that they actively participated in the commissions. The members of the Convent defined themselves as scientific working group. Their goal was to propose several solutions to constitutional problems and not to find political compromises (Bauer-Kirsch 2005). "Above all, they wanted to avoid what they saw as "the serious structural mistakes" of the Weimar constitution, and this professional approach was echoed in the debates of the PC" (Markovitz 2007). Still, it was important for the *Länder* representatives to implement the interests of the *Länder* they represented in the constitution.

3.2.3 The Parliamentary Council

Directly after the meeting of the Constitutional Convent in Herrenchiemsee, the PC constituted itself on 1 September 1958 in Bonn. Within the first week, the PC organised its committees (Niclauss 1998).

In considering the timeline of the deliberations, four phases can be distinguished. The first marks the early and fast work of the PC in the committees (Niclauss 1998). It was dominated by the wish to quickly present a constitutional draft, under the impression that the generosity of the Allies might be rather short-lived. In the second phase, a first intervention of the Allies redirected the work of the PC and it became more apparent that the positions of the parties conflicted heavily with regard to the propositions of the Allies. The third phase of the PC is characterised by the long inter-party negotiations (Niclauss 1998). Regardless of the heavy debates between the parties, the military governors rejected a compromise the parties had finally found. This rejection opened the fourth phase of the *Grundgesetz* debates. A new proposal, however, was also rejected by the occupiers and the negotiations had to be restarted. The SPD, in particular, was not willing to enter compromises going further than the ones already presented (Niclauss 1998).

Finally, in April 1949 the Allies published the Washington Declaration, which presented a more lenient position of the occupiers towards the *Grundgesetz* and towards the propositions from the German drafters. The negotiations took a new turn and the PC worked together with the liaison officers of the Allies on a new compromise. The delegates of the PC voted on the *Grundgesetz* on 8 May 1949 by name. It was accepted with 53 versus 12 votes. The delegates from the DP, the Zentrum, the KPD and six members of the CSU delegation rejected the draft (Niclauss 1998).

The Allies intervened several times in the work of the PC. They published a first statement on the constitutional rules governing public finances in October 1948. A second memorandum followed in November, and in December, a conference between the military governors and a delegation from the PC took place in Frankfurt, where the allies assumed the role of arbitrators between the parties.

With the objection to the big compromise between the parties and the rejection of the second compromise, both in March 1949, the Allies induced a long period of hard negotiations. On 12 May 1949, the Allies agreed to the draft of the *Grundgesetz* from the PC. With the ratification of the *Grundgesetz* in the majority of the Länder parliaments, only Bavaria[3] rejected the draft; on 23 May 1949, the *Grundgesetz* came into effect.

This development raises the question of whether there was any scope for the delegates of the PC to pursue individual interest. The problem that a compromise had to be found, which satisfied the interest all involved actors shaped the options of the delegates in Bonn decisively. The regular intervention of the Western Allies also raises the question how much constitutional export took place.[4]

3.2.4 The Delegates at the Parliamentary Council

The American journalist Theodore White described the Members of the PC as "a collection of waifs, strays, victims, outcasts and resistant to Hitler's politics more devoted to liberty, republicanism and democracy even than ourselves" (Spevack 2001). According to him, the German drafters of the *Grundgesetz* were completely powerless marionettes of the Allies, having gone through several stages of denazification (Spevack 2001). Not only did the Allies intervene with the drafting process of the *Grundgesetz* to shape it after their wishes, but also the members of the PC were, although elected by the Lander parliaments, personalities approved by the Allies and some had strong personal links to their occupiers, e.g. due to migration.

Each *Land* delegated a number of representatives equivalent to their population share. The distribution of seats in the PC for the parties was proportionate to the number of votes they received in total (Möllers 2009). The PC had 65

[3] The Bavarian government has been led by the CSU, which had voted against the *Grundgesetz* also in the PC. They were not content with the degree of centralisation foreseen by the *Grundgesetz*.

[4] An issue which cannot be solved in this study, as it would require a careful comparative analysis of all constitutions coming into question.

members entitled to vote and five delegates from Berlin with observatory status. The Christian Democrats (CDU/CSU) and the Social Democrats (SPD) each sent 27 delegates, the Liberal Party (FDP) five and the Communist Party (KPD), the Center Party (Z) and the German Party (DP) each two. Several replacements occurred during the drafting process. Among the drafters were only four women. The majority of 47 of the members were public servants or had been in the past. The majority of 32 delegates had a judicial background and 11 were economists. More than half of the delegates held a doctoral degree. The average age of the drafters was 55. The Nazi Regime had attracted mainly the young adults; their generation was less represented in the PC after several stages of denazification (Möllers 2009). The background of the members concerning their history in the Nazi regime is of course not representative for the Germans. The majority of the members of the PC had internally or externally migrated or had been part of the active or passive resistance (Möllers 2009). Many came from an intellectual and bourgeois background (Markovitz 2007). "The debates in the PC reflected the elevated class background and education of the members; historical references and literary quotations were bantered back and forth" (Markovitz 2007). They had already experience from the drafting of the Länder constitutions. Three members of the PC had already been involved in the drafting process of the Weimar constitution.

3.3 *On the Interests of the Drafters of the Grundgesetz*

Economic theory has long established that individual characteristics influence behaviour of constitutional drafters. Previous studies found that special interests, either partisan or regional, shape the behaviour of the drafters (Raudla 2010).

Party membership is the best predictor of the interests in the German case, assuming that the individual drafters supported their party's opinion and were selected by their parties, which of course was the case. While the Constitutional Convent at Herrenchiemsee was initiated by the Minister Presidents to guarantee Länder interests in the *Grundgesetz*, the PC was the arena of the parties. The two big parties, the CDU/CSU and SPD, had the greatest weight; yet, their view for a new West German state could not have been more different. On the one hand, the CDU/CSU preferred a federalist, capitalist economic system and a bourgeois democracy. They managed to reconcile their goals to those of the USA. An integration of a West German state into the western sphere was the main goal of the Union parties. The SPD on the other hand supported a socialist organisation of Germany and opposed capitalism in general. Britain, with its Labour Government at the time, was the preferred partner of the SPD. They opposed the division of Germany and were in favour of a more centralised government (Spevack 2001). The FDP objected to the notion of a provisional *Grundgesetz* but favoured a stable and earnest constitution. Under Theodor Heuss, they regularly took a conciliatory position. The DP favoured conservative positions. The Centre Party had a long tradition as a Catholic party in Germany with conservative Christian positions. With the creation of the CDU after the war, it lost its influence dramatically. They supported many of the CDU positions, but were however slightly more socially oriented. Rather marginalized were the members of the Communist party KPD. "In the debates, nobody listened to the Communists. Their surest way of catching the assembly's attention was by way of catcalls" (Markovitz 2007).

It was an early agreement between the CDU/CSU and the SPD that the new constitution should be based on a broad consensus (Elster 1995). This was mainly motivated by the fact that both parties were equally strong in the PC and held the government in an equal number of the *Länder.* Thus, they had to compromise their positions because no party would have been able to gather a sufficiently large majority otherwise.

After party affiliation, the *Länder* were and are definitively the other important interest group in Germany. They exerted their influence mainly at the Herrenchiemsee Constitutional Convent, although the delegates of the PC were dispatched by their *Länder* parliaments. In addition, the ratification of the new constitution was in the hand of the *Länder* parliaments. The interests of the *Länder* were mainly related to the organisation of the federation and associated with the independence of the *Länder* in as many policy areas as possible. The territorial interests were divided between those of the rural population in some of the *Länder,* such as Bavaria or Lower Saxony, and the population in the industrialised regions of Germany, such as the Ruhr area in North Rhine-Westphalia. These interests were taken up by the political parties. The SPD was rather successful among the urban population—the major cities in the Ruhr area as well as Bremen and Hamburg were ruled by SPD governments in 1948—while the CDU was more successful with the bourgeoisie and the conservative rural population. The regional interests did not per se play a dominant role during the negotiations on the *Grundgesetz*; however, they were not completely absent.

4 Description of the Content of the Constitution in Terms of a Power Relation Framework

The following section describes the findings of the content analysis following the coding rules of the codebook of the VOIP.

4.1 Description of the Formal Aspects of the German Grundgesetz

The English version of the *Grundgesetz* counts 21,093 words which is an average length compared to the other constitutions in the project. It has 146 paragraphs and is structured in 14 sections. The *Grundgesetz* has two main parts. The first covers the basic rights from Art. 1 to 19 *Grundgesetz*. It is a particularity of the *Grundgesetz* that the drafters created a section for the basic rights in the very beginning of the constitutional text. This was done to clarify the relationship between the state and the citizen, even before the organisational structure of the state was laid down. In the second part, Art. 20–146 *Grundgesetz*, the organisational standards of the Federal Republic of Germany are formulated (Möllers 2009).

4.2 Presentation of the Statistical Results from the Content Analysis Following the Coding Procedure Presented by the Codebook of the Veil of Ignorance Project

The coding of the German *Grundgesetz* identified in total 1,114 power relations. Among them, 79.2 % have authority as source of power. Wealth and knowledge play a considerably lesser role, which is not surprising in the first place (cf. Table 1). A high share of authority-based power relations would be expected as constitutions structure authorities.

The German constitution has a share of authority-based power relations which is slightly above the mean of the constitutions in the whole project. The question is, whether this high share of authority-based power relations is related to uncertainty.

Table 1 further shows that social power relations have only a small numerical advantage over instrumental power relations in the *Grundgesetz*. Both the types of power and the value from the *Grundgesetz* are above the mean of the constitutions in the project. This leads to the findings for the third variable *V3*. A significant majority of the identified power relations have a positive direction in the *Grundgesetz*. Only 2.8 % of them deny the agent the use of a power resource. The

Table 1 Distribution of power relations in the German *Grundgesetz* by source, type and direction of power (%)

Source of power	
Authority [*V1* = 1]	79.2
Wealth [*V1* = 2]	6.5
Knowledge [*V1* = 3]	5.6
Indeterminate [*V1* = 8]	8.8
Total (*N*)	100.1 (1,114)
Type of power	
Social [*V2* = 1]	51.4
Instrumental [*V2* = 2]	48.6
Total (N)	100.0 (1,114)
Direction of power	
Positive [*V3* = 1]	97.1
Negative [*V3* = 2]	2.8
Indeterminate [*V3* = 8]	0.1
Total (N)	100.0 (1,114)

Table 2 Type of power per source of power in the German constitution (%)

	Social power	Instrumental power	Total (N)
Authority	43.4	35.8	79.2 (882)
Wealth	3.1	3.3	6.4 (72)
Knowledge	1.8	3.8	5.6 (62)
Indeterminate	3.1	5.7	8.8 (98)
Total (N)	51.4 (573)	48.6 (541)	100.0 (1,114)

puzzle concerning the relevance of the variables grows with this finding. Why would one find support for uncertainty according to P1 and P2, even though it is limited, but not according to P3? The very intuitive answer to this question is that one or more of the variables do not capture uncertainty.

Under closer examination, Table 2 shows that in those cases where the power is based on authority, the share of social power relations is higher than the share of instrumental power relations. For the power relations drawing on wealth or knowledge as source of power, this is reversed. The VOIP argues that under uncertainty, constitutional drafters are more concerned about protecting themselves from the abuse of power by others. Therefore, they implement a higher share of authority-based power relations and they are specifically concerned with social power relations. What is found in the German case is a combination of both. Imbeau and Jacob argue that this combined measure is a measure for the opaqueness of the veil of ignorance (Imbeau and Jacob 2015).

A basic proposition of the VOIP is that under uncertainty, constitutional framers will implement rules to avoid a future abuse of power by others. It is interesting to analyse only the basic rights, because they deal without any doubt with the protection of individuals from the abuse of state power. The protection of the individual from state coercion lies obviously in the interest of all citizens and especially in the interest of those who are at the lower end of the power distribution. The *Grundgesetz* has two parts. The first covers only the basic rights and the second part deals with the state organisation of Germany. Thus, it seems to be a suitable endeavour to focus the analysis on basic rights provisions. Even though one could argue that the creation of a whole section concerned only with the protective rights of citizens may be evidence enough for the fact that the framers were indeed very keen to protect individuals from the abuse of power.

Very strong support for the propositions of the VOIP can be expected from the seperate analysis of the statistical findings for these parts. Explicitly comparing the first part of the Grundgesetz (the basic rights) to the second part (the state organisation), the share of authority-based power relations should be higher in the first part than in the second part, the share of social power relations should be increased in the first part in comparison with the second part and the share of negative power relations should as well be larger in the first part than in the second.

As one can see in Table 3, only 110 power relations were identified in the basic rights section. They show a pattern which is distinct from the overall findings as

Table 3 Distribution of power relations in the basic rights section of the *Grundgesetz* by source and direction of power (%)

Source of power	
Authority [$V1 = 1$]	69.0
Wealth [$V1 = 2$]	1.0
Knowledge [$V1 = 3$]	9.0
Indeterminate [$V1 = 8$]	21.0
Total (*N*)	100.0 (110)
Direction of power	
Positive [$V3 = 1$]	89.0
Negative [$V3 = 2$]	11.0
Total (*N*)	100.0 (110)

expected. Authority is in the first part of the *Grundgesetz* only a source of 69 % of the power relations compared to a share of 80 % in the second part. The share of indeterminate sources is considerably higher in the first section of the *Grundgesetz*. Thus, the first expectation concerning the source of power is not met. A very simple explanation for this is that many of the capacities defined in the basic rights section are based on the individual per se and are not derived from his/her political, economic or preceptoral entitlements. The share of social power relations has increased slightly by 1.6 % points. This is as expected but compared to the difference between the two parts of the *Grundgesetz* for *V*1, the result seems negligible.

However, the share of positive power relations also diminishes considerably when only the first part of the *Grundgesetz* is analysed. The protection of the basic rights requires the restriction of state powers. The increase of negative power relations thus is as expected. However, the positive power relations still dominate the text.

The pattern of the variables in the second part of the *Grundgesetz* is in line with the findings for the overall constitution; therefore, a deeper analysis of these findings is omitted here.

The suggestion that the basic rights section yields different results for the variables than the second part of the *Grundgesetz* and the overall text is confirmed. We expected to observe more authority-based power relations in the basic rights part of the *Grundgesetz* than that in the second part of the constitutional document, but we did not find that. This raises the question of how to interpret the result. According to P1, a high share of authority-based power relations is a result of uncertainty, as drafters under uncertainty will implement rules which protect them from the abuse of power by others. The considerations made above, in contrast, suggest that authority-based power relations are either not linked to uncertainty or that there was no uncertainty on the drafters' side during the drafting process.

On the other hand, the share of negative power relations is increased in the first part of the *Grundgesetz* compared to the second part. This difference is as expected and confirms P3, which states that under uncertainty, constitutional framers implement rules to protect individuals from the abuse of power.

Still the results are conflicting and even more puzzling. Why are less authority-based power relations observed in the basic rights section of the *Grundgesetz* than in the state organisational provisions in the second part? Why does the share of social power relations not change at all? Why is the share of negative power relations higher in the basic rights section, although the share of authority-based power relations is reduced? And how can the different findings be reconciled with the theory? Obviously, one or more of the variables does not capture uncertainty and one or more of the propositions of the VOIP has to be reconsidered.

First of all, the share of authority-based power relations may be lower in the basic rights sections, since in this section, the rights of individuals are defined, not the rights of authorities. Thus, even though the basic rights deal with the protection of individuals from the abuse of power, the goal is not served by only analysing this section. Perhaps, it is the fact that this section was created and put ahead of all further provisions which proves more than the content analysis is able to. Second, it is plausible that the share of social power relations may have nothing to say about uncertainty during the drafting process. The findings for the *Grundgesetz* in total are insignificant, and for the basic rights section, it is the same. Third, the negative power relations may be higher in the basic rights part, since basic rights are defensive rights and therefore formulated differently than provisions for the organisation of the state. Still, the share of positive power relations dominates as well in this part of the *Grundgesetz*. Finally, negative power relations may be used in the basic rights section to protect citizens from the abuse of state power, but not in the section of the organisation of the state. There the drafters may have focussed more on defining authority as source of power. However, the VOIP has not yet formulated how the different propositions may be connected.

5 Critical Discussion of the Findings

5.1 About the Different Actors in the Drafting Process

One factor in the discussion is how much room for manoeuvre the delegates had during the drafting process. They knew that not only the majority of the *Länder* parliaments had to accept the draft and that the allies had to consent to it. The Western Allies intervened regularly in the work of the delegates of the PC. There could have been limited scope for the agents to follow their own interest, when this interest was conflicting with the Allies interests, and the Allies had heterogeneous interests as well. Their interactions prove that the matter of the German constitution was highly controversial among them. While the French for example were sceptical towards a unified West German state and preferred a loose federation of the *Länder*, the USA was in favour of a federation following their own model. Both models were not enough for the British, however, who were rather in favour of a strong central organisation. The CDU/CSU was very successful in combining their interest with those of the Americans. In addition, the delegates had to keep in mind that the *Grundgesetz* had to be adopted by a majority of the *Länder*. Thus, a deviation too far from the Herrenchiemsee draft was seen as problematic. The blocking position of the SPD from March 1949 until the end of April 1949 shows that the drafters were not willing to write a constitution only to the liking of the Western Allies. Although some voices in the public often stated that the delegates of the PC were only marionettes of the Allies, it would have been fatal if this critique would have led to the conviction among the Germans that their new constitution was dictated by the occupiers (Elkins et al. 2008).

The regular intervention of the Western Allies influenced the *Grundgesetz*. It is not easy to distinguish from the final constitutional text, to which degree the variables of the VOIP reflect the existence of a veil of ignorance and to which degree they reflect the compromises from the interests of the different veto players.

5.2 Time Considerations

A classic argument in constitutional economics is that the long-term perspective of constitutional rules has the effect that drafters are uncertain about future effects of the rules they implement and that therefore decision-makers approach general interest and may reach agreements more easily in contrast to a situation when all of them try to implement their individual interest (Brennan and Buchanan 1985). It seems that this function is sometimes subsumed under the veil of uncertainty. However, considering the time horizon for rules separately from the veil, the picture becomes complex. Vermeule (2001) counter-argues that it is not obvious from the beginning whether durability of constitutional rules really serves the purpose of distorting individual interests, because it may still be rational for the individual to ignore the future effects and it may be hard to find consent on rules which are hard to change ex post (Vermeule 2001).

It is possible that only the transitory character of the *Grundgesetz* made compromises feasible, which would have been out of reach in case the drafters had expected the *Grundgesetz* to last. The delegates at the Herrenchiemsee Convent and at the PC were perhaps willing to accept formulations or provisions they normally would not have agreed to if they had planned the *Grundgesetz* to be a lasting constitution. It seems likely that the expectation of a quick reunification and therefore a new drafting process of a constitution influenced the behaviour of the drafters and therefore the constitutional text.

6 Conclusion

The test of the Veil of Ignorance Hypothesis suggested by Imbeau and Jacob (2015) analysing the content of a constitution gives only mixed evidence in the German case. The findings from the content analysis of the *Grundgesetz* and the historical background are ambiguous. First evidence from the *Grundgesetz* shows that primarily authority is used as source of power and that the share of social power relations is indeed higher in the constitutional text than the share of instrumental power relations. The advance is, however, so small that it is unclear whether it is relevant. That a constitution would rather limit power than ascribing it is not supported by the findings from the content analysis of the *Grundgesetz*.

Overall a content analysis is an attractive tool to find evidence for a veil of ignorance in the text of a constitution. However, even if evidence could be found that the constitution satisfies the general interest, the complicated structure of the drafting process does not allow for the simple conclusion that the drafters faced a very opaque veil. On one hand, the interaction between several veto players leads to a compromise of the different positions and it is not trivial to evaluate how uncertainty contributed to it. On the other hand, the interpretation of the suggested variables can be questioned. None of them convincingly leads to uncertainty. Authority is what a constitution creates per definition and a constitution organises the competences of the constitutional actors and their relationship. Cultural or language conventions may be the source of the variance and not uncertainty. In addition, there is no objective function formulated. It is not clear what a high share of authority-based power relations is or how much advance social power relations should have over instrumental power relations. Thus, an interpretation of the findings seems arbitrary. Finally, the median voter's interest is not time and space invariant. Each and every society has its own median voter. Comparing the findings over several constitutions would require that one has an idea what the general interest in any society is. Consequently, the observed tendency of the drafters of the constitution to approach the median voter's position cannot be compared between countries. An interesting approach would be to define what could be expected as the interest of the ideal median voter. Defining a median voter for each and every society and measuring how far the different constitutions deviate from this position. Whether this endeavour is promising or accomplishable should be discussed at another instance.

Acknowledgments The author thanks Nora El-Bialy, Julian Boakye-Nyarko, David Börn, Matthias Dauner, Prof. Thomas Eger, Asmaa Ezzat, Patricia Frohberg, Jerg Gutmann, Louis Imbeau, Jun.-Prof. Patrick Leyens, Marwa Mamdouh, Janina Satzer, Prof. Stefan Voigt and Nina Ziesemer for valuable discussions and comments.

References

Bauer-Kirsch A (2005) Herrenchiemsee: der Verfassungskonvent von Herrenchiemsee-Wegbereiter des Parlamentarischen Rates. Inaugural-Dissertation zur Erlangung der Doktorwürde der Rheinischen Friedrich-Wilhelms-Universität zu Bonn. http://hss.ulb.uni-bonn.de/diss_online

Bommarius C (2009) Das Grundgesetz. Eine Biographie, 1st edn. Rowohlt, Berlin

Brennan G, Buchanan JM (1985) The reason of rules. In: Constitutional political economy, 1st edn. Cambridge University Press, Cambridge

Bundeszentrale für politische Bildung (2012) Grundgesetz und Parlamentarischer Rat. http://www.bpb.de/themen/CN4PV2,0,Grundgesetz_und_Parlamentarischer_Rat.html. Accessed 17 Jan 2012

Elkins Z, Ginsburg T, Melton J (2008) Baghdad, Tokyo, Kabul... constitution making in occupied states. William Mary Law Rev 49(4):1139–1178

Elster J (1995) Forces and mechanisms in the constitution-making process. Duke Law J 45(2):364–396

Feldkamp MF, Risse H (2009) Der Parlamentarische Rat. 1948–1949: Akten und Protokolle. In: Der Parlamentarische Rat. 1948–1949: Akten und Protokolle (ed) Deutscher Bundestag. Boldt im Oldenbourg-Verl, München

Frotscher W, Pieroth B (2010) Verfassungsgeschichte, 9th edn. Beck, München

Imbeau LM, Jacob S (2015) Measuring the opacity of the 'veil of ignorance' in constitutions: theory, method and some results. In: Imbeau LM, Jacob S (eds) Behind a veil of ignorance? Power and uncertainty in constitutional design

Markovitz I (2007) Constitution making after National Catastrophes: Germany in 1949 and 1990. William Mary Law Rev 49:1307

Möllers C (2009) Das Grundgesetz. Geschichte und Inhalt. München, Beck

Niclauss K (1998) Der Weg zum Grundgesetz. Demokratiegründung in Westdeutschland 1945–1949. F. Schöningh, Paderborn

Raudla R (2010) Explaining constitution-makers' preferences: the cases of Estonia and the United States. Const Polit Econ 21(3):249–269

Spevack E (2001) Allied control and German freedom. American political and ideological influences on the framing of the West German Grundgesetz. Piscataway, Münster

Stiftung Haus der Geschichte der Bundesrepublik Deutschland (2012) Beobachtungen - Der Parlamentarische Rat 1948/49. http://www.parlamentarischerrat.de/impressum_864.html. Accessed 17 Jan 2012

Vermeule A (2001) Veil of ignorance rules in constitutional law. Yale Law J 111(2):399–433

Chapter 9
Different Veils for Different Governments: The Veil of Ignorance in Shaping the Italian Decentralization

Emma Galli and Veronica Grembi

1 Introduction

We apply the idea of decision-making behind a veil of ignorance in the constitutional phase developed by Buchanan and Tullock (1962) to the process of drafting the Italian Constitution in 1948, especially with respect to the territorial organization of the Italian State. In particular, we address the relevance of opacity and the relative degree of uncertainty of the Italian Constitutional Founding Fathers on the design of the different levels of government. Our main results, based on the content analysis defined as in Imbeau and Jacob (2011) and Imbeau (2009), show that the degree of uncertainty was significantly higher on the decision-making process related to the regional level. The latter, differently from the municipal and provincial level, did not belong to the pre-fascist historical institutional arrangements. We argue that this is among the main reason why the level of opacity referring to the constitutional provisions on intergovernmental relations is higher than the overall uncertainty. We provide also a reconstruction of the main steps that characterized the relations between the State and the periphery from the unification up to now to support our findings.

Through the context analysis, we propose the dilemmas and uncertainties of the idea and enforcement of the Italian regionalism, which characterizes all the historical phases where, from the unification up to today, the organization of the State and the various reforms of the relation between center and periphery were realized. We identify two main attitudes during this historical process. First, we find the idea of Regions, perceived as juxtaposed to the efforts to unify a country which

E. Galli (✉)
DiSSE, University of Rome Sapienza, Rome, Italy
e-mail: emma.galli@uniroma1.it

V. Grembi
Copenhagen Business School, Copenhagen, Denmark
e-mail: veronica.grembi@unicatt.it

L.M. Imbeau and S. Jacob (eds.), *Behind a Veil of Ignorance?*,
Studies in Public Choice 32, DOI 10.1007/978-3-319-14953-0_9

had strong territorial identities and was not always sharing the Piedmont unification strategy and its institutional organization. Second, there is also the necessity of reframing the idea of the State after the fascist period to overcome an excess of centralization by giving more room to the local autonomies which had been penalized in the unification process. After more than 20 years of dictatorship, strongly emerged in the politico-institutional debate, the necessity to reconsider the experience of the liberal State which especially during the last Giolitti[1] Government (June 1920–July 4, 1921) was not able to halt the rise of fascist regime. The introduction of Regions within the Italian 1948 Constitution is regarded as one of the main institutional innovations. However, the uncertainties related to the definition of their legislative and financial competences are among the reasons why they did not fully developed in the last decades of the Italian political life.

The paper is organized as follows. In Sect. 2, we describe the political context in which the Italian Constitution was born. Section 3 addresses the debate about regionalism. In Sect. 4, we present the empirical results based on the content analysis. Section 5 concludes.

2 The Historical Account of the Drafting of the 1948 Constitution

The Italian State was born in the second half of the XIX century through the unification of several existing States under the monarchs of Piedmont. The Founding Fathers believed that the model of a unitary state was necessary for nation building. In fact, there were too many differences among institutions, laws, economies, customs, and languages to maintain a system of sub-national authorities.[2] The organization of the State replicated the model of Piedmont, which, in turn, followed that of Napoleonic France. It included three levels of government: central, provincial, and municipal. This structure stayed in place until the adoption of the Constitution of the Italian Republic in 1948.

The drafting of the constitutional document was the outcome of a political process that began with the institutional referendum of June 2, 1946. After a difficult transitory three-year period (from the end of WWII on April 25, 1945 to the exile of King Umberto II on June 13, 1946), the Italian citizens (older than 21 years) voted in favor of a republican form of government, with 12.7 million of votes versus 10.7 million for the Monarchy. This result was the manifestation of a strong division within the country: The Southern Regions included the islands (Sicilia

[1] Giovanni Giolitti (Mondovì, October 27, 1842—Cavour, July 17, 1928) was a Liberal politician, Prime Minister in many Governments from 1892 to 1921 and he was engaged in the process of democratization of the unitary State and of economic, industrial and cultural modernization of the Italian society between the nineteenth and the twentieth century.

[2] Lower classes in some areas did not speak Italian but only dialects.

and Sardegna), expressed, respectively, 67.4 and 64 % of the valid votes in favor of the Monarchy, while the votes in favor of the Republic were concentrated in the north (64.8 %) and in the center of the country (63.4 %). In other terms, the Northern Regions which had suffered longer the burden of the Nazis' occupation were massively in favor of the Republic, substantially expressing a negative evaluation of the political behavior of the Monarchy, while the Southern Regions, sooner occupied by the Anglo-Americans, were in favor of the Monarchy. Some political analysts argue that at that time, people were not fully able to distinguish the republican form of government from the monarchic one since in Europe until the first part of the twentieth century only France and Switzerland were Republics (Martucci 2002).

In the same circumstance, Italian citizens elected also the *Assemblea Costituente*, an extraordinary legislative body consisting of 556 deputies, which was called to draft the new Constitution, following the example given by the United States (Philadelphia, 1787) and France (between 1789 and 1945).

About 16 political lists were presented such as the *Movimento per l'indipendenza della Sicilia* (which got 4 deputies), the liberal party *Partito d'Azione* (7 deputies), the *Blocco nazionale delle libertà* (16), the *Partito Repubblicano* (23), the *Fronte dell'Uomo qualunque* (30); seven minor parties got less than 2 deputies elected. The three big parties, the catholic party (*Democrazia Cristiana*, DC), the socialist party (*Partito Socialista Italiano di Unità Proletaria*, PSIUP), and the communist party (PCI), with 74.8 % of overall votes elected 207 DC deputies (37.2 % of votes), 115 socialist deputies (20.7 %), and 104 communist deputies (18.7 %).

The Assembly began to work on June 25, 1946, after the election of its President and of the temporary President of the Republic Enrico de Nicola. The Assembly consisted of three sub-committees, the first in charge of the civil and political rights, the second of the constitutional organization of the State, and the third of the economic and social relationships and of a Committee of coordination (the so-called *Comitato dei Diciotto*) which had the responsibility to make homogeneous the different parts of the project. The Committee of coordination ended its work on December 22, 1947, but remained in charge until the political elections held on April 18, 1948. After the promulgation of the President on December 27, 1947, the Constitution of the Republic was enacted on January 1, 1948.

Emerging out of a twenty-year long-lasting fascist dictatorship and a terrible war, the country looked fragmented by ideological, social, and territorial conflicts but unified in the primary goal of establishing a stable democracy where the civil liberties and the democratic participation would be combined for the achievement of a greater social justice.

The political picture which emerged within the *Assemblea costituente* was indeed quite disintegrated, and the 1948 Constitution was the outcome of the agreement between the political parties (in particular the catholic, the socialist, and the communist) that had participated in the *Comitato di liberazione nazionale* (CLN), a political organization which coordinated the resistance against the Nazi-fascist regime from 1943 to 1947.

This circumstance was a guarantee of a Founding Fathers' *super partes* attitude, which produced different majorities aggregated around specific articles. On this respect, Piero Calamandrei, the leader of the *Partito d'Azione* in the Assembly, defined the "far-sighted" Constitution as a text which would not reflect the political disputes of the time but would create an institutional setting allowing the political evolution of the country.

Among the drafters were representatives of the old liberal regime (such as Vittorio Emanuele Orlando and Benedetto Croce), partisan representatives of the *Resistenza italiana* who had fought the Nazi-fascist regime (such as Sandro Pertini), experienced policy-makers (De Gasperi, Dossetti, La Pira, Nenni, Saragat, and Togliatti), jurists (Costantino Mortati and Tomaso Perassi), and young citizens who for the first time participated in the political life of the country and, during the following decades, would have a leading role in Italian politics (Aldo Moro, Giulio Andreotti, Nilde Jotti, and Oscar Luigi Scalfaro). Together they combined the different "souls" represented in the Assembly. The liberal political culture, although in minority in the Assembly, was prevailing in shaping the articles on the natural rights of the individuals, their guarantees against the state (political liberalism), and their economic freedom in production, distribution, and consumption (economic liberalism). The catholic culture, inspired to the social doctrine of the Church, was leading in the recognition of the value of the person, of the family and the various forms of associationism, of the duty of political, economic, and social solidarity. The socialist component was primarily focused on social justice, public education, labor, and economic planning (Bifulco et al. 2006).

The Constitution is a rigid document, which can be modified through a qualified majority of 2/3 of the components of the two Chambers of the Parliament (*Camera dei deputati* and *Senato*) and a double approbation by each Chamber. A referendum is requested if the proposed revisions are approved through a simple majority (art.138).

The first 54 articles of the Italian Constitution (art. 1–12 on Fundamental Principles and art. 13–54 on Rights and Duties of the citizens) represent a modernized version of the French and North-American Declarations of Rights of the XVIII century. Among them are the attribution of the sovereignty to the people (art.1), the principle of equality (art.3), the inviolability of personal freedom (art.13), the right to freely express personal opinions (art.21), the provisions about family (art.29–31), the guarantee of health (art.32), and the right for all citizens to have access to public offices (art.51). Those provisions, which were part of the democratic tradition of the last two centuries, were translated into a constitutional text (Congleton 2011).

The second part of the Constitution concerns the arrangement of the Republic and the definition of the checks and balances system (art. 55–139). The constitutional sequence begins with the Parliament (art.58–82), continues with the President (art.83–91), and concludes with the Government (art.92–96). There is no formal reference to the principle of the division of the powers, and substantially, their organization is not informed by such a principle. The system of the "checks and balances" was interpreted and proposed by the political parties in the *Assemblea Costituente* in the veil of ignorance logic in that the possibility for a member to be, in the future, part of the opposition rather than in the government majority made constituents strengthen the "balances" rather than the "checks" so as to avoid a reinforcement of the government's structure. The direct election of the President of the Republic, whose mandate was to last seven years, was rejected since the "ghost of caesarism" was still alive. He would have the same powers as the King, such as powers of appointment and guidance, and power to dissolve the Parliament. For the Parliament, a perfect Bicameralism was chosen. The Prime Minister was to lead the Government and to promote and coordinate the activities of the Ministers as a *primus inter pares*. This form of government was conceived in a political period characterized by at most seven parties (either member of the opposition or of the majority). Only later would the emergence of a more complex political situation open up to the problems of government instability that still characterize Italy (Martucci 2002).

3 Regionalism in the Political Debate (1860–1948)

In Italy, the intergovernmental relations have been characterized by uncertainty, ambiguity, and pragmatism since the unification in 1861. As we mention above, the need to build a unitary and centralized State lead the Founding Fathers to deny to the pre-unification States not only the federal status but also the role of Regions. At the same time, localism represented a strong government tradition formally recognized in the 1848 *Statuto Albertino* (the Constitution of the Italian Kingdom) that divided the country in Provinces and Municipalities operating, however, under a strict central control. Regions did not exist neither as institutions nor as territories characterized by specific identities or cultural and historical traditions. In the process of reorganizing the State, the necessity to take into account the existence of local interests and peculiarities and the related heterogeneity of local legislation became a priority. In this respect, the idea of establishing Regions appears in the political and institutional debate since the origins of the unitary State (1861) and characterizes the entire life of the country.

A regionalist proposal to reconcile the need of a legislative unification with the diversities of the pre-unitary states was made by the Piedmont Minister of Internal Affairs, Luigi Carlo Farini,[3] in 1860 and subsequently presented to the Chamber of Deputies by the Minister of Internal Affairs Marco Minghetti on March 13, 1861.[4] The objective of Farini's proposal was to coordinate the strong unity of the

[3] Luigi Carlo Farini (Russi, October 22, 1812—Quarto, August 1, 1866) was member of the *Destra Storica* and Prime Minister for a short period between 1862 and 1863. *Destra* and *Sinistra Storica* are respectively close to the idea of nowadays conservative (*Destra*) and progressive (*Sinistra*) parties, even though they do not perfectly coincide with them.

[4] Marco Minghetti (Bologna, November 8, 1818—Rome, December 10, 1886) was member of the *Destra Storica*, twice Minister of Internal Affairs in the government run by Camillo Benso Conte di Cavour in 1861 and Ricasoli in 1862, Minister of Finance in the government run by Farini and twice Prime Minister (March 24, 1863–September 28, 1864 and July 10, 1873–March 25, 1876).

State with the development of the life and liberty of local communities, and progressively to reduce the degree of dependency of Provinces and Municipalities on the central administration. In this perspective, Farini emphasized the need of establishing an intermediate entity, which would be below the political concept of State and above the Province which naturally and historically formed these wider entities. Regions should not be the result of an abstract and artificial design, but rather they would represent those effective natural and historical divisions, "the centers of moral strengths" which, if legitimately satisfied, and not repressed, "could positively contribute to the strength and magnificence of the nation." In his proposal, Regions were characterized by elected bodies, an autonomous administration, and the following competences within the limits imposed by the State's legislation: roads, ports, rivers, social assistance, education, agriculture, and forestry (Atti del Parlamento italiano 1861). Subsequently, in 1861, Minghetti put forward a legislative proposal which designed the establishment of the Regions as clusters of Provinces, with the competences identified by Farini and emphasized the need of equalization in favor of poorer territories, endowed with less infrastructures. Three months after its presentation, and Cavour's death, the legislative proposal was definitely rejected in the Parliament. Again in 1861, Giuseppe Mazzini in his paper "Dell'Unità d'Italia" considered the Region as ancillary in the relation between the Nation and the Municipalities, which are the constitutive and fundamental elements of the new structure of the State. The Nation represented the *association*, the Municipality, the *liberty*. They were both the natural elements of the people. The others were *artificial* and had the only function of facilitating the relations between the Nation and the Municipality and to protect the latter from possible usurpation by the Nation. Mazzini considered the possibility of establishing twelve Regions divided into Districts and consisting in about one hundred Municipalities of large size, which included also the rural population to overcome the dualism between urban and rural areas (Mazzini 1861).

After the defeat of the liberal democratic proposal made by the *Destra storica*, the idea of Region disappeared from the political agenda, except for a few feeble initiatives by the *Sinistra storica*, which includes decentralization in the government platform in 1876. For more than half a century, until the first postwar period, the issue was only reconsidered by single scholars, among which Giuseppe Saredo, member of the Senate in the XVII legislature (1890–1892). In 1886, he prepared a mindful and mature project for the institution of the Regions based on the idea that Italy presented a combination of unitary and regional elements as far as interests, conditions, traditions, and needs were considered, showing a picture of variety in the unity. He considered the Italian State strong enough in its political unity to confer the Regions a wide administrative autonomy; in his view, each Region was able to take care of its own interests and locally to provide public services. This would simplify the activity of the State, reduce its burden, limit people's contribution to national taxation, enhance civil participation, appraise the competence of local policy-makers, and strengthen the political institutions by giving different populations both the benefits of the unity and of a legitimate autonomy. Like Minghetti, Saredo was aware of the necessity and importance of resource equalization among the Regions that should be guaranteed by the State (Boneschi 1946: 101). Saredo's proposal ended with De Pretis' death.

The first postwar period was characterized by a strong resume of the political initiative on regionalism because of two major factors: the emergence of regional political parties (i.e., the *Partito sardo d'azione*) and the creation of a mass party by Luigi Sturzo,[5] the *Partito popolare* that had a regionalist agenda (Boneschi 1946: 101). In line with most of the regionalists, Sturzo conceived regionalism as opposed to federalism and the Region as a convergent, rather than divergent, entity of the State. The Regions should be elected–representative, autonomous–autarchic, and administrative–legislative entities, by encompassing within their territorial limits local collective interests (Sturzo 1921).

After the long parenthesis of fascism, the debate on regionalism re-emerged in 1944–1945 and intensely continued through the contributions of many scholars. Among them, Jemolo, member of the Commission for the reorganization of the State, suggested the possibility to give the Regions wide legislative competences, either exclusive or concurrent with the State (1945: 13–31); instead, Salvemini strongly opposed the idea of Region in favor of the autonomy and self-government of Provinces and Municipalities (1945: 357).

On November 13, 1946, Gaspare Ambrosini, President of the Committee for the regional autonomy, presented a project on the establishment of Regions (unanimously approved on November 8) to the sub-commission of the Commission for the Constitution (*Assemblea Costituente*). After illustrating the main points of the debate on regionalism from Farini and Minghetti to Saredo and Sturzo, he examined four models of Region: (1) the most extreme, which envisages a federalist system; (2) the administrative decentralization, which is the closest to the already existing organization of the State; (3) the institutional and autarchic decentralization, which implies the attribution of some of the central government's competences to sub-national elected authorities; (4) the further advancement of the status of the Region from an administrative authority to a legislative one with exclusive and concurrent competences in sectors of local interest, to be exercised within the limits of the Constitution and of the fundamental legislation of the State and financial autonomy. The latter was the preferred solution, approved by the Commission for the Constitution (Assemblea Costituente 1946).

The Regions were finally introduced about one century later when the process of democratization, on the one hand, and the need to modernize the administrative sector, on the other, created the conditions for the establishment of wider units of government with functions of development and planning. The 1948 Constitution foresees the principle of a decentralized organization of the State identifying three levels of sub-national governments (Regions, Provinces, and Municipalities) that are autonomous and necessary (art.114). It favors local autonomy (art.5), defining the Provinces and the Municipalities as autonomous entities within the principles established by the general laws of the Republic, with administrative functions

[5] Luigi Sturzo (Caltagirone, November 26, 1871—Rome, August 8, 1959) was a priest and politician who founded il *Partito popolare* to give a voice to Catholics in politics and create a catholic and social alternative to the socialist movement.

(art.128–129) and establishing a further level of government, the regional one (art. 5 and Title V of the Constitution). The Founding Fathers introduced the "autonomist principle" among the fundamental principles of the Constitution (Vandelli 2004: 21–24) by devoting only a few articles to the Provinces and the Municipalities which had a solid and deep-rooted tradition as well as an administrative role. As expected, most of the provisions of Title V were devoted to the newly created Regions, perceived as more politically relevant because of their legislative competences.

Italy was thus divided in 20 Regions. Five of them, the first to be established between 1948 and 1963, enjoy a special statute (*Regioni a Statuto Speciale*, or RSS), because of their multilingual status, borderline position, or particularly low level of development. The remaining 15 Regions characterized by an "ordinary statute" (*Regioni a Statuto Ordinario*, or RSO) were established in 1970, 22 years after the constitutional provision. Several Italian constitutional lawyers and political scientists (e.g. Putnam 1993) argue that the creation of the regional governments in 1970s constituted a response to the stalemate in national politics, where the Communist Party, which represented more than 1/3 of the electorate, could not participate in government activities because of its incompatibility with the Italian set of alliances. Regional governments could provide communist politicians with a chance to govern certain areas of the country without interfering with foreign policy. At the same time, the experience of administrating regional governments could make Italian politics more oriented toward administration than ideology (Veronese 2007). In the 1970s, however, the Parliament was still defining the powers of the Regions, and the financial relations between regional and local authorities were still not clear since the Regions were still limited by the existing centralism and the persistent localism (Baldi and Agostini 2011).

4 The Content Analysis on the Italian Constitution: A Focus on the Sub-national Level

The Italian Constitution counts 126 articles divided in 6 sections, preceded by 12 articles addressing the fundamental principles related to civil and fundamental rights. It counts 10,836 words which, analyzed according to the method explained in Chap. 4 (Imbeau and Jacob 2015), can be translated in 488 power relations. 4.1 % of them rely on wealth, 6.1 % on knowledge, whereas the majority,

Table 1 Sources and types of power in the Italian Constitution

		Type of power		Total
		Social power	Instrumental power	
Source of power	Authority	182	176	358
	Wealth	8	12	20
	Knowledge	13	17	30
	Indeterminate	40	40	80
Total		243	245	488

73 %, relies on authority (see Table 1). In the Italian Constitution, instrumental and social relations are completely balanced counting 50 % each. This means that agents are given or taken the competence to act on things or on people in an equal measure. Consistently with the other case studies, the direction of power is negative only for 0.04 % of the 488 detected relations (see Table 2).

In Tables 3, 4 and 5, we provide a similar analysis with a special focus on the main political agents described in Sect. 2: the President of the Republic, the Parliament, and the Government. Among the three, the higher number of power relations defines the Parliament (see Table 3), while for all three of them, the source of power is authority (see Table 4). Distinctions are detectable once we look at the type of power: For the President of the Republic, the majority of power relations are social, while they are instrumental for the Parliament, and there is not a strong majority in the case of the Government defined by an equal number of social and instrumental power relations (see Table 5). Finally, the direction of

Table 2 Direction of power in the Italian Constitution

		Direction of power		Total
		Positive	Negative	
Source of power	Authority	346	12	358
	Wealth	20	0	20
	Knowledge	30	0	30
	Indeterminate	74	6	80
Total		470	18	488

Table 3 Distribution of the power relations among political agents

Political agents	Number of power relations	%
President of the Republic	36	7.38
Parliament	74	15.16
Government	42	8.61
Others	336	68.85

Table 4 Sources of power among political agents

Source of power	Authority	Wealth	Knowledge	Indeterminate
President of the Republic	32	0	2	2
Parliament	64	0	7	3
Government	37	0	1	4

Table 5 Types of power among political agents

Type of power	Social power	Instrumental power
President of the Republic	21	15
Parliament	28	46
Government	21	21

the power is in any case completely positive (see Table 6). This analysis confirms what we have stated at the end of the Sect. 2 on the fear of the Founding Fathers of a strong government.

We then calculate the values of V1 (Source of power), V2 (Type of power), and V3 (Direction of power) on three subsets of power relations concerning the sub-national level of governments. The first subset is based on the overall sample of power relations dealing with Regions, Provinces, and Municipalities, even if they are not directly mentioned as agents in the granted power relation. We define this subset as the sub-national level set. The second and the third samples contain information, respectively, only on Regions, Provinces, and Municipalities. These samples identify only the power relations in which the identity of the agents is clearly stated. They are defined as regional and *provincial and municipal level.* The goal of our analysis is to provide a comparison of the content analysis on these subsets with the values obtained from the analysis on the overall constitutional text, which we define, the national level.

Table 7 shows the number of power relations per subset of levels of government and samples, where it is apparent that the 24 % of the national power relations concern sub-national levels.

In Table 8, we present the number of power relations according to their source, type, and direction. It is worthwhile to notice that only three power relations are indeterminate when dealing with Regions, while the number rises to twelve when the level of government is provincial and municipal. The type of power is mainly social for Regions, while it is mainly instrumental for Provinces and Municipalities. However for both level, the direction of power is overwhelmingly positive.

The results are consistent with our hypothesis. The source, the type, and the direction of the power relations are almost identical when the national level

Table 6 Direction of power among political agents

Direction of power	Positive	Negative
President of the Republic	35	1
Parliament	74	0
Government	42	0

Table 7 Distribution of the power relations among levels of government*

Level of government	Power relations
National level	488
Sub-national level	115
Regional level	60
Provincial and Municipal level	53

*The sub-national level does not represent the sum of regional and municipal relations, since some articles deal with both at the same time.

Table 8 Distribution of power relations according to their source, type, and direction*

		Power relations		
		Sub-national level	Regional level	Provincial and Municipal level
Source of power	Authority	83	53	29
	Wealth	13	1	12
	Knowledge	3	3	0
	Indeterminate	16	3	12
Type of power	Social power	62	36	25
	Instrumental power	53	24	28
Direction of power	Positive	110	55	53
	Negative	5	5	0

*The sub-national level does not represent the sum of regional and municipal relations, since some articles deal with both at the same time.

analysis is compared to the analysis run on the sub-national level. The levels of opacity and therefore uncertainty are equivalent: 72 % of power relations are based on authority at the sub-national level and 73 % at the national level, 54 % of them are social rather than instrumental relations in the sub-national level versus a 50 % at the national level, and the direction of the relations is negative in the same percentage (0.04) (see Table 9).

Results change substantially once the analysis moves on the different identity of the sub-national level agents. The index calculation relying only on the regional relations shows a substantially higher level of uncertainty faced by the constitutional fathers not only compared to the national level but also to the level strictly related only to the municipal and provincial. The level of opacity of the latter is lower than those presented for the regional issues. This is consistent with the fact that the constitutional drafters were quite aware of the municipal realities and interests, whereas the definition of the political balances for Regions was much more uncertainty.

Table 9 Power relations in the sub-samples

Level of government	Power relations		
	Source % authority	Type % social	Direction % negative
National level	0.73	0.50	0.04
Sub-national level	0.72	0.54	0.04
Regional level	0.88	0.60	0.08
Provincial and Municipal level	0.55	0.47	0.00

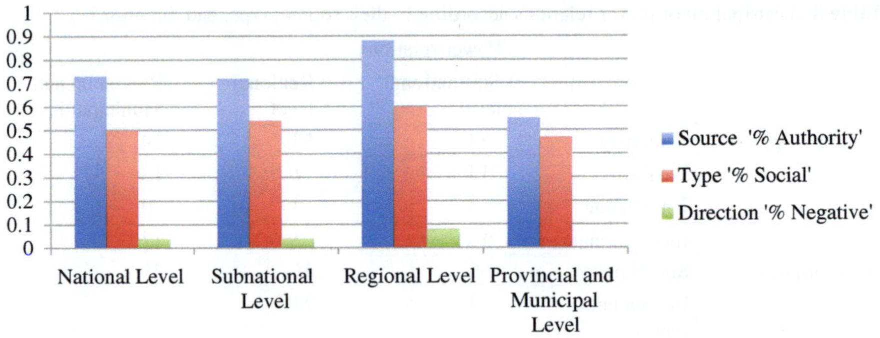

Fig. 1 Power relations per level of government

Figure 1 provides graphical representation of the evidence shown in Tables 8 and 9. Overall the national and the sub-national level appear balanced. Within the sub-national level, differences between the regional level on one side and the provincial and municipal level on the other are striking.

5 Conclusion

In this chapter, we test the Veil of Ignorance hypothesis on a specific issue, which has characterized the Italian political debate since the birth of Italy as a unitary country in 1861: The creation of Regions as an intermediate level of government between the State and the local authorities. The empirical analysis runs through the methodology described in Chap. 4, confirms that the level of opacity, which characterized the choice made by the Founding Fathers on the regional issue was higher than the overall level of constitutional opacity. We explain this outcome as a function of a double level of debate within the Italian institutional history. A first level is related to the concerns of the Founding Fathers of the unitary country, who considered the introduction of a regional level an attempt to the unitary design. A second level belongs to the Founding Fathers of the 1948 Constitution, who had to deal with the reconstruction of a democratic country after 20 years of fascist dictatorship. In this perspective, the recognition and advancement of the preexisting local autonomies together with the introduction of the Regions represented a guarantee of the democratization process.

However, this spirit was betrayed during the enforcement of the Constitution and it was reaffirmed in the 1990s, in particular during the XIII Legislature (1996–2001), when the experience of the so-called First Republic born after WWII collapsed due the political scandals of the Clean Hands (Mani Pulite) judiciary investigation. The rise of a Second Republic in 1994 was hailed as the possibility to fully realize and expand the potentialities of the original regionalist project of the Founding Fathers, only partially enforced in the First Republic history. As a consequence, a new constitutional reform reinforcing the role and the competences of the Regions was enacted in 2001. Again, this new Constitutional design, federalist in spirit, remained unenforced due, as in the past, to political reasons.[6] The story of regionalism in Italy seems to be conflicting in its nature: On the one side, the institutional design provides a proper structure for decentralization, on the other the political consequences of a full implementation of an autonomous regional level are not really wanted most likely because of the consequences in terms of accountability of a greater legislative and financial autonomy.

References

Assemblea Costituente (1946) Commissione per la Costituzione. II Sottocommissione. Resoconto Sommario delle Sedute dal 26 luglio 1946 al 1 agosto. Camera dei Deputati, Roma

Atti del Parlamento italiano (1861) Sessione del 1860 dal 2 aprile al 28 dicembre 1860 (VII legislatura). Raccolti e corredati di note e di documenti inediti da Giuseppe Galletti e Paolo Trompeo, Tipografia eredi Botta, Palazzo Carignano, Torino, pp 66–67, In: Longobardi E (ed) Regionalismo e Regioni in Italia 1861–2011. Gangemi, Roma

Baldi B, Agostini C (2011) Le Regioni tra Decentramento e Federalismo. In: Longobardi E (ed) (2011) Regionalismo e Regioni in Italia 1861–2011. Gangemi, Roma

Bifulco R, Celotto A, Olivetti M (a cura di) (2006) Commentario alla Costituzione. UTET giuridica, Torino

Boneschi M (1946) Le libertà locali. Milano, Rosa e Ballo editori

Buchanan JM, Tulloc G (1962) The Calculus of Consent. Ann Arbor, University of Michigan Press

Camera dei deputati—Legislatura VII-Sessione 1861–62, Raccolta dei documenti stampati per ordine della Camera, vol 1, eredi Botta tipografi della Camera elettiva, Torino, 1863. In: Longobardi E (ed) (2011) Regionalismo e Regioni in Italia 1861–2011. Gangemi, Roma

Congleton R (2011) Perfecting parliament: constitutional reform, liberalism, and the rise of western democracy. Cambridge University Press, Cambridge

Imbeau LM (2009) Testing the veil of ignorance hypothesis in constitutional choice: a walk talk approach. J Public Finance Public Choice 26(1):3–21

Imbeau LM, Jacob S (2011) Is the veil of ignorance in constitutional choice a myth? An empirical exploration informed by a theory of power. In: Marciano A (ed) Constitutional mythologies. Springer, New York

Imbeau LM, Jacob S (2015) Measuring the opacity of the 'veil of ignorance' in constitutions: theory, method and some results. In: Imbeau LM, Jacob S (eds) Behind a veil of ignorance? Power and uncertainty in constitutional design. Springer, New York

Jemolo AC (1945) Il decentramento regionale. Quaderni del Partito d'Azione 11:1–31

Martucci R (2002) Storia costituzionale italiana. Carocci editore, Roma

Mazzini G (1861) Dell'Unità d'Italia, in Scritti editi e inediti di Giuseppe Mazzini, vol III, Imola, Cooperativa Tipografico-Editrice Paolo Galeati, 1907, pp 302–335. In: Longobardi E (ed) Regionalismo e Regioni in Italia 1861–2011. Gangemi, Roma

[6] Even if an attempt to enforce the 2001 reform was done in 2009 through the provisions of an ordinary legislation which were suspended as a consequence of the public finance priorities due to the international financial crisis.

Putnam RD (1993) Making democracy work. Civic traditions in modern Italy. Princeton University Press, Princeton
Salvemini G (1945) Federalismo, regionalismo e autonomismo. In La Critica politica, VII (10), pp 357–365
Sturzo L (1921) Speech on the Regions, October 23. III National Congress of the Partito Popolare Italiano, Venice, Italy
Vandelli L (2004) Il sistema delle autonomie locali. Il Mulino, Bologna
Veronese B (2007) How do institutions shape policy making? The transition from parliamentarism to presidentialism in Italian local governments. In: Padovano F and Ricciuti R (eds) italian institutional reforms: a public choice approach, Springer, New York

Chapter 10
Constitutional Convulsions in Modern Greece

George Tridimas

Abstract Over the twentieth century, Greece shifted from monarchy to republic in a sequence that involved civil war, dictatorship, rigged referendums and several constitutional revisions. This experience is used to examine the changing profile of power relations of the post-WWII monarchical and republican constitutions. A pattern of increasing authority, instrumental and positive power relations is observed. Of those, only the former trend is compatible with the definitional propositions of the VOIP.

Keywords Constitution · Monarchy · Republic · Power · Modern Greece

JEL classification D7 · N4

Since gaining her independence in 1832, Greece has experienced major constitutional changes including absolute monarchy, constitutional monarchy and parliamentary republic, intercepted by coups, foreign occupation, civil war and dictatorship. From 1844 onwards, Greece has had six different constitutions, the most recent in 1975 that has already been revised three times. In comparison with other democratic transitions from royal to parliamentary rule over the last two hundred years, Greece displays an almost unique constitutional profile of oscillations from monarchy to republic back to monarchy and again to republic. This rich experience is used to explore the evolving pattern of power relations determined by the constitutional writers.

G. Tridimas (✉)
Department of Finance, Accounting and Economics,
Ulster University Business School, Newtownabbey, Co, Antrim BT37 0QB, UK
e-mail: G.Tridimas@ulster.ac.uk

L.M. Imbeau and S. Jacob (eds.), *Behind a Veil of Ignorance?*,
Studies in Public Choice 32, DOI 10.1007/978-3-319-14953-0_10

The study is structured as follows. Section 1 presents the profile of constitutional developments in modern Greece emphasising the waxing and waning fortunes of the monarchy under different political contexts. Section 2 reflects on the role of the military and the use of referendums for changing the constitution. Section 3 uses the VOIP measure of power relations developed by Imbeau (2009) and Imbeau and Jacob (2011, 2015), to investigate the changing profile of power relations of the five post-WWII constitutional documents, the monarchical one of 1952, the republican of 1975 and its three revisions in 1986, 2001 and 2008. Section 4 concludes.

1 Brief Constitutional History of Greece [1]

1. *From absolute monarchy to crowned democracy: 1832–1909*

After the war of independence against the Ottoman Empire, 1821–1828, Greece was recognised as an independent state in 1832. Otto Wittelsbach, a Bavarian prince, was chosen as king by the three "protecting powers" of Britain, France and Russia that helped Greece win her independence. Otto brought with him a large entourage of Bavarian advisors and troops for setting up the administration of the new state and guaranteeing his own protection, factors that caused significant friction among his subjects. First, he ruled as an absolute monarch facing ever rising tensions: fiscal indebtedness, failed land reform, internal security threats from violent brigands and political malcontents, the question of autonomy of the Greek Orthodox Church (with him, a Roman Catholic, as its head) from the patriarchate of Constantinople and the perennial foreign policy question of liberating ("redeeming") the Greeks living in Ottoman territories. In 1843, a military rebellion forced him to grant a constitution.[2] The 1844 Constitution, based on the 1830 French and 1831 Belgian constitutions, provided for a constitutional monarchy where the legislative power was exercised by the king (who also had the right to ratify legislation), by the parliament and by the senate, whose members were appointed for life by the king. The king retained the right to choose and remove ministers and judges. Remarkably, the constitution introduced universal male suffrage for men above the age of 25 years in possession of land or exercising a profession. It also mandated that the next king of Greece had to be Christian Orthodox. The very last sentence of the text provided that "the observance of the

[1] Short accounts of the political and social history of modern Greece can be found, respectively, in Clogg (1986) and Gallant (2001), while the edited volume sponsored by Greek Parliament (2004) offers a concise analysis of the constitutional texts.

[2] The background to the popular revolt was that in July 1843, Greece defaulted on her external debt and was forced to cut public spending. The latter hit particularly hard civil servants and military staff who initiated the uprising of September 1843.

constitution is devoted to the patriotism of the Greeks", a declaration of the responsibility of citizens to protect the constitution, which has been repeated in all subsequent constitutions, but proved a dead letter given the number of times the constitution was violated. After repeatedly disregarding constitutional government, Otto was deposed in 1862 following a military rebellion.[3]

In 1863, George Glücksburg, a Danish prince, was chosen as king by the protecting powers, an appointment subsequently approved by the Greek parliament. A new more liberal constitution came into effect in 1864, proclaiming Greece a "crowned democracy", a democracy with a monarch.[4] The constitution, modelled on the Belgian 1831 and Danish 1849 constitutions, established the principle of popular sovereignty, specified that the king had only the powers bestowed on him by the constitution and abolished the senate. It barred salaried public employees from becoming MPs but not serving army officers. The king retained the right to appoint and dismiss ministers and to call or dissolve the parliament, but the dissolution had to be countersigned by the cabinet, while it also provided for the establishment of parliamentary "examination committees", the analogue of contemporary select committees that check and report on the work of government departments. After a period of political instability, the principle that the government must enjoy the "manifest confidence" of the parliament was adopted in 1875 under the premiership of Ch. Trikoupis, while in 1877, universal suffrage was extended to all adult males. The period of political stability that followed was interrupted by national default in 1893 and ended with a humiliating military defeat by the Ottomans in 1897.

2. *From Monarchy to Republic: 1909–1974*

In 1909, a military rebellion forced a new constitution that came into effect in 1911 under the premiership of the liberal politician E. Venizelos. It provided for tenured civil servants, public prosecutors and lower judicial officials, stronger protection of various rights and specifically personal security, equality in tax burdens, the right to assemble, the inviolability of the domicile and state-financed compulsory school education. It also provided for easier terms of property expropriation to serve the public "benefit" (rather than "need" as it was the case before), such as allocation property to landless farmers after compensation determined by the courts. Other provisions included the establishment of an electoral court for resolving electoral disputes, employment incompatibilities for serving MPs (including that of serving military officers), the establishment of the state council as the highest administrative court and the strengthening of judicial independence. King George was assassinated in 1913 after Greece emerged victorious from the

[3] Interestingly, opposition to the king had also been preceded by an external default in 1860.

[4] The Greek language lacks separate words for "democracy", the system of government where political decisions are made by the people through a competitive electoral process, and "republic", the form of state where the head of state is not hereditary, which is also translated as "democracy".

Balkan wars of 1912–1913 against the Ottoman Empire (resulting in significantly increasing her territory) and was succeeded by his son Constantine I. The king (the first Christian Orthodox king) insisting that Greece remained neutral in the WWI clashed with the Prime Minister, E. Venizelos, who argued for Greece to fight with the entente. The rift precipitated a deep national schism dividing the country into two bitterly opposed camps of royalists and anti-royalists. Constantine gave up the throne in 1917 but without formally abdicating and went into exile with his eldest son, crown prince George. He was succeeded by his second son Alexander, who died unexpectedly in October 1920. The alliance of pro-royalist parties won the November 1920 election and promptly invited Constantine to return to the throne. He declared that he would do so only after being recalled directly by the people. A 99 % majority for his return was officially recorded in the December 1920 referendum.[5] However, following defeat of the Greek forces in Asia Minor by Turkey in August 1922, the military staged a coup which overthrew the pro-royalist government and forced Constantine to abdicate in September 1922. He left Greece and was succeeded by his son George II.

With mounting social and economic problems, the anti-royalist current grew so strong that in 1923, King George II was forced to take "leave of absence" and in March 1924, the government of the socialist A. Papanastasiou passed a parliamentary resolution abolishing the monarchy, a change ratified in a subsequent referendum. After long delays, a new constitution came into effect in 1927. It provided for legislative power to be exercised by the parliament and a senate with veto powers. It explicitly adopted the principle of parliamentary majority by stating that the cabinet must "enjoy the confidence of the parliament", and for the first time, it referred to the prime minister as the person chairing the cabinet. It also provided for an elected president as head of state, chosen by the parliament and the senate. The president was politically unaccountable, did not possess legislative authority and could dissolve the parliament only with the approval of the senate. The constitution established certain social rights such as protection of work, the family and press freedom. The republic was associated with economic hardship (including an external debt default in 1932) and weak and unstable parliamentary governments intercepted by four coups in 1925, 1926, 1933 and 1935, each one associated with cycles of reprisals and purges in the civil service and the military. The 1935 election following a failed putsch of anti-royalist officers was not contested by anti-royalist parties and resulted in a huge pro-royalist parliamentary majority. King George II was restored to the throne after a new blatantly rigged referendum returned a 98 % vote for the monarchy. A year later, in 1936, dictatorial rule was imposed with the approval of the king.

In 1941, Nazi Germany overran the Greek forces and King George II left Greece. By 1944, two different camps were vying for control, the internationally recognised, government-in-exile, which was loyal to the king, and the resistance

[5] It is thought that even though the actual size of the majority was manipulated, there was sufficient support for Constantine's return to win in a fair ballot (see Clogg 1986).

groups in Greece dominated by the strongly anti-monarchical communist party. In the 1946 parliamentary elections, the leftists and the communists abstained and the alliance of royalist parties gained a substantial parliamentary majority against the liberals. King George returned after another (fraudulent) referendum in favour of the monarchy held in September 1946. Although the monarchy did not enjoy much support, there was widespread opposition to a communist rule and the monarchy was seen as a safeguard against a communist takeover (see Clogg 1986). The king died a few months later in 1947 and was succeeded by his brother Paul I. The civil war ended in 1949 with the victory of the nationalist–royalist forces, and a new constitution came to effect in 1952. It retained the fabric of the crowned democracy and reaffirmed the parliamentary form of government as in the 1927 charter. Written in the aftermath of the civil war, it included several illiberal provisions including a ban on civil servants strikes and some forms of censorship. Further, on the proposal of the cabinet, it allowed the king to suspend articles regarding personal freedoms and to introduce extraordinary courts. Two interpretative clauses made voting compulsory and recognised the right of women to elect and get elected. The country entered a period of economic reconstruction and comparative political stability although there were some disputes between the king and the long-serving conservative Prime Minister C. Karamanlis.

After Paul's death in 1964, the throne passed to his son Constantine II, who in 1965 clashed with the centrist prime minister G. Papandreou bringing on the resignation of the latter and triggering off a period of political instability. In April 1967, a military coup suspended the constitutional order. Following an unsuccessful counter-coup in December 1967, Constantine II fled Greece. The military regime abolished the monarchy in 1973 after a discredited referendum, held under martial law. The dictatorship collapsed in July 1974 as a result of mounting economic problems and a failed coup it instigated in Cyprus that led Greece and Turkey to the brink of war. A "national unity government" was sworn in, which before holding parliamentary elections, it legalised the Communist party, an action that marked the modernisation and full normalisation of Greek political life. In December 1974, the constitutional question was settled when a new, clean referendum was held that recorded a 69 % vote in favour of republic.

3. *Republic and Constitutional Revisions: After 1975*

In 1975, the conservative government led by C. Karamanlis passed a new constitution, built on some of the principles of the 1927 and 1952 documents and the 1949 West German and 1958 French constitutions. It introduced a "presided parliamentary republic" providing for a president elected by the parliament in a secret vote requiring a two-thirds majority.[6] The president was endowed with a range of important

[6] If no candidate obtains the latter, the required majority is reduced to three-fifths; if that fails, the parliament is dissolved. After the election, a candidate must receive a three-fifths majority of the votes in the new parliament to be elected as president. If that is not achieved, a simple majority is required; failing that, the candidate receiving a plurality of votes is deemed as elected president.

powers. In the case of a hung parliament and after the leader of the party with the highest number of MPs had failed to secure a vote of confidence, the president could give an exploratory mandate for forming a government to the leader of the party with the second highest number of MPs, any other MP or a non-MP thought as able to muster a parliamentary majority. Similarly, if the prime minister resigned or lost a vote of confidence, the president could appoint a MP who was not a party leader to form a government and ask for a vote of confidence, or a non-MP who would then dissolve parliament. The president could also dismiss the cabinet and appoint a new government as described before. In addition, in cases of an "obvious disharmony" (a rather vague term) between the parliament and the popular feeling, or government instability, or on the proposal of the cabinet, the president could dissolve parliament and call elections. Finally, the president was also given the power to call a referendum on issues of national interest (which could nevertheless be overturned by a simple majority of the parliament), call and chair the cabinet in exceptional circumstances and address the people directly. To some extent, such prerogatives formalised but also limited some of the implicit powers exercised by the king in the royalist constitutions. Such extensive presidential powers may conflict with the principle that the acts of government must always enjoy a parliamentary majority. In other respects, the constitution strengthened democratic principles. For the first time, it recognised formally the right of Greeks to form and join political parties and formally prescribed the convention that the leader of the party with an absolute majority of seats in the parliament is appointed as prime minister (although as already mentioned, it allowed the president to use his discretion in case of a hung parliament). It also included a number of individual and social rights, welfare provisions, restrictions on private property and free enterprise to serve the public interest, and provisions for the participation of the country in international organisations and the European Economic Community that reduced national sovereignty. In the light of the previous violations of the constitutional order, the last article of the constitution declared that its observance is "entrusted [instead of "devoted"] to the patriotism of the Greeks who shall have the right and the duty to resist by all possible means against anyone who attempts the violent abolition of the Constitution", strengthening the responsibility of the citizens to protect the constitution.

In 1985, as the term of the then president of the republic, C. Karamanlis, came to the end, and in the middle of partisan disputes about the election of a new president, the socialist government of A. Papandreou initiated the procedures for constitutional revision. An amended constitution came to effect in 1986 with new provisions regarding the president. First, the parliamentary vote for the election of the president was changed from secret vote to roll call. Since candidates for the presidency are nominated by political parties and voted by the parliament, this shift effectively increased the power of the nominating party leaders. The discretionary powers of the president regarding the choice of prime ministers in case of a hung parliament, dissolution of the parliament and calling a referendum, although they had not been exercised in the preceding eleven years, were transferred to the cabinet. The changes reinforced the parliamentary character of the republic vesting more powers in the hands of the party leaders and especially the prime minister and conferred to the president the role of a figurehead. A second consensual constitutional revision took place in 2001, completing a process that had formally started in 1997 and supported by both the socialist government and the conservative opposition. The revision introduced new individual rights and organisational rules that bolstered the welfare state, refined professional incompatibilities of MPs (requiring that they shall have no paid employment outside the parliament), detailed impeachment procedures for ministers, prohibited ownership by the same person of both media business and public procurement business, upgraded local government and enshrined the political independence of a number of public sector agents.[7] It also undertook an extensive reform in the field of justice that covered the functions and administration of courts and the constitutional review of policy. A total of seventy-nine articles were amended, and in the majority of the cases, the amendments were accepted by four-fifths of all the parliamentarians. A third modest revision was enacted in 2008. The conservative government at the time proposed a series of amendments (including a lift on the ban on private universities), but only a few minor proposals received the required votes in the parliament, notably those regarding the abolition of the restrictions on the professions compatible with serving MPs introduced by the 2001 amendment, and budgetary procedures that mandated special treatment of the insular and mountainous regions of the country in the design of development policy.

The constitutional convulsions from monarchy to republic are summarised in Table 1. In the climate of the 1820s, when Greece gained her independence, her head of state and government was invested in the hands of a hereditary monarch. Domestically too, lacking a national royal house, a foreign prince seemed acceptable to the various factions vying for control and the population at large as a way to bring an end to political infighting. Thereafter, the shift from absolute to constitutional monarchy (one constrained by rules) and the liberal reforms from 1875 to 1911 show that Greece followed the pattern of constitutional developments witnessed in the West during the nineteenth and early twentieth centuries. This is aptly analysed by Congleton (2011), who documents that parliaments gradually acquired more policy authority at the expense of the king in a process of constitutional exchanges. In the course of the latter, which are most likely during unsettled economic, political and social circumstances, the king trades policy making authority to parliament in exchange for tax revenues and guarantees for the dynasty. At the same time, parliaments also became more representative as the franchise was extended to poorer classes. Lacking its own constitutional tradition, Greek constitutional writing has been influenced by principles embodied in Western European constitutions. More importantly, all six constitutions of the 1844–1975 period were written in response to political and social upheavals. If longevity is a measure of institutional success, the 1864 constitution is the most

[7] These included the Data Protection Authority, the Confidentiality of Communications Authority, the National Council for Radio and Television, the Civil Service Appointments Authority and the Office of the Citizen's Advocate (Ombudsman).

Table 1 Summary of constitutional developments

Form of state and regime	Period	Monarch reign	Constitution (Y)
Absolute monarchy	1832–1843	Otto 1832–1843	
Constitutional monarchy	1843–1862	Otto 1843–1862	1844 (20)
Crowned democracy national schism 1915–1917	1863–1924	George I 1863–1913 Constantine I 1913–1917 Alexander 1917–1920 Constantine I 1920–1922 George II 1922–1924	1864 (47) 1911 (13)
Republic	1924–1935		1927 (8)
Crowned democracy	1935–1974	George II 1935–1941	a
Dictatorship 1936		George II 1946–1947	b
German occupation 1941–1944		Paul 1946–1964	1952 (15)
Civil war 1944–1949		Constantine I 1964–1967	
Military dictatorship 1967–1974			
Republic	1974–present		1975 (38) Revised: 1986, 2001 and 2008

Y Number of years the constitution has been in effect
a 1911 Constitution reinstated in 1935. *b* 1911 Constitution reinstated in 1944

successful as it survived for 47 years,[8] followed by the 1975 one, which including three revisions is now 38 years old. Assuming that citizens retain the constitution that advances their interests, then the shortlived constitutions of 1911, 1927 and 1952 manifestly failed to do so. Clearly, for over a hundred years, the biggest source of constitutional convulsions has been the disputes about the form of the government, monarchy or republic and the powers of the head of state vis-à-vis those of the elected prime minister, fuelling uprisings and military interventions leading to repeated rounds of constitutional revision.

2 Constitutional Writing, the Military and Referendums

As circumstances change, future generations of citizens may wish to change the rules and principles that govern them. Recognising this need, the constitutional drafters provide for procedures for constitutional amendment. Revisions enacted by applying the relevant procedures for amendment are de jure revisions, while

[8] This is by no means certain since preservation of the constitution may simply reflect the rigidity of the procedures for amending it.

those that do not follow such rules are de facto revisions.[9] In a nutshell, the de jure rules for constitutional revision in Greece require that the sitting parliament votes by a supermajority (currently 3/5) to amend specific articles and the proposed amendments pass by a simple majority of the next parliament. All articles of the constitution may be revised except of the so-called fundamental ones. Fundamental provisions are those that describe the form of government (monarchy or republic), respect and protection of the value of the human being by the state, equality before the law and inviolability of personal liberty, and the exercise of legislative, executive and judicial powers. Revision is not permitted before the lapse of a certain period from a previous revision, currently five years.[10] However, as the previous section documented, despite its character as "fundamental", the form of the government, monarchy or republic has been changed several times and articles about individual rights and the exercise of government were violated in cycles of extra-constitutional political disputes, civil war and military interventions. None of the revisions that led to the constitutions of 1864, 1911, 1927, 1952 and 1975 was carried out according to the rules provided by the existing constitution; they have all been de facto revisions that broke the rules. Only the 1975 constitution has been de jure revised (three times).[11] This section elaborates on the effects of the military on Greek constitutional developments and the use of referendums to approve constitutional changes.

Table 2 summarises the military interventions into Greek politics and the constitutional developments that followed them. In the first instance, the practice of allowing serving officers to stand for parliament (abolished after the 1909 Constitution) contributed to the politicisation of the armed forces and their indiscipline. As already discussed, the military uprisings forced Otto to sign the 1844 Constitution and led to his departure in 1862. Over the period 1909–1936, a total of nine military revolts, putsches and counter-putsches took place. However, with the exception of the short 1925–1926 dictatorship, the officers did not establish dictatorial rule. Nor were they pursuing a particular political ideology; coups were mounted by both pro-royalist and liberal officers. Veremis (1997: 7) writes "the scope of most interwar coups was limited to redressing personal grievances, promoting professional interests or replacing one civilian government with another. Officers became arbiters of the struggle between the Liberal and Conservative parties although they were ultimately controlled by them." It is also worth noting that on several occasions, officers (both pro-royalist and anti-royalist) involved in coups eventually resigned from the military and became active in electoral politics.

[9] In addition, significant but implicit constitutional re-writing may take place through judicial review of the constitutionality of laws and administrative acts carried out by the courts (see Voigt 1999). This type of implicit constitutional change for the case of Greece is left for future research.

[10] The 1844 monarchical constitution did not provide for amendment, while the revision provisions of the 1864 constitution were considerably stricter requiring large supermajorities and the consent of three successive parliaments.

[11] For an extensive discussion of the questions of legitimacy and methods of constitutional amendment, see Mueller (1996), Chap. 21 and Mueller (1999).

Table 2 Military interventions and constitutional developments

Year	Military intervention	Constitutional consequence
1843	Revolt against King Otto	Constitution of 1844
1862	Revolt against King Otto	Otto deposed
1909	Coup	Constitution of 1911
1916	Coup in Northern Greece by anti-royalist officers	National Schism
1922	Military revolution after Asia Minor catastrophe	King Constantine abdicates
1923	Military counter-revolution by pro-royalist officers	Republic proclaimed—1924
1925	Coup by General Pangalos	Dictatorship by Pangalos
1926	Coup against Pangalos to restore democracy	Constitution of 1927
1933	Coup against pro-royalist government—fails	
1935	Coup against pro-royalist government—fails	Monarchy restored
1936	Dictatorship backed by the military and the King	
1967	Coup	Dictatorship
1974	Dictatorship collapses after failed coup in Cyprus	Republic proclaimed Constitution of 1975

However, after the end of the civil war, the junior and middle rank officers saw themselves as an independent political force. As a result, rather than deferring office powers to politicians, the leaders of the 1967 coup established a military regime. The military regime drafted two constitutional documents. The first in 1968 retained the monarchy, while the second in 1973 abolished it. They contained a large number of illiberal clauses. Even though both were "approved" in rigged referendums, they were never put into effect, as the military government did not repeal the state of emergency declared upon taking power. These documents have been null and void. After the restoration of democracy in 1974, the military ceased to pose any threat to the republican constitutional order. Thus, despite an interfering military, none of the six Greek constitutions that came into effect was written by a military dictator.

Turning to the use of the referendum, it bears noting that ever since King Constantine decided to legitimize his 1920 return by referendum, all constitutional changes regarding the restoration or abolition of the monarchy were sanctioned by the same procedure (see Table 3 for summary data).

The 1920, 1924, 1935 and 1946 referendums rubber-stamped the preceding parliamentary votes called on the behest of the government rather than being genuine popular contests, while the military government did not sanction a free vote in 1973. On the contrary, in 1974, there was no parliamentary vote on the monarchy; the fortune of the latter was decided by the referendum, the only one that passed the test of free and fair election.[12] It is noteworthy that referendums were used to settle the question of the form of the state rather than asking voters to approve or

[12] See Tridimas (2010) for a detailed political economy analysis of the 1974 referendum.

Table 3 Referendums on the Monarchy

Date	% Votes For		Outcome	Implication
	Monarchy	Republic		
1920	98.97	1.03	Constantine I returns	
1924	30.02	69.78	Republic proclaimed	1927 Constitution
1935	97.87	2.13	Monarchy restored	1911 Constitution reinstated
1946	68.40	31.60	Monarchy restored	1952 Constitution
1973	21.56	78.44	Republic proclaimed	1973 Constitution–not activated
1974*	30.82	69.18	Republic proclaimed	1975 Constitution

* Referendum result not contested by the losing side

reject the proposed constitution. Ratification of the constitution has always been the preserve of the parliament. Interestingly, no other constitutional or political issue has been settled by referendum.[13] A possible explanation of the de facto amendments of the pre-1975 constitutions may be the rigid constitutional revision procedures that they had legislated. Inflexible procedures are inevitably slow. Since the constitution sets the rules for making policy, denying opportunistic short-run majorities the capacity to destabilise the constitution is not without advantages.[14] However, inability to respond to fast changing circumstances may lead to breaking the rules and de facto constitutional rewriting. Revision of the constitution by a standing parliament saves time and uses the relevant expertise of the parliament, but according to Mueller (1996) such efficiency, gains are more than offset by corresponding political costs. When faced with several pressing tasks at the same time (constitutional writing, urgent issues of domestic and foreign policy and so on), the existing parliament may fail to deal with them satisfactorily. Moreover, sitting parliamentarians who are seeking re-election may not be prepared to set aside the short-run interests of their constituencies in order to advance the long-run interests of the country. Constitutional writing will then violate what Mueller calls "the first law of constitution writing—those who are likely to hold office under the new constitution should not be involved in its writing lest they draft a constitution to serve *their* interests and not those of the citizens" (Mueller 2005: 65—emphasis in the original).

On this account, it is worth highlighting the partisan identity of the authors of the 1975 and 1986 constitutions. The constitution of 1975 promoted the president

[13] It is ironic that the referendums called before the 1975 Constitution had no constitutional basis, while no referendum has been called after the procedure of holding one was formally incorporated in the 1975 charter. On the contrary, in November 2011, a call by the then PM, G. Papandreou, for a referendum to approve the austerity measures required to tackle the Greek sovereign debt crisis was not only aborted but also led to the resignation of the prime minister.

[14] Britain, however, offers the counter-example where an unwritten constitution can be changed by ordinary legislation and yet constitutional crises are rare.

to a significant political actor. Both C. Tsatsos, who drafted the 1975 constitution, and C. Karamanlis, who was prime minister at the time of its ratifications enjoying a parliamentary majority of more than 2/3, were conservative politicians who went on to become presidents. One may then surmise that the 1975 constitution was written with a view of the future political role of the leading politician at the time. On the other hand, the 1986 constitution was authored by the socialist government of A. Papandreou and legislated for a president with ceremonial duties. In the period 1981–1985, Papandreou as prime minister "cohabited" with C. Karamanlis as president. Again, when the opportunity arose, ideologically for a left leaning politician, as well as politically, it made sense for him to legislate for an institutionally weak president and concentrate power in the hands of the prime minister.

3 Power Relations in the Post-WWII Greek Constitutions

Using the Imbeau–Jacob head-count measures of power relations, Table 4 presents the summary of the composition of power relations by source, type and direction in the five Post-WWII constitutional texts of 1952, 1975, 1986, 2001 and 2008. The second panel of the Table shows the results from testing the three definitional propositions of VOIP. Namely, the larger the uncertainty at the stage of constitutional writing, the larger the proportion of (1) political power rather than economic or preceptoral power relations; (2) social rather than instrumental power relations and (3) negative rather than positive power relations. The test is carried out by assuming that in a random division of power relations, the expected proportion of power relations based on authority would be equal to the proportion of power relations based on the two other sources and hence equal to ½; the proportion of social and instrumental powers would be equal; and the expected proportions of positive and negative relations would be equal too. The third panel, Table 6, shows the χ^2 values from testing the hypothesis that the composition of power relations by

Table 4 Power relations in post-WWII Greek constitutions by year *breakdown by category*

	%	1952	1975	1986	2001	2008	Mean	Mean/R
Source	Authority	79.78	79.73	80.45	78.28	78.35	79.13	79.06
	Other	20.22	20.27	19.55	21.72	21.65	20.87	20.94
Type	Instrumental	36.39	45.22	45.72	55.11	54.80	49.00	50.36
	Social	63.61	54.78	54.28	44.89	45.20	51.00	49.64
Direction	Positive	89.76	93.73	93.84	94.62	94.60	93.78	94.21
	Negative	10.24	6.27	6.16	5.38	5.40	6.22	5.79
N		371	829	844	893	887	3824	3453

Mean Average of all five constitutions 1952–2008
Mean/R Average of four republican constitutions 1975–2008
N Total number of power relations

Table 5 Hypothesis testing χ^2 from testing VOIP under monarchical and republican constitutions

Hypothesis: equal proportions (½) of	Monarchy 1952	Republic (Mean/R)
1 Authority and other power relations	131.64	371.84
2 Social and instrumental power relations	27.50	0.0454
3 Positive and negative power relations	234.56	674.87

Critical value of χ^2 at 0.01 with 1 DF = 6.63

Table 6 Hypothesis testing χ^2 from the differences between monarchical and republican constitutions

Hypothesis: monarchical and republican constitutions have equal proportions of	χ^2 (DF = 1)	Probability of acceptance
1 Authority power relations	0.08	$0.75 < P < 0.90$
2 Social power relations	20.38	$P < 0.005$
3 Positive power relations	7.78	$P \approx 0.005$

Critical value of χ^2 at 0.01 with 1 DF = 6.63

source, type of power and direction is the same for both the monarchical and the (mean of the four) republican constitutions.

1. *The time profile of the number of power relations*

In the first instance, the findings of Table 4 reveal that the total number of power relations has more than doubled from the 1952 to the more recent constitutions. The former was a shorter document with a standardised length of 17 pages against the latter analogues, all 32 pages long almost twice the size. The number of power relations increased from 371 to 829 in 1975, a staggering 123 % increase. Subsequently, revisions also changed the number of power relations, by 1.8 % in 1986, another 5.8 % in 2001 and a fall of 0.7 % in 2008. What explains the increase in the number of power relations from earlier to more recent constitutions?

Three explanations are proposed. In the first instance, the general trend towards democratisation—more liberal provisions—as the country moved away from monarchy towards parliamentary republic may account for the observed trend. Political liberalisation translated into more rights for the citizens and lengthier formal descriptions of such rights. A second explanation may be the worldwide tendency over the last half century towards the "judicialization of politics",[15] that is, the use of legal means and procedures, and especially referral to domestic and also international courts, to resolve political conflicts. The spread of property ownership, trade expansion, economic integration and broadening consumer choice led to the decline of social class as the main determinant of voting behaviour. Successful resolution of several policy issues calls for technical expertise that transcends traditional

[15] See among others Shapiro and Stone Sweet (2002) and Ferejohn (2002).

partisan allegiances. This again has led to more detailed enumeration of the competencies of the arms of government, their powers and obligations towards the citizens as well as the rights of citizens for redress. A third reason for the expansion of power relations, more specific to Greece, may be the wish of the drafters to respond decisively to the public discontent arising from inefficient and often corrupt public administration: Given that constitutional rules last longer than ordinary legislation, a constitutional amendment signifies that the drafter is committed to change things the way described by the constitutional amendment.[16]

2. *Sources of power*

Looking at the composition of the power relations, it is first observed that for both monarchical and republic constitutions, authority relations dominate as they comprise on average 79 % of the total of relations identified. The chi-square ratios reveal that for both the monarchical and the republican constitutions, we reject unambiguously the hypothesis that the proportion of authority power relations equals the proportion of the other sources of power relations (see the first row of Table 5). Moreover, the hypothesis that the proportion of authority relations is the same across the different constitutions cannot be rejected at the usual acceptance level (see the first row of Table 6).[17] The overwhelming presence of authority as a source of power is in accordance with the proposition that constitutional writers are primarily concerned with political power.

3. *Types of power*

On the other hand, the picture for the second definitional proposition, that is, uncertainty causes constitutional drafters to concentrate on social power relations instead of instrumental, is considerably more complicated. Inspecting the division of power by type, we observe an intriguing picture where the proportion of instrumental power is increasing overtime at the expense of social power so that eventually their relative sizes are reversed (3rd and 4th lines of Table 4). In the 1952 monarchical constitution, there are almost twice as many social powers as instrumental (63.61 % of the total), as argued by the VOIP view. However, this pattern changes dramatically with the republican constitutions; the relative number of instrumental powers gradually increases, so that the 2001 and 2008 constitutions provide for more instrumental powers than social powers. We therefore observe a complete reversal of the pattern identified under monarchy. Accordingly, this finding refutes the definitional proposition regarding the effect of uncertainty on the balance of social–instrumental power relations. The chi-square ratio from the

[16] Eleftheriadis (2005), however, argues that such deficiencies are better tackled by using the criminal law system rather than constitutional amendments, especially if the intended objective is transparency in public administration.

[17] Nor can the hypothesis that the proportion of authority relations is the same across the five different constitutions can be rejected as it yields a χ^2 ratio of 1.03 with 4 degree of freedom (not shown).

hypothesis that the proportion of social and instrumental power relations are equal in the 1952 constitution is 27.50 implying that the hypothesis cannot be accepted, while it falls to 0.0454 for the mean of the republican constitutions, implying that it cannot be rejected. In addition, the hypothesis that the 1952 monarchical constitution and the average of the four republican constitutions contain the same proportion of instrumental relations is decisively rejected as it yields a χ^2 ratio of 20.38 with 1 D.F, $P < 0.005$ (second row of Table 6). We then infer that with every change, the republican constitutional writer gave the power holder proportionately more power to act on things and events and less power to act over other actors.

4. *Direction of power*

Finally, over time the proportion of positive relations has increased from 90 % in 1952 to an average of more than 94 % in the post-1975 republican era. The hypothesis that the ratios of positive and negative power relations are equal to each other is decisively rejected for both monarchy and republic (see the third row of Table 5). The finding of a significantly larger proportion and modestly increasing positive relations is in contrast to the definitional proposition that the constitutional writer tends to limit power. Comparing the monarchical and republican constitutions, we find that the hypothesis that the 1952 monarchical constitution and the average of the four republican constitutions contain the same proportion of positive relations yields a χ^2 ratio of 7.78 with 1 DF that carries a probability of acceptance of approximately 0.5 % (3rd line of Table 6) and is therefore rejected.

All in all, Greek constitutional writing is consistent with the VOIP argument that higher uncertainty leads to more authority power relations, inconsistent with the proposition that uncertainty leads to more negative power relations and supports the proposition that uncertainty leads to more social power relations only in the case of monarchy but rejects it in the case of republic. In addition to the latter difference, there are more positive power relations in the republican constitutions than in monarchy, while the proportion of authority power relations is more or less the same across the different constitutional orders.

What factors may explain the observed pattern and most importantly the remarkable reversal of the composition of power relations by type and the large increasing number of positive power relations? It is the contention of this paper that the change from the monarchical 1952 constitution, which was considered as illiberal, to the parliamentary republic order and the subsequent extensions of individual freedoms and rights after the 1967–1974 dictatorship go a long way towards offering an explanation. Political liberalisation that confers freedoms to individuals, a parliamentary republican rule that explicitly describes what state organs are permitted to do (rather than implicitly deferring to the monarch), adoption of the principles of the welfare state that expands the scope of state activities and the requirement to transpose laws and regulations of the European Union to domestic legislation, as well as the attempts to force the public administration to respond to public discontent from inefficient and corrupt practices, led to the observed explosion of the number of power relations and to the increase in instrumental powers. Therefore, in changing from monarchical to parliamentary republic institutional order, and in inaugurating a clean break from the repressive military regime, the Greek constitutional writer assigned new instrumental powers.

Insofar as the increase in the number of positive and instrumental power relations is the result of granting more rights, one may query why so many new rights where included in the more recent constitutions. A possible answer is suggested by Mueller's (1991) work on constitutional rights. He argues that citizens wish to protect certain individual rights when the cost suffered by the citizen who is denied a right is very large relative to the gain of the others when the right is denied, and when the constitutional writers are uncertain whether they will be protected or harmed by that right. Then, conferring to citizens inviolable constitutional rights to undertake certain actions offers them the same strong protection of their interests as does the unanimity rule of decision making, with the added benefit of lower decision-making costs than the unanimity.

As a corollary, constitutional writing may be determined not only by uncertainty about the future, but is also informed by past experiences of the drafters. That is, drafters who went through the adverse effects of particular constitutional rules or lack thereof of explicit rules, when they have the opportunity, they will frame a constitution that leaves out such rules and includes provisions that are expected to prevent the emergence of circumstances that generated the adverse consequences, as well as institutions that may advance their own interests. For example, if the previous constitution comprised clauses that explicitly or implicitly enabled the monarch to interfere in politics in a partisan way, or facilitated repression, when amending the constitution, the writers will seek to remove ambiguities, list in more detail procedures and courses of action, possibly set up new organisational forms and add extra protections. Hence, although uncertainty about what may happen in the future tends to increase social and negative powers relations, knowledge of what has happened in the past may increase instrumental and positive power relations.

4 Conclusions

Since gaining her independence in 1832, Greece has had six constitutions in 1844, 1864, 1911, 1927, 1952 and 1975, the latter revised in 1986, 2001 and 2008. After surveying the constitutional profile of Greece, the present study examined two related issues. First, it investigated the pattern of power relations in five post-WWII Greek constitutions in the period 1952–2008, a time span that covers the monarchical constitution of 1952 written after the end of a vicious civil war won by the nationalist side against the communists, a republican constitution passed in 1975 after the collapse of military government and the abolition of monarchy by referendum, and three revisions of the latter. An inexorable trend of increasing authority, instrumental and positive power relations has been recorded. The former is compatible with the proposition that uncertainty about their future political position leads constitutional drafters to write constitutions that focus on political power rather economic or preceptoral power. The observations that in the post-1975 republican constitutions, the number of instrumental power relations exceeds that of social and that the number of positive power relations is larger than the number of negative, and increasing for successive republic constitutions contradicts the rest of the basic propositions of the VOIP.

Over a period of almost two hundred years, constitutional drafting has been an endogenous process. The initial 1844 constitution was the result of national liberation, and political liberalisation and was influenced by its contemporary European analogues. Constitutional writing proceeded as existing charters were unable to cope with unexpected challenges; in so doing, it built on previous experiences and borrowed from other European constitutions. All in all, the hypothesis that constitutional writing in Greece was the result of disinterested framers designing institutions behind a veil of ignorance to cope with uncertainty receives less than solid support, while there seems to be support for the conjecture that constitutional writing responded to the experiences and reflected the interests of whoever held the political advantage at the time of writing.

References

Clogg R (1986) A short history of modern Greece. Cambridge University Press, Cambridge

Congleton RD (2011) Perfecting parliament: constitutional reform and the origins of western democracy. Cambridge University Press, New York

Eleftheriadis P (2005) Constitutional reform and the rule of law in Greece. West European Polit 28:317–334

Ferejohn JA (2002) Judicializing politics, politicizing law. Law Contemp Probl 65:41–68

Gallant TW (2001) Modern Greece. Hodder Arnold, London

Greek Parliament (2004) Thirty years from the 1975 constitution. The Greek constitutions from Rigas to today. (In Greek)

Imbeau LM (2009) Testing the « veil of ignorance » hypothesis in constitutional choice: a « walk-talk » approach. J Pub Fin Pub Choice 26(1):3–21

Imbeau LM, Jacob S (2011) Is the "veil of ignorance" in constitutional choice a myth? an empirical exploration informed by a theory of power. In: Marciano A (ed) Constitutional mythologies, new perspectives on controlling the state. Springer, New York, pp 53–70

Imbeau LM, Jacob S (2015) Measuring the opacity of the 'Veil of ignorance' in constitutions: theory, method and some results. In: Imbeau LM, Jacob S (eds) Behind a veil of ignorance? power and uncertainty in constitutional design, New York, Springer

Mueller DC (1991) Constitutional rights. J Law, Econ Organ 7:313–333

Mueller DC (1996) Constitutional democracy. Oxford University Press, Oxford

Mueller DC (1999) On amending constitutions. Const Polit Econ 10, 385No396

Mueller DC (2005) Constitutional political economy in the European Union. Public Choice 124:57–73

Shapiro M, Stone Sweet A (2002) Constitutional judicial review. In: Shapiro M, Stone Sweet A (eds) On law, politics and judicialization. Oxford University Press. Oxford, pp 138–148

Tridimas G (2010) Referendum and the choice between monarchy and republic in Greece. Const Polit Econ 21:119–144

Veremis T (1997) The military in Greek politics: from independence to democracy. Black Rose Books, London

Voigt Stefan (1999) Implicit constitutional change—changing the meaning of the constitution without changing the text of the document. Eur J Law Econ 7:197–224

Chapter 11
Is the Swiss Constitution Really Constitutional? Testing the "Veil of Ignorance" Hypothesis over Time

Karin Ingold and Frédéric Varone

1 Introduction

In this chapter, we suggest an empirical analysis of the power distribution outlined in the current Swiss constitution. We furthermore concentrate on the historical evolution of the constitutional text. We compare three points in time: the original Federal constitution of 1874, its complete revision in 1999, and finally the text in force in 2011.

Switzerland can be considered as some kind of a special case. While we can confirm the first hypothesis outlined in the "veil of ignorance" research program, namely that political power relations dominate over economic and perceptoral power, we obviously have to reject the second and third hypotheses. Empirical results confirm that direct democratic instruments—where Swiss citizens through their voting right (i.e., mandatory vote for all constitutional amendment) also become the constitution drafters and adopters—seem to reduce drafting uncertainties. This might explain why the Swiss constitution is dominated by instrumental over social power relations (hypothesis 2) and why it rather ascribes than limits power (hypothesis 3).

After outlining the historical background from the Federal constitution's genesis and adoption in 1874 until today, we present the content analysis of the 2011 constitutional text. In the fourth section, we then systematically test the three overall hypotheses and show the evolution of power relations in the Swiss constitution. In the last section, we compare results from the versions of 1874, 1999, and 2011. Finally, we conclude highlighting the major results and explanations that make Switzerland and its constitutional text a special case.

K. Ingold (✉)
University of Bern, Bern, Switzerland
e-mail: karin.ingold@ipw.unibe.ch

F. Varone
University of Geneva, Geneva, Switzerland
e-mail: Frederic.Varone@unige.ch

K. Ingold
The Swiss Federal Institute of Aquatic Science & Technology, Eawag, Dübendorf, Switzerland

L.M. Imbeau and S. Jacob (eds.), *Behind a Veil of Ignorance?*,
Studies in Public Choice 32, DOI 10.1007/978-3-319-14953-0_11

2 Historical Background: The Constitutions of 1848 and 1874

Modern Switzerland is created with the promulgation of the constitution of September 12, 1848. The constitution lays the foundation stone for the new Federal nation-state which emerged from a very loose confederation of 25 independent cantons considering themselves Sovereign states. Since 1815, a conference of cantons' delegates—called the "*Diet*"—was empowered to implement the "*Federal Pact,*" a treaty guaranteeing the independence of each canton and, at the same time, their mutual assistance. However, the *Diet* was not a real Parliament and the *Federal Pact* could not be regarded as a formal constitution either (Kölz 2006: 167). Furthermore, no Federal Government was elected at that time to exercise executive powers (Linder 1994: 5).

The constitution of 1848 marked thus a paradigmatic institutional change. It was adopted in response to the "*Sonderbundkrieg,*" a quick civil war opposing Protestants (or Progressives) to Catholics (or Conservatives) in November 1847. The conflict between a majority of protestant and industrializing cantons, on one side, and a minority of catholic and rural cantons, on the other side, crystallized around the traditional role devoted to the Catholic Church in public affairs, and the strengthening of the central power within the cantons' confederation. Protestants were in favor of a laic State and power centralization; they tried unsuccessfully to overthrow the Government of Lucerne by force when, in 1844, the Jesuits took over the secondary education in this canton. In reaction, seven conservative cantons—namely Schwyz, Uri, Unterwalden, Lucerne, Zug, Fribourg, and Valais—formed the so-called *Sonderbund* (i.e., literally the "separate league") and negotiated a separate treaty to protect their common interests and rights. They wanted to preserve the traditional role of the Church, and they were also skeptical about any centralization process which could lead to the formation of a Federal Government. The progressive cantons demanded the dissolution of the *Sonderbund*, but it was only in 1847 that the *Diet* declared this "separate league" to be a violation of the *Federal Pact*. The conflict then escalated into a 27-day—but almost bloodless—civil war. Finally, the *Sonderbund* was ended after a major battle taking place in Lucerne: The Catholic *Sonderbund* members surrendered after their defeat against the Federal troops. The various cantons, which had been engaged in this religious conflict, then united to form a single nation-state (i.e., a real Federation replacing the confederation of cantons in place between 1815 and 1848; see Linder 1994: 6).

The victorious Progressives were logically the leading drafters of the Federal constitution of 1848. Their proposal provided (1) for Federal authorities including a Parliament (*Federal Assembly*), a Government (*Federal Council*), and a judicial power (*Federal Supreme Court*); (2) a federalist structure of the Swiss State with three levels of power (i.e., Federal, cantonal, and municipal), with subsidiarity as guiding principle and, consequently, with the necessity to have an explicit constitutional base for every new policy competency delegated by the cantons to the

Federal power; and (3) a mandatory vote by the people and by the cantons to introduce, or to refuse, any new constitutional amendment. This constitution's draft was submitted to a popular vote in the various cantons. In September 1848, the *Diet* declared the constitution adopted as a large majority of people and cantons had accepted it.

The Swiss constitution of 1848 is directly influenced by its counterpart in the United States (US). As a matter of fact, several claims of the Catholic cantons against power centralization were similar to the grievances expressed by anti-federalist forces in the USA a few decades before (Linder 1994: 6). As a compromise solution between Progressives and Conservatives, the 1848 Swiss constitution finally combines the democratic principle (i.e., one person, one vote) with the federalist principle (i.e., one canton, one vote) (Linder 1994: 16–18). For example, the *Federal Assembly* is organized as a two-chamber system based on the American model: The *National Council* represents the people, while the *Council of States* represents the cantons. Furthermore, this parliamentary bicameralism is perfect insofar as both chambers are equal: The *Federal Assembly* can only exercise its powers through the agreement of both chambers. The strong power of the "upper chamber" should thus protect the Catholic minority from unilateral decisions taken by the Protestant majority. The same institutional balance between democracy and federalism is also at work when it comes to changing the Federal constitution. In order to be adopted, a constitutional amendment that is submitted to citizens in the form of compulsory referenda always requires a "double majority" of both the people (majority exceeding 50 % of the voters) and the cantons (i.e., majority of 13 cantons at least).

The constitution of 1848 was then revised at several occasions, either partially (1866, 1891, 1921, etc.) or entirely (in 1874 and 1999 only). The global revision of 1874 did not change the structure of the Swiss Federation per se but extended the direct democracy beyond the existing mandatory popular vote that had to be organized on every constitutional amendment proposed by the *Federal Assembly* and *Federal Council*: "The system was extended in 1874 with the introduction of the optional referendum for laws (1874), with the popular initiative (1891) and the referendum for international treaties (1921). (The year 1977) brought a first extension of direct democracy in foreign policy, and in 2003, a second reform opened the optional referendum for all substantial international treaties" (Linder 2009: 66–67).

Of particular interest here is the *popular initiative* that allows for a total or partial revision of the Federal constitution[1] and generally takes the form of a formu-

---

[1] Note that Swiss citizens may *not* propose a new law or to modify an existing law through a popular initiative. But 50,000 citizens or eight cantons may launch an *optional referendum* against federal laws, urgent statutes exceeding one year of validity, or, under certain conditions, international treaties. This optional referendum requires only a simple majority of the people in order to succeed (i.e., to prevent the entry into force of the tackled law). Approximately 7 % of the legislative production that is eligible for an optional referendum is effectively challenged in the ballot via this direct democratic instrument.

lated draft (i.e., concrete proposal of a constitutional amendment). Launching a popular initiative requires 100,000 signatures. To be accepted (i.e., to modify the constitution), the initiatives require a "double majority" of both the people and the 26 cantons forming today the Swiss Federal system. Note that the *Federal Assembly* can propose a counterproposal to the popular initiative on which the citizens also vote at the same time. In the case of an initiative and a counterproposal, a third question is added, asking citizens which of the two they prefer.

Owing to popular initiatives, on one side, and to the proposals directly formulated by the *Federal Assembly* and *Federal Council*, on the other side, the Swiss constitution was subject to continual changes over time. In a nutshell, no less than 140 constitutional amendments were accepted since 1874. From a historical perspective, we observe an increased use of popular initiatives (i.e., proposals formulated by citizens) and mandatory referendum (i.e., proposals formulated by the Federal Parliament and Government) since World War II. In particular, the more frequent activation of direct democracy has been related to the growth of the Federal "welfare state" (see Linder 2009 for a detailed account of this long-term evolution). As every new policy competency gained by the Federal authorities needs a formal constitutional base (see the compromise negotiated in 1848 and presented above), there were several popular votes on specific policy issues. These partial revisions of the Federal constitution concerned, for example, the guarantee of private property rights and land use planning, the development of public infrastructures (i.e., transportation, energy, and communications), education and research, health care, the consolidation of social insurances, economic and labor market regulation, the adjustment of fiscal policies, environmental protection, defense and external affairs, and morality issues such as abortion and biomedicine. The gradual addition of more than one hundred ad hoc amendments unsurprisingly led to a patchwork and to internal incoherencies of the Federal constitution of 1874. The Federal authorities thus decided to revise it completely in the mid-1960s. This revision process took more than four decades to eventually translate into a new fundamental text in 1999. Even if this new constitution is a global revision of the former text of 1874, it does not, however, change the institutional structure of the Swiss Federal nation-state. It shall be considered as an update of the 1874 constitution without changing it in substance. The new version of the Federal constitution was approved by popular and cantonal vote on April 18, 1999, and it came into force on January 1, 2000. The following section recapitulates the milestones and outputs of this long decision-making process.

3 Genesis of the Constitution of 1999

We first address the historical context of the new constitution's genesis and then present the interests of its drafters and adopters. Section 4 will discuss its core elements in terms of power relations, as conceptualized in the theoretical chapter of this volume (Imbeau and Jacob 2015).

3.1 Drafting and Adopting the Constitution of 1999[2]

Several attempts completely to revise the Federal constitution failed before the 1960s. In September 1935, for example, 72 % of voters and 22 cantons rejected a popular initiative calling for a new constitution. In 1966, the *Federal Assembly* finally accepted two parliamentary motions asking for a major constitutional revision. Two expert groups, directed by a *Federal Councilor* (i.e., an elected member of the Federal Government), were designated to elaborate a first draft of the new constitution. The so-called *Furgler commission*[3] presented its proposal in November 1977. This draft was submitted by the Government to an open public consultation procedure. About 885 reactions coming from the cantons, political parties, interest groups, trade unions, private firms, NGOs, associations, etc., were collected, analyzed, and weighted. This external consultation helped identify five main conflictual issues, namely (1) the limitation of private property rights and economic freedom, (2) the institutional relations between the Federation and the cantons, (3) the people's right to launch a popular initiative, (4) the constitutional review of Federal laws by the *Federal Supreme Court*, as well as (4) new social goals and rights. The latter corresponded mainly to unwritten fundamental human rights that were recognized by the *Federal Supreme Court*'s extensive case law and that were already guaranteed in the European Convention on Human Rights (ECHR), which Switzerland ratified in 1974.

Notwithstanding this impressive preparatory work, the revision process was strongly delayed when Rudolf Friedrich was elected as successor to Kurt Furgler in the *Federal Council*. But 1986–1987 brought a new start: The *Federal Assembly* urged the Government to pursue the formal update of the constitution, and Elisabeth Kopp took over the head of the Ministry for Justice and Police. Great expectations accompanied this personal change in the Federal Government.

However, the whole revision enterprise was soon frozen, once again, when the Government decided to change its strategy toward the European integration. Concretely, the *Federal Council* decided to participate in the European Economic Area (EEA) and, furthermore, to apply for full accession to the European Union (EU). In accordance with the Federal constitution, entry to the EEA required a mandatory referendum. On December 6, 1992, a day which became to be known as the "Black Sunday," the Swiss citizens rejected a popular vote, and in contradiction to their Government's position, joining the EEA. Through this refusal, Switzerland found itself with a disadvantageous access to the single European market. Since membership to the EU had proved to be unviable due to domestic opposition, the Government pursued a strategy of "sectoral bilateral agreements

---

[2] This historical sketch is mainly based on the yearly accounts of Swiss politics exposed in the "*Année Politique Suisse*" since 1976.

[3] Kurt Furgler was President of the *Federal Council* in 1977 and at the head of the Justice and Police Ministry.

with EU" with the aim to counter economic isolation. In parallel to this European policy, the revision of the Federal constitution was relaunched to stimulate an internal reform of Swiss institutions and their anchorage in the Federal constitution.

In June 1994, the *Federal Council*—with Arnold Koller as new Minister in charge of the Justice and Police Ministry—proposed a revised draft of the Federal constitution. This new governmental proposal suggested (1) doubling the number of signatures required for a popular initiative and an optional referendum, (2) strengthening the role played by the cantons in foreign affairs, (3) implementing the freedom of information and transparency principles in public administration, and, last but not least, (4) guaranteeing social goals and human rights. Note that the constitutional review of Federal laws by the *Federal Supreme Court* was abandoned in this new proposal.

After a second public consultation procedure organized in 1995, the draft went to the parliamentary commissions of the *Federal Assembly* in 1996. The MPs did not change dramatically the content of the text that had been elaborated by the *Federal Council* and integrated the remarks formulated during the public consultation procedure, with the notable exception of direct democratic rights: The MPs preferred to keep the *status quo ante* (i.e., lower number of signatures necessary for validating a popular initiative or an optional referendum). So, exactly 150 years after the birth of modern Switzerland, the Parliament approved the new constitution on December 11, 1998, with a very large majority in the *National Council* (i.e., 134 Yes, 14 No, and 31 abstentions) and unanimity in the *Council of States* (i.e., 44 Yes). This constitutional text was then submitted to a popular vote. On April 18, 1999, 59.2 % of the voters and 13 cantons accepted the new Federal constitution, which came into force on January 1, 2000.

3.2 Interest of Drafters–Adopters

In the Swiss context, it is quite difficult—if not simply impossible—to clearly distinguish between the drafters and the adopters of the Federal constitution of April 1999. Much preparatory "drafting" work was realized by successive expert groups directed by a member of the Federal Government (1977–1995) and then discussed by specialized parliamentary commissions in both chambers of the *Federal Assembly* (1996–1998). However, these rather "closed" and internal institutional venues were complemented by two very open and external consultation procedures (1977–1980 and 1994–1996), during which all political and non-political actors had the opportunity to articulate their opposition to the drafted text and, furthermore, to propose alternative contents and formulations.

These extensive public consultation procedures are essential in the Swiss political system, which is often interpreted as an emblematic case of "consensus democracy" (Lijpahrt 1999). Specifically, actors opposing a constitutional change may use direct democratic voting campaigns to challenge the new constitutional provisions proposed by the political elites. Voters may overturn formal decisions made by the Government and the parliamentary majority through a negative vote at the *mandatory referendum*. Uncertainty for the dominant political coalition is thus introduced to the constitutional decision-making process through the use of direct democracy. The threat of being defeated at the ballot box, and thus of blocking any change to the constitutional *status quo*, acts like a Damocles' sword pending over the whole constitution's revision process. As a general consequence, direct democracy has led to power-sharing institutions and to a large governmental coalition (according to the seminal hypothesis formulated by Neidhart in 1970; see also Papadopoulos 2001 and Vatter 2009).

There are also tangible impacts of direct democracy on the particular decision-making process investigated here: The constitutional considerations and specific positions of all political and non-political actors, which might otherwise (successfully) oppose any constitutional change during a referendum campaign, are already integrated at the pre-parliamentary phase of the decision-making process—where the initial constitutional proposals are elaborated—in order to avoid an *ex post* defeat in the popular vote. The mandatory referendum is thus a key institutionalized veto point that can be used by opponents to any constitutional change and can be labeled as a "veto player referendum" (Tsebelis 2002: 125).

All in all, it does *not* make sense, when analyzing the Swiss case, to undertake a separate analysis of the interests promoted by the constitution's drafters on the one hand and by its adopters on the other hand. Instead of such a double analysis, we proceed hereafter to the identification of the main cleavages between the actors who supported, versus those who opposed, the Federal constitution submitted to popular vote. This empirical analysis is based on an *ex post* survey of 1,203 Swiss citizens that was realized in April and May 1999. This empirical sample is representative of the different linguistic regions and cantons of Switzerland, as well as of the education level, professional occupation, age category, and gender distribution within the whole population (see Delgrande and Linder 1999). Five results of this statistical analysis are relevant for our interpretation of actors' interests:

1. First, the French- and Italian-speaking cantons were stronger supporters of the new constitution (with approval rates of 79 and 74 %, respectively) than the German-speaking cantons (61 %). Furthermore, the rural municipalities within the German-speaking part of Switzerland were the most reluctant to accept the new constitutional provisions (54 %).
2. Two socioeconomic factors are important to understand the final outcome of the vote: Younger citizens who had benefited from a higher education level (i.e., higher preceptoral power) and who earned a higher revenue (i.e., higher economic power) showed the highest approval rates. It is also noteworthy that other socioeconomic characteristics of the survey respondents (i.e., gender, religion, and civil status) have no explanatory power.
3. Voters who are affiliated to or sympathizers of the political left (i.e., Social Democrats) or the center right parties (i.e., Christian Democrats and Liberals)

supported the constitutional revision. On the contrary, 83 % of the voters belonging to the radical right end of the partisan spectrum (i.e., Swiss People's party) opposed the global revision of the Federal constitution. This major cleavage between all political parties, on one side, and the extreme right, on the other side, is also reflected by the values defended by the opponents to the constitution's revision: They neither support the political and cultural openness of Switzerland (i.e., no integration in the EU) nor do they accept equal opportunities between Swiss citizens and foreigners.

4. Apparently, the federalist structures and processes of the Swiss political system were not a decisive issue at stake. The statistical analysis shows no significant difference in the voting behavior of centralists and federalists.
5. Last but not least, citizens who do not trust the Federal Government and who are not satisfied with the present functioning of the Swiss democracy casted a NO-vote.

In summary, the authors of this study concluded that opponents to the constitutional revision were those who were attached to fundamental national myths formulated in the past: They were proud of their nationality and very much attached to the traditional political institutions. Their NO-vote translated an obsession with issues of identity: They were afraid of a dissolution of their country and the citizenship. Their decision was therefore not an expression of dissatisfaction with the constitution's content, but more a symbolic vote. It is why specific points or paragraphs outlined in the amended text were rarely explicitly criticized (Delgrande et al. 1999: 24).

4 Content of Today's Constitution

Here, we present the general architecture of the new Federal constitution and we proceed to an in-depth analysis and test of the three major hypotheses guiding this research.

Hypothesis 1	There are more concerns for political power than for economic or preceptoral power in a constitution
Hypothesis 2	There are more concerns for social power than instrumental power in a constitution
Hypothesis 3	There are more concerns for negative than positive power relations in a constitution

In Sect. 5, those results are then compared to the power relations of 1874 and 1999. This allows us then to gain more knowledge on how the Swiss constitution evolved.

4.1 Description of the Constitutional Text

Today's Federal constitution contains approximately 24,654 words (in the French version that was coded here) and 197 articles, and it is structured in 6 sections. The Preamble and Title 1 (articles 1–6) define the characteristic traits of the *Swiss State* on its three levels of Government, namely Federal, cantonal, and municipal. Title 2 (articles 7–41) is entitled "Fundamental Rights, Civil Rights and Social Goals." These articles establish a comprehensive and directly enforceable *Bill of rights* (e.g., right to life and personal freedom, right to privacy, freedom of religion and conscience, freedom of assembly, guarantee of ownership, exercise of political rights, and acquisition and deprivation of citizenship). Furthermore, this second section also defines a set of social goals, such as access to social security, to health care, to a suitable accommodation on reasonable terms, and to education and protection against the economic consequences of old age, invalidity, unemployment, and maternity. Title 3 (articles 42–135) presents the general principles for the *allocation and fulfillment of State tasks* by the Federation, the cantons, and the municipalities. This third section stipulates which authorities are—exclusively or jointly—competent for the main policy domains: security and defense, education and culture, environment and spatial planning, public works and transport, energy and communications, economy and employment, social security and public health, finance, etc. Title 4 (articles 136–142) is dedicated to political rights in general and to the instruments of *direct democracy* in particular (i.e., popular initiative and mandatory or optional referendum). Title 5 (articles 143–191) presents the composition, prerogatives, and standard operating procedures of the Parliament (*Federal Assembly*), the Government (*Federal Council*), and judicial authorities (*Federal Supreme Court*). Finally, Title 6 (articles 192–195) contains transitional provisions as well as the rules of the game for any upcoming partial or total revision of the Federal constitution.

4.2 Statistical Results from the Content Analysis

We found 931 power relations defined in the current Federal constitution. Two-third of these relations concern political power; only 10 % relate to economic power relations and 5.7 % to preceptoral power relations (see Table 1). The dominant source of power is thus authority; wealth and knowledge sources are by far less prominently defined and considered.

Furthermore, the constitution drafters emphasized instrumental (62.9 %) rather than social power relations (36.8 %). That means concretely that agents are given or taken the competence to act on things or events, rather than the competence to act over other actors or people.

Table 1 Characteristics of power relations in the Swiss constitution of 2011 (percentage)

Resource of influencing party	
Authority	62.4
Wealth	10.1
Knowledge	5.7
Indeterminate	21.8
Total (N)	100.0 (931)
Type of power	
Instrumental	62.9
Social	36.8
Indeterminate	0.2
Total (N)	99.9 (931)
Direction of power relation	
Positive	98.5
Negative	1.5
Total (N)	100.0 (931)

And interestingly, only a negligible amount of power relations limits the competence of agents (1.5 %). A large majority of power relations (98.5 %) give agents the capacity to act over events or people. The Swiss constitution generally assigns, rather than limits, the capacity of agents. This fact will be explored more in detail in the following sections.

4.3 Which Agents Are Identified in the Constitution?

We will outline hereafter the agents who are mostly engaged in power relations as defined in the current Swiss constitution. In the federalist context of Switzerland, it makes furthermore sense to identify the institutional level (Federal, cantonal, and municipal) those actors belong to.

As outlined in Table 2, at 34.4 %, the Swiss confederation is the agent most often engaged in power relations. Furthermore, the confederation is always linked to other agents (social power), but never to events or things (instrumental power). At the national level, the other two most active agents are the Swiss Government (i.e., the Federal Council) and the Swiss Parliament (i.e., the *Federal Assembly*), engaged in 7.4 and 6.3 % of power relations.

The cantons are the second most involved agents in the constitution with 12.4 % of the power relations. Municipalities are only mentioned three times (0.3 % of power relations).

Obviously, another very important agent is the Sovereign, namely the people (who may be called to the ballot box to vote on a popular initiative or referendum). Different expressions exist in the constitution to name the Sovereign. We outline

Table 2 Most important agents involved in positive and negative power relations (percentage)

	Positive	Negative	Total
Federal level			
Confederation	34.4	0	34.4
Federal Council	7.2	14.3	7.4
Parliament	6.2	7.1	6.3
Cantonal level			
The cantons	12	28.6	12.4
Municipal level			
Municipalities	0.3	0	0.3
The Sovereign			
The people	2.7	7.1	2.8
Every person	2.9	0	2.9
Citizen	1.8	0	1.8
Others	32.5	42.9	32.7
Total (N)	100.0 (917)	100.1 (14)	100.0 (931)

in Table 2 the most common ones: People are mentioned 2.8 %, «Anyone» 2.9, and the citizen 1.8 % when it comes to define the power distribution in the Swiss constitution.

4.4 Which Capacities Do These Agents Have?

Overall, Table 3 provides us with three important insights. First, for all power sources, instrumental power always dominates both social and negative power relations. Second, the percentage of social power within each power source (authority, wealth, and knowledge) gets smaller as we go from authority to wealth to knowledge: In political power relations, 43.2 % are social relations and therefore concern at least two agents, a source and a target; for economic and preceptoral power, only 35.9 and 32.1 %, respectively, is social relations. Third, no social relation is formulated negatively: All limiting power relations are expressed when an agent is in relation with a thing or an event.

Of the power relations that express the capacity to act over other agents (*positive social power*), 71.72 % concern political, 9.62 % economic, and 4.96 % preceptoral power relations. Therefore, we observe the same split between dominant authority, and a minority of wealth and knowledge power sources.

But the question here is not only who the "sources" of power relations are, e.g., the actors who exercise power over other actors, but also who are the "targets" of power relations. As illustrated in Table 2, the confederation is engaged in 34.4 % of all power relations. But whose power is enhanced? Upon a closer look at the current Federal constitution, one notices that more than half of all positive

Table 3 Positive and negative power directions per source of power

	Positive	Negative
Authority		
Instrumental	321 (56.4 %)	12 (100 %)
Social	246 (43.2 %)	0
Wealth		
Instrumental	59 (64.1 %)	2 (100 %)
Social	33 (35.9 %)	0
Knowledge		
Instrumental	36 (67.9 %)	0
Social	17 (32.1 %)	0

relations that are coming from the confederation target the power of the cantons. The cantons on their side mostly target the power of the communes (around one-fourth of their power relations) and the confederation (again around one-fourth of their power relations). These relationships reflect both the Swiss "functional federalism" (i.e., the confederation formulates the public laws, while the cantons implement them) and the principle of subsidiarity (i.e., explicit delegation of powers from the cantons to the confederation for every policy sector newly regulated by the Federal level of power).

The Government and the Parliament target each other in most of their power relations. The Parliament furthermore often ascribes power to the Sovereign (one-fourth of its relations).

4.5 Which Capacities Does the Text Take from These Agents?

To answer this question, we need to consider only negative power relations. Generally, and as outlined in Table 1, negative power relations are very rare and therefore the exception. And very interestingly, social power is never defined in a negative way (see Table 3). This means that no power relation is restricting in the current Swiss constitution when it comes to acting over other people. Furthermore, no negative power relation at all is defined within the category of preceptoral power (see Table 3).

From all relations where an agent is restricted in his/her capacity to act over an event or thing (*instrumental power*), 85.7 % concern political and 14.3 % economic power relations. The very few negative power relations (14 in total) are thus dominantly present within the category «authority» as the source of power. Table 4 illustrates who is limited in its instrumental power.

It is not a surprise that the cantons competences are—even though rarely—overall the most frequently limited. Article 3 of the Swiss constitution gives the

Table 4 Limiting power relations (only instrumental)

	Article	Number of negative relations
Federal level		
Federal Council	144/162	2
Parliament	162	1
Cantonal level		
The cantons	39/127/134	4
The Sovereign		
The people	138	1
Others		
Foreigners	121	3
Judge	144	1
Chancellery	162	2
Total		14

overall sovereignty to the cantons if this sovereignty is not explicitly limited within the constitution as this is the case four times. Furthermore, it is interesting to see that also foreigners are limited in their action and that this is made explicit in the constitution. Overall, foreigners are mentioned 10 times, while three times their freedom of action is limited (Article 121).

5 Hypothesis Testing and Evolution Over Time

5.1 Power Distribution in Today's Constitution

The results presented above clearly show that the Swiss constitution contains a large amount of political power relations, and much less economic or preceptoral power relations. We can thus clearly confirm the first research hypothesis. Swiss constitution drafters–adopters seemed to be a more uncertain about the distribution of authority than of wealth or knowledge. Expressed differently, they were more certain about their future economic or preceptoral positions, than their political roles in the society.

Further, we have to reject the second and third hypotheses for the Swiss case. Constitution drafters–adopters tend to enhance instrumental rather than social power (hypothesis 2) and tend to ascribe rather than to limit power over events or people (hypothesis 3). We identified 63 % of instrumental and only 37 % of social power relations. But most strikingly, 98.5 % of the power relations enhance agents' power over others or on events/things. This leads us also to the conclusion that the theoretically deduced hypothesis 3 (for the overall research project), stating that the constitution tends to limit rather than to ascribe power, has to be definitely rejected for the Swiss case. Note that this generic hypothesis is also falsified in other countries, in Canada for instance (as demonstrated by Imbeau and Jacob 2011).

5.2 Power Distribution Over Time

Based on the above-outlined results and the developments during the last century that led to the successive revisions of the constitution, we suggest here a comparative investigation of three versions of the constitutional text: the original Federal constitution of 1874, the amended constitution of 1999, and today's version (2011). When doing that, it makes much sense to consider—besides the degree of uncertainty of the *constitution drafters*—also that of *Swiss citizens*. As all amendments to the Federal constitution have to be accepted by the people (i.e., mandatory popular vote with double majority of the people and the cantons), Swiss citizens' degree of uncertainty seems to be crucial too when investigating constitutional power relations.

We still assume that constitution drafters *and* the Swiss citizens were, at the moment of adoption of the constitution, under a certain "veil of ignorance." But the pure fact that citizens intervene in constitution drafting and that we do not have a clear-cut in Switzerland between drafters on one side and adopters on the other leads us to the assumption that *over time* uncertainty was reduced.

Overall, and as outlined in Table 5, Swiss constitution drafters tend to be in general more uncertain about their future political positions rather than their economic or preceptoral positions in society. We therefore can confirm hypothesis 1 over the whole period of analysis. However, a slight reduction of uncertainty can be observed, as the difference between the three power resource types gets lower. Furthermore, those results confirm the major changes to the constitution outlined above (Sect. 3). They concern mostly authority issues such as institutional and procedural definitions of competences, of direct democratic and citizens' rights, and of Federal laws. Only few amendments concerned property or social rights redefinitions.

The reduction of uncertainty over time is further confirmed by the fact that instrumental power—even though always dominant in the Swiss constitution (see again Table 5 and the rejection of hypothesis 2)—gets more important over time and in relation to social power relations.

Table 5 Comparison over time (in percentage)

	1874	1999	2011
Resource of influencing party			
Authority	83	72	62
Wealth	6	14	10
Knowledge	7	4	6
Type of power			
Instrumental	53	54	63
Social	47	46	37
Direction of power			
Positive	90	96	98
Negative	10	4	2

It seems that the Swiss constitution was not changed in the view of the least privileged individual in society (as suggested by the overall hypothesis 3). On the contrary, changes seem to go in the direction of ascribing rather than limiting the power of people. This fact got more accentuated over time until the stage where, today, almost all power relations are positively formulated in the constitutional text. We have three major arguments for explaining this diachronic evolution. First, and as outlined in Sect. 3, better educated citizens with higher revenues voted in favor of the new constitution; less privileged people mostly voted against. Second, direct democratic instruments strongly reduce uncertainty: During the extensive public (pre-parliamentary) consultation phase, not only the constitution drafters, but also diverse private and public representatives of economic and civil society interests were invited to comment on the constitution project. Together with the popular vote, this leads to the situation where a majority of people are defending their own interests rather than the ones of the less privileged people. And third, the Swiss constitution is subject to continual changes over time, as 100,000 Swiss citizens may launch a popular initiative to amend partially the Federal constitution. The mere existence of this direct democratic instrument also means that the long-term perspective of constitutional choices (underlying the Buchanan and Tullock hypothesis) is not perfectly given in the Swiss case. As a matter of fact, more than 140 constitutional amendments were accepted since the first constitution of 1874. Furthermore, the Swiss citizens may only modify the constitutional text through a popular initiative, but they may not propose a new law or modify an existing law through a popular initiative (see footnote 1 above). In a nutshell, the distinction between constitutional choices (choice of rules), on the one hand, and "in-period" choices (choices within rules), on the other hand, is not clear-cut in Switzerland. All in all and confirmed by our longitudinal analysis, we conclude that power in general, and political power in particular, is rather ascribed than limited in the Swiss constitution.

6 Conclusion

What did we learn about the Swiss case? Swiss constitution drafters–adopters—including the Swiss citizens—seemed to be more certain about their economic and preceptoral power positions; this is why they emphasized political power relations. However, their uncertainty was generally limited: They did not adopt the preferences of the less privileged individual which resulted in the fact that they rather ascribed than limited power in general, and political power in particular.

We highlight the fact that our preliminary results are compatible with previous studies on partial revisions of the Swiss constitution. Dietmar Braun has studied in detail the new equalization scheme and revision of competences between the Federal Government and the cantons "Neuer Finanzausgleich" (NFA) that was accepted by the Swiss people in November 2004 (Braun 2009). This major change concerns seven articles of the Federal constitution and more than thirty laws about the respective policy tasks of the Federation and the cantons, the intensified collaboration between the cantons, the horizontal and vertical fiscal equalization schemes, etc. Braun (2009) concluded that this constitutional debate over NFA remains a "mixed motive game" (Vanberg and Buchanan 1989): It combines a two-step procedure that was strategically crafted by the political elite. The first phase was a general discussion about the principles of the NFA reform. It was based on "arguing," behind the veil of ignorance (that was "crafted" by the reform leaders) as the cantons could not know in detail and with certainty the concrete outcomes of the NFA. Rather, the second phase was a classical "bargaining" process, focusing on the distributive outcomes (in the respective cantons) of the concrete application of the NFA principles adopted during the first phase. In one word, Braun (2009) convincingly argued that the careful separation of arguing and bargaining was a key factor for the success of the NFA reform: "The veil of ignorance helps to raise the level of discussion to arguing, but it cannot transform selfish interests into common good interests. The constitutional debate remains a mixed motive game throughout the whole process" (Braun 2009: 331).

References

Braun D (2009) Constitutional change in Switzerland. Publius J Federalism 39(2):314–340

Delgrande M, Linder W (1999) *Analyses* des votations fédérales du 18 avril 1999, VOX Nr 67, GfS et IPW Université de Berne

Imbeau LM, Jacob S (2011) Is the "veil of ignorance" in constitutional choice a myth? An empirical exploration informed by a theory of power. In: Marciano A (ed) Constitutional mythologies: new perspectives on controlling the state. Springer, New York, pp 53–69

Imbeau LM, Jacob S (2015) Measuring the opacity of the 'veil of ignorance' in constitutions: theory, method and some results. In: Imbeau LM, Jacob S (eds) Behind a veil of ignorance? Power and uncertainty in constitutional design. Springer, New York

Kölz A (2006) Histoire constitutionnelle de la Suisse moderne. Stämpfli, Berne

Lijpahrt A (1999) Patterns of democracy: Government forms and performance in thirty-six countries. Yale University Press, New Haven/London

Linder W (1994) Swiss democracy, possible solutions to conflict in multicultural societies. St. Martin's Press, New York

Linder W (2009) The impact of direct democracy on public policies: a historical perspective. In: Stéphane N, Frédéric V (eds) Rediscovering public law and public administration in comparative policy analysis: a tribute to Peter Knoepfel. Presses polytechniques et universitaires romandes, Lausanne, pp 63–77

Neidhart L (1970) Plebiszit und pluralitäre Demokratie. Eine Analyze der Funktion des schweizerischen Gesetzesreferendums. Bern, Francke

Papadopoulos Y (2001) How does direct democracy matter? The impact of referendum votes upon politics and policy-making. West Eur Polit 24(2):35–58

Tsebelis G (2002) Veto players: how political institutions work. Princeton University Press, New Jersey

Vanberg V, Buchanan JM (1989) Interest and theories in constitutional choice. J Theor Polit 1(1):49–62

Vatter A (2009) Lijphart expanded: three dimensions of democracy in advanced OECD countries? Eur Polit Sci Rev 1(1):125–154

Chapter 12
The Thickness of the Veil of Uncertainty and Its Effects on Constitution-Making in Post-communist Transition: The 1992 Constitution of Estonia

Ringa Raudla

1 Introduction

Studying constitution-making during post-communist transition can be regarded as particularly insightful for testing the veil of ignorance hypothesis proposed by Buchanan and Tullock (1962) because of the manifold transition that took place in these countries. These countries were simultaneously moving from one-party system to multi-party system, from command to market economy, and from government unconstrained by laws to the rule of law (see Sunstein 1991: 371). Hence, one would expect constitution-makers in these countries to have been facing extreme uncertainties with regard to their future power positions. This chapter examines constitution-making in one particular transition country—Estonia. After the declaration of independence (from the Soviet Union) in 1991, the constitutional assembly (CA) drafted a new constitution for the restored republic. What makes the Estonian case special compared with other instances of constitution-making in Central and Eastern Europe during the transition period is that the 1992 Constitution of Estonia was prepared by a separate CA (rather than by an existing legislature) *and* the resulting constitution was approved by means of a referendum, implying that it could be viewed almost an "ideal" case if viewed in the light of normative propositions for constitution-making brought out in the literature on constitutional political economy. Therefore, the Estonian constitution-making can be considered to be a particularly interesting case for constitutional political economy in general and for exploring the opaqueness of the veil and its effects on the content of the constitution in particular.

This paper will explore what kind of motivations of the framers can be inferred from the text of the Estonian constitution as discourse (about power relations) and

R. Raudla (✉)
Ragnar Nurkse School of Innovation and Governance,
Tallinn University of Technology, Tallinn, Estonia
e-mail: ringa.raudla@ttu.ee

L.M. Imbeau and S. Jacob (eds.), *Behind a Veil of Ignorance?*,
Studies in Public Choice 32, DOI 10.1007/978-3-319-14953-0_12

how opaque was the veil of uncertainty behind which the members of the Estonian Constitutional Assembly (1991–1992) drafted the new constitution.[1] According to the theoretical framework proposed by Imbeau (2009) and by Imbeau and Jacob (2011, 2015), if the veil of uncertainty in constitution-making is opaque, the predominant power relations in the constitution should be based on political power, pertain to social relations and be concerned with *denying* capacities to act (rather than *attributing* capacities to act). Thus, this paper examines to what extent these theoretical propositions are corroborated in the Estonian case.

This chapter is structured as follows. The first section gives an overview of the historical setting in which the CA was convened, how the constitution was drafted and what the motives and objectives of the framers were. The second section describes the content of the Estonian 1992 Constitution in terms of the power relations framework and addresses the following sub-questions: (a) What proportion of power relations in the Estonian constitution is based on political power (as opposed to economic power and perceptoral power)? (b) Among the power relations, what is the proportion of social and instrumental power relations? (c) Is the Estonian constitution concerned more with negative or positive power relations? The third section discusses the findings of the Estonian case study in the light the theoretical propositions of the Veil of Ignorance Project. The final section concludes.

As will be shown, the Estonian constitution does indeed emphasize power relations based on *authority*, but at the same time, it is more concerned with *positive* power relations than with *negative* ones and entails a lower proportion of *social* power relations than could be expected behind the veil of uncertainty. This paper also shows that, while for the most part, the opacity of the veil does indeed facilitate the reaching of agreements, there can also be situations where the transparency of the veil can contribute to reaching agreements among the framers, and conversely, that in some situations or issue areas, the veil can be so thick that the uncertainties involved make it very difficult to reach consensus. The Estonian case also points to the importance of the prevailing normative discussions on constitutionalism at the time of constitution-writing and to the role of path-dependencies in shaping the content of the constitution.

2 Historical Context of the Drafting and Adoption of the Constitution

2.1 The Historical Setting: The Decision to Convene the Constitutional Assembly

The decision to convene the CA (together with the Declaration of Independence) on August 20, 1991 can be considered as the culmination point in Estonia's struggle for independence from the Soviet Union, which had already started at the end of 1980s.

[1] The main sources of information for the case study in this chapter were the verbatim reports of the plenary sessions of the CA, the memoirs of the members of the Assembly, archival materials and secondary materials describing and discussing the constitution-making in Estonia.

The Supreme Council of Estonia made use of the power vacuum in the Soviet Union—created by an attempted coup d'État in Moscow—and seized the opportunity to restore Estonia's independence and hence end the Soviet occupation, which had lasted since 1940.[2]

The task of drafting a new constitution for the country was given to the CA, which was to include members from the two competing parliamentary bodies in Estonia at the time: the Supreme Council and the Estonian Congress (30 from each body).[3]

The Supreme Council (105 members) had been elected in the first multiparty parliamentary elections in 1990 by the electorate that consisted of all adult inhabitants registered in Estonia.[4] The Estonian Congress (499 members) had been elected in 1990 by all who had been citizens of Estonia prior to the Soviet occupation (and their adult descendants). These parallel elections to two different representative bodies mirrored the competition of two different pro-independence groups in Estonia, which had begun already in 1988–1989, when the more active movement toward independence started (Raitviir 1996: 353; Pettai 2001). On the one hand, the Estonian Popular Front advocated a more compromise-oriented approach to re-establishing Estonian independence, implying the utilization of the existing political institutions, gradual takeover and reform of the existing organs of state power, formal secession from the Soviet Union, and the proclamation of a *new* Estonian Republic. On the other hand, the movement called the Citizens' Committees (consisting of the Estonian Heritage Society, the Estonian National Independence Party (ENIP), and the Christian Union) vehemently disagreed with such a "conciliatory" strategy; instead, they called for setting up new institutions and *restitution* of the pre-war Estonian Republic (on the basis of legal continuity). As a result of the elections to these two bodies, the Popular Front became a dominant force in the Council, while the National Independence Party, together with the Estonian Heritage Society, became an important power in the Estonian Congress. Although the Estonian Congress remained a kind of "shadow parliament" to the Supreme Council (which had de facto powers and passed the laws), it was supported by the public and could not be ignored by the Council on important issues (Pettai 2001: 112–114; Taagepera 1993, Chap. 7; 1994: 213–214; Raitviir 1996: 353; Lauristin and Vihalemm 1997: 90).

The freely elected Supreme Council provided an opportunity for the Estonian political elites to experiment with democratic institutions. Altogether, it was a curious mix of elements of Western democracy and residues from the Soviet past. For example, although in principle the political system in place in 1990 was parliamentary

---

[2] The two-day putsch in Moscow was organized by reactionary members of the Communist Party of the Soviet Union, who opposed the reform program advocated by Gorbachev (which, inter alia, entailed the granting of larger autonomy to the individual republics). For a detailed discussion of the coup, see, for example, Dunlop (2003).

[3] The description of the constitution-making in Estonia in 1991–1992 draws on Raudla (2010a: 254–256).

[4] As Taagepera (1991: 479) notes, the competitive parliamentary elections that took place in Estonia in 1990 were comparable to a situation in Denmark in 1943, where also free elections were organized in the presence of foreign occupation powers.

democracy and the parliamentary majority appointed the cabinet, the members of parliament were not allowed to become cabinet ministers. There was no de jure head of state, although the Chairman of the Presidium of the Supreme Council (Arnold Rüütel) came to serve as a de facto head of state in 1990 and 1991. Legislative activity of the new parliament was bogged down by quorum and majority requirements, which were unrealistically high—another leftover from the Soviet-type system (Taagepera 1991: 478). Despite these hurdles, the Supreme Council managed to pass a significant number of laws, some of which (e.g., on the head of state, the parliament, the electoral rules) amounted to a temporary constitution (Taagepera 1991: 480). Parallel to the work of the Supreme Council, the Estonian Congress also debated constitutional issues and commented on the laws adopted by the Council.

The decision of the Supreme Council to convene the CA has been termed as a "miracle compromise" (Pettai 2001: 111), since it succeeded in striking a balance between the diverging plans of the Supreme Council and the Estonian Congress on the question of how to proceed with constitution-making. Until then, some members of the Supreme Council had suggested that the Supreme Council should be declared a constitution-making body, while the leaders of the Estonian Congress demanded new elections for a CA or, alternatively, re-enacting the 1938 Constitution, which had been the last constitution in force before Estonia was occupied (Pettai 2001: 114).[5]

In sum, the constitution-making in Estonia was to take place in the context of high uncertainty as Estonia was in the early phase of a manifold transition. Internationally, it was not clear how the breakup of the Soviet Union would evolve and what implications these developments would have for Estonian foreign and internal politics. Domestically, while some of the political delineations had already been formed, the party landscape was still in the process of being formed, which, in turn, made strategic calculations more difficult for the actors involved. Further, with regard to socioeconomic issues, the uncertainty was even more pronounced. Given that during the Soviet regime, private property had been limited and privatization process had not been clearly outlined yet, it would have been rather difficult for the framers to evaluate their own socioeconomic position in the future.

2.2 *The Constitutional Assembly at Work: The Drafting of the Constitution*

The elections to the CA took place on September 7, 1991, in the Supreme Council and the Estonian Congress. The resulting composition of the Assembly mirrored relatively proportionally the strength of the different groupings in the two bodies (Taagepera

[5] Although at the time of the declaration of independence, the "official" constitution in Estonia was the "Constitution of the ESSR", this was generally regarded as "a meaningless scrap of paper", disregarded in practice (Taagepera 1994: 212–213). According to Taagepera (1994: 213), the ESSR Constitution was so despised by the Estonian politicians that no one recommended it even as a "possible starting point for the constitutional debate".

1994: 217). Among the total of 60 CA members, about 20 were from the Popular Front, another 20 could be labeled as national radicals, 13 were various Estonian moderates and reform Communists, and 7 were representatives of the Russians.[6]

Altogether, the CA of Estonia met at 30 different sessions between September 1991 and April 1992. The Assembly's work was divided between plenary sessions and committee work. The committees were to focus on more detailed discussions of the topics and the issues that could not be resolved within the committees were brought to the plenary session.

At the second session of the CA, two draft constitutions were submitted. The first one had been drafted by a working group of legal experts led by the Minister of Justice Jüri Raidla. The second draft was the 1938 Constitution of Estonia. By the end of September, three further draft proposals were submitted. The main competing drafts were the draft of Raidla and his team (putting forth a more presidential system) and the draft of Jüri Adams (putting forth a more parliamentary system by mending the 1920 Constitution of Estonia with some more balanced provisions and incorporating some provisions from the 1938 Constitution).[7] In October, the CA chose the draft of Adams (a member of the Estonian Congress and the chairman of the ENIP) as the basis for further deliberations (with 29 vs. 22 votes).

At the end of October 1991, a delegation of foreign experts from the Council of Europe attended the Assembly's sessions and voiced their opinions on the draft. The first draft of the constitution was released to the public on December 21, 1991. One of the committees was given the task to sort through the proposals submitted by the public and accommodate these proposals, where they considered appropriate (for a more detailed discussion, see Raudla 2010b).

In January 1992, the Supreme Council decided that the CA should continue its work but cooperate more closely with Raidla (the Minister of Justice) and his expert group, who had been involved in formulating the more presidential draft (but which had been rejected by the CA) (Aaskivi and Pärnaste 2002: 60). As a result of the cooperation, several additions were made to the draft, in particular to the chapter on the fundamental rights and duties (Hänni 2002: 164).

In February, the CA approved the draft[8] it had formulated by then and sent it to the Supreme Council, who, in turn, sent it back to the CA, claiming that it did not correspond to the preferences of the Estonian people (especially on the question of how to elect the president) and that it did not have the support of the majority of the Assembly.

[6] Given that the membership of the Supreme Council and the Estonian Congress overlapped to some extent, then there was overlapping membership also among the members of the CA: among the 30 representatives elected from Supreme Council, 15 were also members of the Estonian Congress, among the 30 representatives elected from the Estonian Congress, 3 were also members of the Supreme Council (Aaskivi and Pärnaste 2002: 49).

[7] As Adams (2002) admits in his memoirs, he wrote this draft essentially in 1 week. Still, he had been interested in constitutional issues for a longer time and had written several memoranda concerning constitutional issues to the Estonian Congress during 1990–1991. As pointed out by Pettai (2001) and Taagepera (1994), Adams had no formal training in law, but a degree in forestry. Because of his dissident background, he had been working as a boiler-man.

[8] By a margin of 32–3 votes, with 6 abstentions.

According to the decision of the Supreme Council, the CA was to "coordinate" its draft with the expert group consisting of Council's lawyers and prepare a revised draft by mid-April (Taagepera 1994: 226–227; Aaskivi and Pärnaste 2002: 68; Adams 2002: 151; Hänni 2002: 166). The CA obliged, although mostly in form rather than substance, as witnessed by the fact that as a result of this "coordination," only minor wording changes were made to the draft constitution, but, in terms of content, no extensive changes were made. In particular, the CA was not willing to give in on the issue of how the President should be elected: it stayed with its initial choice of having the president elected by the parliament (and, if the parliament fails to achieve 2/3 majority, by an electoral body composed of members of the legislature and representatives of the local governments). The only more substantive change was the right given to the president to appeal to the Supreme Court after his veto is overridden by the parliament. The Assembly reaffirmed its support for the draft constitution at the 30th session (on April 10, 1992), and the Supreme Council decided to put the Constitution to referendum. On June 28, 1992, the Constitution was approved in a referendum where only Estonian citizens could vote. The list of citizens included 669 080 persons; 446 708 took part in the referendum, of whom 91 % voted in favor of the Constitution.

It is worth mentioning here that together with the core text of the Constitution itself, the CA also worked on what was called the implementation law (the so-called Chap. 17 of the constitution) which entailed provisions on how to phase in and implement the new constitution. The most controversial aspect in preparing the implementation law was the proposal to "block former Communist power-holders from running for office during the first ten years" (Taagepera 1994: 225). After heated debates on the issue, the CA concluded that it was "too political for a constitution-making body to decide" and proposed to the Supreme Council to include it as a separate question on the constitutional referendum ballot (Pettai 2001: 126). However, by the time the implementation act was submitted to popular referendum this "lustration" provision had been dropped. The implementation act also foresaw different rules for the first elections of the parliament and the President. The first parliament was to be elected only for 2.5 years (instead of 4). The President was to be elected for 4 years (instead of 5) and according to a different election procedure: in the first round, the public could directly vote for the candidates, and if no candidate received more the 50 % of the votes, the parliament would elect the president. The different method for the first election of the President was introduced in order to appease the public, but also several members of the Supreme Council and the Government, who favored direct elections of the president.

2.3 *The Framers of the Estonian Constitution: Their Motivations and Objectives*

The constitution-making in Estonia in 1991–1992 was characterized by a complex configuration of actors with various powers. The representatives from the existing legislature (the Supreme Council) and the Estonian Congress had agenda-setting, deliberative power, and voting power. The Supreme Council as a whole had process-guiding powers. The local constitutional experts who were involved in the work of the assembly through advisory functions (although they did not have voting powers as such) had some agenda-setting powers and powers emerging from their expertise. The foreign constitutional experts had the power of persuasion and were regarded with great respect by the Estonian framers because of their assumed neutrality and long-term expertise (see also Raudla 2010a). And, in the end, the Estonian citizens had the power to approve or reject the constitution in a referendum.[9]

Altogether, the framers came from either the existing political elite (e.g., the representatives of the Supreme Council) or emerging elite (the representatives of the Estonian Congress), among whom several had been dissidents under the Soviet regime. In other words, the members of the CA were, to a large extent, holders of significant political and perceptoral powers. It can be conjectured that a significant proportion of them expected to become members in the future parliaments and governments and thus hold positions of power—especially political power and perceptoral power. With regard to the position of wealth, then because of the transition from one economic system to another, the framers had only limited possibilities to foresee their future positions: There were simply too many uncertainties surrounding the regime change.

It is worth noting here that despite the fact that about one-third of the population in Estonia was made up of Russians, they were, to a large extent, excluded from constitution-making. Although seven Russian-speakers were formally members of the CA, they found it difficult to participate in its work because they did not speak Estonian, which was the working language of the CA. According to Taagepera (1994: 221), the Russian members "did not seem to have much interest in details, apart from the rights of citizens and noncitizen residents." In addition, as Pettai (2001) notes, the Russians were also unmotivated to participate in constitution-writing because the citizenship laws adopted in the autumn of 1991 foresaw that Estonian citizenship would be automatically granted only to the citizens of the inter-war republic and their descendants (and thus declaring the 500,000 Russians living in Estonia non-citizens). Thus, the Russian representatives were not overly enthusiastic to work on a constitution for a country where they would be non-citizens.

The "subjective motivations" of the Estonian framers varied to a significant degree. Some of the framers (from ENIP) argued for the restoration of the inter-war republic, together with the 1938 constitution: for them, the 1938 Constitution carried a symbolic importance as it would have implied the continuity of the Estonian Republic and signaled to the world that the Soviet occupation had been illegal. Most of the framers, however, viewed the 1938 Constitution as problematic (since it had been written within the context of an authoritarian regime) and called for finding a balance between the ultra-democratic 1920 Constitution and the super-presidential 1938 Constitution. In general, when reading the verbatim notes of the CA, one gets the feeling that the framers, for most part, did indeed set out to find

[9] As Raudla (2010b) argues, though, the probability of rejection was rather low.

the most "fitting" constitution for the Estonian context, while drawing on Estonia's own historical experiences with the different inter-war constitutions, the experience of other countries and the propositions of constitutional law and political science. In fact, at the first session of the CA, the members had to give an oath to the effect that they would leave aside day-to-day politics when deliberating the draft constitution. And indeed, the verbatim records show that to a large extent the deliberations took place at the level of "constitutional theories" rather than being expressed in the form of naked "interests" (Raudla 2010a).[10] As Pettai (2001: 138) puts it, CA's "attention was focused on how institutions could be structured through incentives and deterrents to produce reasonable and balanced effects."

The retrospective evaluations of the members of the Assembly (in their memoirs) indicate diverging views about the extent to which the discussions were dominated by current politics and interests. On the one hand, Kask (2002: 178) states:

> The important component of the success of the Assembly was the atmosphere that was not dominated by the politics of the day, there were attempts to interrupt it but these attempts were relatively unsuccessful. The discussions both in the Assembly and the committees were often very heated but were carried less from the political fights of the day than we had been afraid of.

On the other hand, Adams (2002: 139) argues that:

> Of course, it was natural that a majority of the members of the Assembly looked at their work not only on a theoretical level but also from the point of view of current politics and practical future implications for themselves.

Indeed, there were a number of issues where the day-to-day politics (and "objective interests") entered the constitution-making, namely in the choice between parliamentarism and presidentialism, the powers of the president and the mode of electing the president (directly by the public or by the parliament). As can be seen from Table 1, however, the preferences of the framers with regard to the powers of the president were far from being uniform. The only grouping which appeared to have strongly uniformed preferences was Free Estonia, consisting of top leaders of the Communist Party and managers of state factories. They all favored a strong president because of their connection to Arnold Rüütel, the most likely first President.[11]

Within ENIP, the dividing lines between those preferring presidentialism over parliamentarism were driven by very different considerations: The ENIP members who preferred presidentialism did it mostly because they were in favor of restoring the 1938 Constitution. More moderate members of the ENIP and also the members of the Estonian Heritage Society were more in favor of parliamentarism.

When looking at the debates in the CA, the main argument of the proponents of parliamentarism in the CA was that parliamentarism is more conducive to the survival of a young democracy; references were often made to the studies by Matthew

---

[10] For the distinction between "constitutional theories" and "constitutional interests," see Vanberg and Buchanan (1989).

[11] As Taagepera (1994: 213) notes, presidentialism was also "philosophically more congenial for Soviet-trained managers."

Table 1 Group preferences for presidentialism versus parliamentarism in the constitutional assembly

Party/grouping	Preferences
ENIP	More radical members favored presidentialism (i.e., restoration of the 1938 constitution), more moderate members parliamentarism
Estonian heritage society	Mostly favored parliamentarism, some members presidentialism
Popular front	Preferences with regard to the presidential versus parliamentary system varied
Free Estonia	Preferred presidentialism
Russians	Preferred presidentialism

Shugart and his colleagues (including Rein Taagepera, who was himself a member of the CA). It was feared that strong presidentialism would give rise to conflicts between the president and the parliament, leading to instability. Based on the verbatim records of the debates in the Assembly alone, one could conclude that the empirically proven constitutional theories and the desired goal of a stable democracy played a major role in the constitutional choice between presidentialism and parliamentarism. The memoirs of the members of the CA, however, point to a different conclusion. As a prominent member of the CA, Kask (2002: 180) admits in his recollections of the work of the Assembly that the constitutional preference of the majority of the Assembly for a strong parliamentary system was driven by the current interests of the members rather than by the weight of the arguments. Lang (2002: 219), who was an expert to the Assembly, states that in preparing the Constitution, there was a competition between the different forces who wanted to secure their power for the future: "Therefore, every legal construction that concerned the mechanisms of power were viewed through a political prism." Hänni (2002: 164), another prominent member of the Assembly, notes that although the members of the Assembly had given an oath not to consider the issues of current politics, these considerations rose high in discussions over the institution of president. A number of CA members (both from the Congress and the Council) have admitted that they did not want to design a strong institution of the president, since they did not like Arnold Rüütel, the most likely candidate for that position and the party he was affiliated with (see, e.g., Kask 2002: 180; Lang 2002: 219; Hänni 2002: 164). Arnold Rüütel himself was formally a member of the CA but could not take part in its discussions very actively, given his obligations to act as de facto head of state. Still, through his position as the head of the Supreme Council, Rüütel could influence the reactions of the Council to the draft constitutions (Raudla 2010a: 259). Supported by several groupings in the Council who wanted to secure that Rüütel would become the first president, the Council repeatedly sent the draft constitution back to the Assembly and demanded that the CA revised the articles concerning the institution of president (Laar 2002; Ruutsoo 2002a, b).

After the debates on the choice between parliamentarism and presidentialism and the powers of the president, the most heated discussions arose on the issue of how the president should be elected. For most part, it seemed that those who favored Rüütel as president supported the election of the president by the public (given how popular Rüütel was among the public at large) and those who disliked the idea of him becoming a president advocated indirect elections of the president. The CA's insistence on indirect elections (i.e., by the parliament) was also one of the reasons why the Supreme Council kept sending the draft constitution back to the CA. As pointed out in Sect. 2.2, eventually, the issue was "resolved" by prescribing a different mode of electing the president for the first election taking place after the adoption of the constitution. Ruutsoo (2002a: 204) argues that this provision was "engineered" by the representatives of the Congress with a goal to guarantee that Rüütel would not become president. The supporters of Rüütel, however, still expected him to become the president, even with a system like that. This shows that there were some opaque "spots" even in the relatively "thin" veil that covered the institution of the president: It was still difficult for the framers to foresee how many presidential candidates there would be, how exactly the distribution of public support for the candidates would look like, and what the composition of the first parliament would be.

While the debates over the election-mode of the president were permeated by current politics and "objective" interests of the framers, then on many other issues, their decisions were driven by constitutional theories and the desire to put together a good constitution for Estonia. For example, as Raudla (2010a) argues, despite the prevalence of delegates from the existing legislature in the CA, the judiciary was given extensive constitutional powers and guarantees of autonomy.[12] The general attitude among framers was that guaranteeing the independence and autonomy of the judiciary was extremely important for establishing a genuinely democratic order and avoiding the politicization of courts, which had characterized the Soviet period. With regard to constitutional review, Pettai (2005: 93) notes that during the discussions of the CA, "the need for some kind of constitutional review was never disputed", and the debates were confined to the specific "mechanics" of how the procedures and institutions would look like. As Raudla (2010a: 259) notes, the discussions on constitutional review in the CA appear to provide evidence for the arguments by Shapiro (1999: 218), who suggested that constitutional review has been adopted by framers in many countries partly because it has become to be perceived as an obligatory component of constitutionalism.

3 Description of the Content of the Estonian 1992 Constitution in Terms of a Power Relation Framework

The 1992 Constitution of Estonia is made up of 168 articles (11,181 words in English) and it is divided into 15 chapters. Three chapters pertain to the powers of the parliament, president, and cabinet (encompassing 52 articles) and the longest chapter (48 articles) entails the bill of rights. The remaining chapters are shorter and are concerned with foreign relations, local government, courts, defense, and finances.

[12] According to Salzberger and Voigt (2002: 41) among the eight CEE countries they studied, the Estonian constitutional court has the highest de jure independence. Furthermore, Estonia is the only country in CEE where judges are guaranteed life tenure by the constitution.

Table 2 Characteristics of power relations in the Estonian 1992 constitution

Source of power	Frequencies	Percentage
Authority	427	80.57
Wealth	5	0.94
Knowledge	38	7.17
Indeterminate	60	11.32
Total	530	100.00
Type of power		
Instrumental	256	48.30
Social	274	51.70
Total	530	100.00
Direction of power		
Positive	504	95.09
Negative	26	4.91
Total	530	100.00

The content analysis of the Estonian constitution shows that it provides for altogether 530 units of power relations, which is quite close to the average of the sample of 16 countries analyzed in the Veil of Ignorance Project (564.6). At the same time, the density of power relations in the Estonian constitution is 47.4, which is very close to the sample average (46.7). Table 2 provides an overview of the power relations found in the Estonian constitution, broken down by the direction of power, source of power, and type of power.

Altogether, with regard to the *source* of power, 80.6 % of the power relations are based on authority (which is higher than the sample average of 75 %), 0.9 % are based on wealth and 7.2 % on knowledge. Based on these ratios, one would argue that the Estonian constitution was drafted behind a rather opaque veil (at least to a large extent, this was indeed the case in Estonia as shown above in Sect. 2 although there were also some transparent spots in the veil).

With regard to the *type* of power, the division of social and instrumental power is almost equal, with social power recorded in 48.3 % of the units and instrumental power in 51.6 % of the units (this coincides with the sample average). Given the opaqueness of the veil in the Estonian case (as demonstrated by the high ratio of power relations based on authority), one would have expected the ratio of social power relations to be higher.

Concerning the *direction* of power, in 95.1 % of the units the direction of power is positive and only in 4.9 % of the units it is negative (which is a little higher than the sample average of 3.8 %). Based on the framework of the VOI Project, one would have expected the ratio of negative power relations resulting from constitution-making behind the veil of uncertainty to be higher.

The main agents identified in the constitution are the parliament (the Riigikogu) and its membership, the President, the Government (i.e., the cabinet of ministers), the courts, and the Chancellor of Justice. In addition, in the bill of rights part of the Constitution, the citizens and residents of Estonia are the main agents, in their capacity to use their rights (and hence "everyone" and "Estonian citizens" or other

Table 3 The powers of the main agents in the Estonian constitution (number of occurrences)

	Total	Type		Direction	
		Instrumental	Social	Positive	Negative
Riigikogu (the parliament)[a]	111	57	54	107	4
The president	84	31	53	82	2
Government[b]	86	39	47	81	5
Courts[c]	34	13	21	33	1
The chancellor of justice	17	15	2	17	0
Everyone	42	35	7	41	1
Estonian citizens	15	12	3	15	0

[a]Including members of parliament
[b]Including cabinet ministers and state agencies
[c]Including courts, supreme court, and judges

specified groups of individuals have been identified as agents). Table 3 provides an overview of the main agents and the power relations associated with these agents in the Estonian constitution.

The main capacities of the Riigikogu are to adopt legislation, to authorize the candidate for Prime Minister to form the Government, to elect the President, and to appoint to office the Chief Justice of the Supreme Court, the Auditor General, and the Chancellor of Justice (and other high offices). As can be seen from Table 3, with regard to the power relations that the constitution attributes to the parliament, just below half of the power relations are based on social power (53), just above half are based on instrumental power (57). The main capacities of the President are to represent Estonia in international relations, to proclaim laws, to review the constitutionality of laws, and to make proposals to the parliament for appointments to high offices such as the Chief Justice, the Chancellor of Justice, and the Auditor General. Again, an overwhelming proportion of the power relations is positive.[13] The main capacities of the Government are to execute the policies and to administer the implementation of laws and issue regulations. In the case of government, the constitution foresees 47 social power relations and 31 instrumental power relations; 81 positive power relations and 5 negative power relations.[14] The courts are attributed predominantly social power relations and only one provision refers to negative power.[15] It is interesting to note that while for the parliament, instrumen-

[13] The negative powers are expressed in the following provisions: The Chairman of the Riigikogu acting as a president may not declare extraordinary relations of the Riigkogu and may not refuse to proclaim laws.

[14] Negative power relations can be found in Article 26, stipulating that state agencies "shall not interfere with the private or family life of any person; Article 42, stipulating that the state agencies" shall not gather or store information about the belief's of an Estonian citizen against the citizen's free will; Article 100, which states that members of Government shall not hold any other state office, nor belong to the management board or supervisory board of a commercial enterprise).

[15] Article 147, which states that judges "shall not hold any other elected or appointed office, except in the cases prescribed by law".

tal power relations dominate, then for the government, the president and the courts, social power relations are more frequent. In the bill of rights, in 40 cases "everyone" is identified as an agent and they have been accorded capacities in terms of positive power relations. In 15 units, the Constitution, instead of stating "everyone," accords rights to the Estonian citizens (those rights mostly pertain to political rights like voting, membership in parties, etc.).

4 Discussion

The veil of uncertainty influenced constitution-making in Estonia at different levels. First, it can be argued that the decision of the Supreme Council to convene a CA—a separate entity that would also involve the representatives of the Estonian Congress—for drafting the constitution (rather than having the constitution written by a committee of the Supreme Council) was made possible by the extreme uncertainties that characterized the situation of Estonia and its government during the putsch in Moscow in August 1991. Before the coup, the divisions between the different representative bodies and the groupings they entailed ran deep and Estonia was "seemingly nowhere near ready to undertake the solemn and consensus-obliging task of constitution-making" (Pettai 2001: 112). However, the demonstration of unity between the Supreme Council and the Estonian Congress was needed to secure both domestic and international credibility of the declaration of independence. In order to reach the compromise, both sides were willing to make concessions that would have been difficult (or even impossible) during the times of "normality," which is why it has been termed a "miracle compromise" (Pettai 2001: 115). By agreeing to share the constitution-making with the Congress, the Supreme Council ceded a significant amount of its formal power and gave up the proposal to declare the Council as a constitution-making body. In return for being included in the making of the new Constitution, the representatives of the Congress gave up their ideas of re-enacting the 1938 Constitution or calling for general elections of a new constitution-making body. Taagepera (1994: 216) remarks that after the threat of the coup passed, some representatives on both sides began to feel they had conceded too much, but the agreement had already been signed. Given that the resolution to convene the Assembly was in the same decision with the declaration of independence, contesting one would have jeopardized the other.

With regard to the work of the CA itself, the making of the 1992 Constitution by the CA in Estonia was driven by a complex configuration of subjective motivations, objective interests, constitutional theories, symbolic considerations, and historical experiences. As Raudla (2010a, b) emphasizes with regard to the role of institutional and partisan interests in the constitution-making in Estonia, there is certainly some evidence for their influence, these factors cannot account for the "entire story." A mix of additional considerations (theories of political science, the substance of inter-war constitutions and the types of polities these previous constitutions gave rise to, symbolic considerations, and the prevailing international discourse on constitutionalism) have to be taken into account in order to understand the causal mechanisms behind the proposals, choices, and decisions of the Estonian framers. In other words, as Raudla (2010b: 74) notes, the Estonian case provides evidence for "the interaction between strategic calculations and symbolic meanings that the actors attach to particular choices in the making of the constitution." Thus, while strategic calculations certainly played a role in delineating the powers of the parliament and the president (and the preference for a strong parliament was certainly influenced by the fact that most of the framers were members of legislature-type body at the time of constitution-making), then various symbolic considerations shaped constitutional choices as well. For example, the symbolic meanings attached to the inter-war constitutions played an important role in the institutional choices. Because the 1938 Constitution was seen as overly authoritarian, many of the framers were reluctant to copy the presidential system it had entailed. At the same time, because the inter-war constitutions had another symbolic connotation—that of re-asserting the continuity of the Estonian statehood and sovereignty—the members of the CA did "borrow" a significant number of provisions from these constitutions. Also, the desire to establish a clear break with the Soviet heritage shaped a number of institutional choices, like granting strong guarantees of independence for the judiciary.

As the constitutional political economy literature in general and the VOIP framework would have predicted, in the Estonian case those issue areas where the veil appeared to be *the least opaque* gave rise to the most *extensive* discussions. These were the areas where it took the longest to reach a compromise among the framers: the mode of electing the president and the powers of the president. Given the popularity of the head of state (Arnold Rüütel) during the work of the CA, many framers thought that he would become the first President. That, in turn, motivated his proponents to argue for strong presidency and his opponents for a presidential institution with relatively limited powers.

On the other hand, one can also argue that in some areas of debate, it was the *reduction* of uncertainty that *facilitated* agreement in the CA. This was particularly the case with the adoption of the citizenship law by the Supreme Council (already during the beginning of the work of the CA), which foresaw the granting of automatic citizenship only to the citizens of the inter-war Estonian Republic and their descendants. That effectively meant that a significant proportion of the Russian-speaking inhabitants would be excluded from participating in national elections and the Assembly was essentially crafting a political system that "would be dominated and run by Estonians" (Pettai 2001: 120). That in turn meant, as Taagepera (1994) and Pettai (2001) note, that the members of the CA did not have to think about arrangements that would have accommodated the Russian-speaking population (e.g., in the form of consociational governance structures), which, one can argue, made the reaching of "agreements" on the constitutional structures easier. As Pettai (2001: 120) puts it, "the subsequent process was in fact more akin to writing a constitution for a homogeneous nation-state than for the multiethnic republic that the country actually was." Thus, it appears that in some situations *reduced* uncertainty can facilitate the reaching of constitutional agreements. This, at least at first sight, appears to go against the predictions of the constitutional political economy literature. However, one should not forget that this higher "certainty" was achieved in Estonia by effectively excluding a sizable minority from political decision-making and hence could not be viewed as a consensus (which is a recommended decision rule in the constitutional political economy framework).

What is also interesting in the Estonian case is that although there was extremely high uncertainty with regard to the future positions of wealth and economic power among the framers (both on individual and group level), the number of power relations that pertain to wealth is very limited in the constitution. One possible explanation is that the framers in Estonia had a pretty clear idea of what kind of elements should be included in the constitution and viewed the constitution primarily as a document that deals with the delineation of political authority rather than economic aspects of social life. In addition, one could argue that extreme economic uncertainty—when the framers do not even know how the entire economic system is going to look like in the near future—can render it difficult to reach consensus on those power relations that have to do with wealth. Because of the prevailing uncertainty (or one could even say ignorance) with regard to how the market economy would operate and to what kind of outcomes it would lead to and how the state-market nexus would look like, it was probably very difficult for the framers to theorize—even in general terms—what the effects of provisions pertaining to wealth relations could be, how the causal mechanisms could play out, etc. In other words, because of the lack of "constitutional theories" in that regard, it was difficult for the framers to even start a negotiation or bargaining process over constitutional provisions concerning power relations based on wealth.

It is also worth noting that even provisions concerning social rights in the Estonian constitution are rather constrained. Despite the opaqueness of the veil (and hence uncertainty with regard to their own position in the future), the framers were reluctant to include provisions pertaining to extensive welfare entitlements in the constitution. As Pettai (2001: 123) explains, this was in part due to "the legacy of Soviet socialism, which many liberal-minded Estonians did not remember fondly."

Evaluating the Estonian constitution-making in the light of the propositions of the contractarian approach suggesting that constitutional choice should take place behind the "veil of uncertainty," which in turn is facilitated by the generality and durability of rules, an interesting feature of the Estonian case is that the "thin veil" behind which the discussions on the implementation law of the constitution took place actually facilitated reaching agreement on some provisions of the constitution negotiated behind a "thicker veil." As mentioned above, the "implementation act" of the constitution (the so-called Chap. 17) foresaw different rules for the first elections of the Riigikogu and for the President. The different method for the first election of the President (especially having the first round as direct election by the public) was introduced in order to appease the public, but also several members of the Supreme Council and the Government, who favored the direct election of the president. The more "official" explanation for this option was that since the party system in Estonia was still in the process of being formed it would have been hard to expect that the political groupings in the parliament could immediately agree on a common President. Given that the constitution requires a 2/3 majority in the parliament for electing the President, it was suggested that the political system was too young to achieve such compromises only after the very first election. The implementation chapter was meant to "facilitate a gradual habituation to the new system" (Pettai 2001: 125). Altogether, the Estonian case shows, when there are some upstream and/or downstream constraints on the framers (who, as a result of these constraints, have to consider whether the produced document will pass through the institution acting as the constraint), a distinction between rules for the long term and rules for the short term can help to facilitate agreement. The Supreme Council (acting as an upstream authority) repeatedly sent the draft constitution back to the CA and sought to persuade the Assembly to strengthen the powers of the president (alongside with the requirement to replace indirect elections of the president with direct elections). The implementation law, with its different rules for the first election, facilitated the acceptance of the constitution by the upstream authority. Thus, curiously, the Estonian case shows that adopting two sets of "constitutional" provisions—"thick veil" provisions that take effect in a longer term and "thin-veil" transitional provisions that are enacted immediately—can facilitate the achievement of agreement between the conflicting parties (like between the CA and the institutions acting as upstream or downstream constraints on the constitution-making body).

What also seems to go against the propositions of the contractarian approach in the Estonian case are the provisions in the implementation chapter according to which, for 3 years following its adoption, constitutional amendments could be made with relaxed majorities in the parliament or initiated by popular initiative (requiring 10,000 signatures).[16] This was seen as necessary to allow flexible adaptation to changing circumstances, but from the point of view of the contractarian approach, it would have reduced the "durability" and "stability" of expectations, which are supposed to facilitate the thickness of the veil and the achieving of an agreement.

5 Conclusion

Altogether, the Estonian case corroborates the prediction of the veil of ignorance framework outlined by Imbeau (2009), and Imbeau and Jacob (2011, 2015) with regard to the proposition that predicts that in the context of uncertainty, the framers focus on those power relations that are based on authority (rather than

[16] In 1994, as a result of the popular initiative, a constitutional amendment proposal was submitted to the Riigikogu: it suggested introducing the direct election of the president and the right to receive old-age pension according to the work contribution of the person. In the parliament, this initiative did not find support.

on knowledge or wealth), but the case appears to go against the proposition that behind an opaque veil the framers write more negative power relations into the constitution. Also, the theoretical prediction stating that behind the veil of uncertainty, framers would include more power relations based on social power than instrumental power in the constitution was not borne out in the Estonian case. Whether this can be counted as evidence that there were some transparent holes in the predominantly opaque veil or whether the theoretical proposition itself should be revised would warrant further discussion in theorizing over the effects of the veil of ignorance.

As a whole, the case study indicates that constitution-making in Estonia took place in the midst of high uncertainty and that influenced the content of the constitution. The analysis above indicates that, while for most part, the *opacity* of the veil can indeed facilitate the reaching of *compromise*, there are situations where the *transparency* of the veil contribute to reaching *agreements* among the framers and, conversely, that in some situations or issue areas, the veil can be *so thick* that the uncertainties involved make it *very difficult to reach consensus.*

As the constitutional debates over the mode of electing the president indicate, the relative transparency of the veil (i.e., the predictability of the effects of particular constitutional rules on constellations of power in the immediate post-constitutional phase) can make it difficult to reach consensus on what the best rules would be for the long term. In the Estonian case, this conundrum essentially led to the adoption of the implementation act of the constitution (which foresaw different rules for the first post-constitutional election). Thus, the Estonian case demonstrates that in some cases, adopting two sets of "constitutional" provisions—"thick veil" provisions that take effect in a longer term and "thin-veil" transitional provisions that are enacted immediately—can facilitate the achievement of agreement between the conflicting parties involved in constitution-making.

The Estonian case also shows that *even* in the case of extreme uncertainty with regard to future positions of wealth—as prevailed at the wake of the transition period, with transition from planned economy to market economy—the framers may be reluctant to include a significant number of power relations based on wealth. Even if, in theory, the uncertainty with regard to future wealth position of the framers could make it easier to reach agreement on power relations based on wealth, the constitution-makers at a particular space and time may be more influenced by what they think should be included in a constitution and what the constitution should signal to the population at large and even to the international community.

In the Estonian case, the framers considered it important to focus on those power relations that are based on authority, because, in many ways, this is what the prevailing constitutional theories (and the international constitutional discourse) at the time "told" them to focus on. Also, given that the main reference constitutions the Estonian CA drew on—the inter-war constitutions of Estonia and the constitution of Germany—also focused on power relations that were based on authority, there were also some important lesson-drawing and path-dependence effects at play here.

References

Aaskivi Ü, Pärnaste E (2002) Kronoloogia: EV Ülemnõukogu. Eesti Kongress, Põhiseaduse Assemblee (chronology: the supreme council, the Estonian congress, the constitutional assembly). In: Pärnaste E (ed) Põhiseaduse Tulek. Kogumik (the coming of the constitution). Justiitsministeerium, Kirjastus SE&JS, Tallinn

Adams J (2002) Eelnõu sünd ja saatus (the birth and the fate of the draft). In: Pärnaste E (ed) Põhiseaduse Tulek. Kogumik (the coming of the constitution). Justiitsministeerium, Kirjastus SE&JS, Tallinn

Buchanan J, Tullock G (1962) The calculus of consent University of Michigan Press, Ann Arbor

Dunlop JB (2003) The August 1991 coup and its impact on Soviet politics. J Cold War Stud 5(1):94–127

Hänni L (2002) Põhiseaduse sünd redaktsioonitoimkonnast nähtuna (the birth of the constitution seen from the side of redaction committee). In: Pärnaste E (ed) Põhiseaduse Tulek. Kogumik (the coming of the constitution). Justiitsministeerium, Kirjastus SE&JS, Tallinn

Imbeau LM (2009) Testing the «veil of ignorance» hypothesis in constitutional choice: a «walk-talk» approach. J Public Finan Public Choice 26(1):3–21

Imbeau LM, Jacob S (2011) Is the "veil of ignorance" in constitutional choice a myth? An empirical exploration informed by a theory of power. In: Marciano A (ed) Constitutional mythologies: new perspectives on controlling the state. Springer, Dordrech, pp 53–69

Imbeau LM, Jacob S (2015) Measuring the opacity of the 'veil of ignorance' in constitutions: theory, method and some results. In: Imbeau LM, Jacob S (eds) Behind a veil of ignorance? Power and uncertainty in constitutional design. Springer, New York

Kask P (2002) Järelmõtteid Põhiseaduse Assamblee tööst ja rollist (reflections on the work and role of the constitutional assembly). In: Pärnaste E (ed) Põhiseaduse Tulek. Kogumik (the coming of the constitution). Justiitsministeerium, Kirjastus SE&JS, Tallinn

Laar M (2002) Assamblee (assembly). In: Pärnaste E (ed) Põhiseaduse Tulek. Kogumik (the coming of the constitution). Justiitsministeerium, Kirjastus SE&JS, Tallinn

Lang R (2002) Mõned mõtted seoses põhiseadusega (some thoughts on the constitution). In: Pärnaste E (ed) Põhiseaduse Tulek. Kogumik (the coming of the constitution). Justiitsministeerium, Kirjastus SE&JS, Tallinn

Lauristin M, Vihalemm P (1997) Recent historical developments in Estonia (1987–1997). In: Lauristin M, Vihalemm P (eds) Return to the western world. Cultural and political perspectives on the Estonian post-communist transition. Tartu University Press, Tartu

Pettai V (2001) Estonia: positive and negative institutional engineering. In: Zielonka J (ed) Democratic consolidation in Eastern Europe, institutional engineering. Oxford University Press, Oxford

Pettai V (2005) Democratic norm building and constitutional discourse formation in Estonia. In: Czarnota A, Krygier M, Sadurski W (eds) Rethinking the rule of law after Communism. Central European University Press, Budapest

Raitviir T (1996) Eesti Üleminekuperioodi valimiste (1989–1993) võrdlev uurimine (elections in Estonia during the transition period (1989–1993): a comparative study). Teaduste Akadeemia Kirjastus, Tallinn

Raudla R (2010a) Explaining constitution-makers' preferences: the cases of Estonia and the United States. Const Polit Econ 21:249–269

Raudla R (2010b) Constitution, public finance and transition. Peter Lang, Frankfurt

Ruutsoo R (2002a) Tähelepanekuid riikluse ja riikliku mõtlemise sünnist (remarks on the birth of the stateness and constitutional thinking). In: Pärnaste E (ed) Põhiseaduse Tulek. Kogumik. Justiitsministeerium, Kirjastus SE&JS, Tallinn

Ruutsoo R (2002b) Presidendi institutsiooni taustast ja kujundamisest 1992. aasta Põhiseaduses. Meenutusi ja arutlusi aastaist 1991–1992 (the background and the making of the institution of president. Memories and discussions from 1991–1992). In: Toomla R (ed) Presidendiraamat (the book on president). Tartu Ülikooli Kirjastus, Tartu

Salzberger EM, Voigt S (2002) On the delegation of powers: with special emphasis on central and Eastern Europe. Const Polit Econ 13:25–52

Shapiro M (1999) The success of judicial review. In: Kenney S, Reisinger W, Reitz J (eds) Constitutional dialogues in comparative perspective. St Martin's Press, New York

Sunstein C (1991) Constitutionalism, prosperity, democracy: transition in Eastern Europe. Const Polit Econ 2(3):371–394

Taagepera R (1991) Building democracy in Estonia. PS Polit Sci Polit 24(3):478–481

The Constitution of the Republic of Estonia. 1992. The English version can be accessed at:www.riigiteataja.ee/en/eli/530102013003/consolide

Taagepera R (1993) Estonia: return to independence. Westview Press, Boulder, San Francisco, Oxford

Taagepera R (1994) Estonia's constitutional assembly, 1991–1992. J Baltic Stud 25(3):211–232

Vanberg V, Buchanan JM (1989) Interests and theories in constitutional choice. J Theor Polit 1(1):49–63

Salzberger EM, Voigt S (2002) On the delegation of powers: with special emphasis on Central and Eastern Europe. Const Polit Econ 13:25–52
Shapiro M (1990) The success of judicial review. In: Kenney S, Reisinger W, Reitz J (eds) Constitutional dialogue in comparative perspective. [illegible]
Sunstein C (1991) Constitutionalism, prosperity, democracy: transition in Eastern Europe. Const Polit Econ 2(3):371–394
Taagepera R (1993) Building democracy in Estonia. PS Polit Sci Polit 26(3):478–481
The Constitution of the Republic of Estonia (1992) The document is available (accessed [illegible]) at www.riigiteataja.ee/akt/633949?leiaKehtiv
Taagepera R (1993) Estonia: return to independence. Westview Press, Boulder, San Francisco, Oxford
Taagepera R (1994) Estonia's constitutional assembly, 1991–1992. J Balt Stud 25(3):211–232
Vanberg V, Buchanan JM (1989) Interests and theories in constitutional choice. J Theor Polit 1(1):49–62

Chapter 13
Constitutional Choices Turned into Simple In-Period Choices: A Power Relations Reading of the Chadian and Cameroonian Constitutions

Thomas Cedric Eboutou

In the constitutional political economy literature, an important element of distinction between constitutional choices and regular politics choices is that the former involve a great deal of uncertainty and are said to be made behind a "*veil*": the veil of ignorance. However, the hypothesis that constitutional choices are made behind the veil of ignorance has mostly received a theoretical treatment.

The Veil of Ignorance Project (VOIP) proposed by Imbeau (Imbeau and Jacob 2015, 2011; Imbeau 2009) is mainly an empirical endeavor. It seeks to test the presence of a "*veil*" at the time of the making of constitutions and suggests, in order to do so, that we read constitutional texts in terms of power relations. That a constitutional text deals more with political power than economic or preceptorial power (H1), that it is most concerned with social power than instrumental power (H2), and that it tends to restrict power more than to ascribe power (H3) can be viewed as indications of the presence of a "*veil*" during the drafting/adoption of that constitution. Heuristically, the VOIP follows a logic known as abduction.[1] This abduction logic is strengthened as we make our inferences in light of the historical context of the drafting and adoption of a constitution.

The purpose of this case study is to implement the VOIP framework using the Chadian and Cameroonian constitutions to tell whether or not they were adopted behind a veil of ignorance. Beyond the methodological interest, one can derive a practical interest from this undertaking. Indeed, one can learn valuable lessons on how to design settings suitable to the making of democratic constitutions. This case study has the following structure: First, we present the major events that led to the current Chadian and Cameroonian constitutions; second, we present a power relation-based content analysis of those constitutions; and third, we discuss our findings.

[1] For further discussion on that concept and how it applies to the VOIP, see Imbeau (2009).

T.C. Eboutou (✉)
HEC, Université de Montréal, Montréal, Canada
e-mail: eboutouthomas.ancien@gmail.com

L.M. Imbeau and S. Jacob (eds.), *Behind a Veil of Ignorance?*,
Studies in Public Choice 32, DOI 10.1007/978-3-319-14953-0_13

1 Constitution Making in Context

The purpose of this section is to shed light on the context of different constitutional phases that Chad and Cameroon went through up to the adoption of their current constitutions. In that regard, the two countries have a quite similar trajectory except that Chad's political history was marked by more violence and instability. Both countries were under French tutelage before 1960: Chad as a colony and a part of Cameroon as a mandate.[2] Following the Second World War, France initiated a gradual process of decolonization of its colonies that would ultimately result in their independences in 1960. At their independences, Cameroon and Chad adopted constitutions that resembled very much that of the French Fifth Republic: Obviously, the drafters and adopters of those first constitutions wished to see their new countries become and evolve as democracies.

At the time of their independences, there were legitimate concerns about the viability of the new nations: Many feared that the young countries would implode because of their ethnic and religious heterogeneity. As a consequence, the first executives of Chad and French Cameroon, respectively, Francois Tombalbaye and Ahmadou Ahidjo, prioritized among other things the reinforcement and the consolidation of national unity. In fact, they would later use that objective as a pretext to arrogate more constitutional powers and turn their nascent democracies into autocratic presidentialist regimes.

In Chad, it did not take too long before "centrifuge forces" blew off "national unity." Northerners felt underrepresented in Tombalbaye's government[3] and criticized his autocratic leanings: In 1962, he promulgated a new constitution instituting a unique-party system and strengthening his powers as president. They reacted by forming in June 1966 a coalition of rebellions (Front de Libération Nationale du Tchad) against him, and Chad entered a cycle of civil wars and coups that lasted until recently.[4] The coalition overthrew and killed Tombalbaye in 1975, suspended the constitution, and instituted a military regime led by General Felix Malloum. In 1982, General Hissen Habré a dissident of the coalition seized power after a coup and promulgated an interim constitution. Habré then became the president of a divided country with several regions under the control of warlords; he resorted to violence and brutality to restore his authority over the country.[5] His dictatorial regime lasted for eight years till the Idriss Deby's coup in 1990.

[2] After World War I, the German colony Kamerun (later Cameroon) was divided into two parts; the eastern part was mandated to France and the western part to Great Britain by the League of Nation. From a legal point of view, Eastern Cameroon was a League of Nation mandate, but in reality, it was administered by France like a colony.

[3] Tombalbaye was a Christian from the South.

[4] In 2008, the current president Idriss Deby defeated in extremis, a rebellion with the help of the French army.

[5] Habré's regime is notorious for human rights abuses; Habré is now on trial for the crimes committed under his regime.

Contrary to his predecessor, Deby promised democracy to Chadians in his take-over speech. In fact, the geopolitical context at the time somewhat pressured him to do so. Indeed, France's president Mitterrand at La Baule introduced the principle of conditional aid toward France former colonies in exchange of political and institutional reforms. Several Western donors later adopted the same policy. In addition, the collapse of the Berlin Wall in 1990 ignited among African people strong desires for democracy and liberties. In the early 1990s, almost everywhere on the continent, people were rioting and marching against the authoritarian and dictatorial regimes that had oppressed them almost since the independences.

In Chad, some leaders of the civil society and political parties' leaders suggested the organization of a National Conference, a sort of political forum to discuss a thorough reformation of the state. That idea received strong support from the people, and in 1991, Deby promised to convene the Sovereign National Conference to draft a new constitution. He appointed at the end of that year a first committee of eighty members with the task of setting the conference agenda, proposing its rules and procedures, selecting the participants, and specifying the logistics (Buijtenhuijs 1993). The public opinion was, however, unsatisfied with the composition of that committee which it thought was partisan: The committee chair was one of Deby's army general, and many members were in some way close to him (Buijtenhuijs 1993). To ease up the tension, Deby appointed a second preparatory committee called the Tripartite Committee (members came from the three main groups of the polity): Five members representing the public authorities (from which the chair was chosen), five others the political parties (including Deby's party and the opposition), and two the civil society. The Tripartite job was to discuss, "second-read" and eventually amend the first preparatory committee's report. The Sovereign National Conference scheduled to take place in 1992 finally started in January 15, 1993, and sat until April 12, 1993. There was a great confusion about how many people exactly attended the conference and even potential historical sources diverge on that issue (May and Massey 2000). Officials at the time said 830; Buijtenhuijs[6] on the first day of the conference for the election of the presidium found 846 voter cards of which only 822 could be accounted for. According to Buijtenhuijs' accounts (Buijtenhuijs 1993: 46–56), there were seven categories of delegates as follows:

- 116 public officials (ministers, prefects, mayors, etc.),
- 256 representatives of political parties (eight for each registered party and one for political parties in the process of being registered),
- 31 delegates from human rights and youths organizations,
- 99 delegates from professional corporations, unions, cultural, and humanitarians organizations,

[6] The Dutch political scientist was invited to attend the conference as an observer and followed the conference from a vantage point.

- 168 delegates representing the people of Chad: sultans, chiefs representing cantons, farmers, and representatives from the diaspora,
- 8 delegates from religious groups: two Catholic bishops, two Protestant pastors, and four Muslim leaders,
- 144 Chadian notables, a heteroclite groups made up of former ministers, ambassadors, academicians, state corporations executives, former high-ranking military officers, etc.

During the debates, three themes received paramount attention from the delegates: the decisions/voting rules of the conference, its procedures, and its competencies (Buijtenhuijs 1993: 67). As far as the decision rules were concerned, the Tripartite Committee suggested the general rule of consensus and the voting by showing of hand. Delegates opponent to Deby's viewed that voting method as an intimidation technique and wanted a secret ballot. Deby's partisans argued in return that the voting method proposed was just a way to avoid electoral frauds. That controversy lasted for 10 days. Finally, it was agreed that only voting for official positions would be secret. The procedures were very much discussed for obvious practical reasons, but also because many delegates did not want the conference to be chaired by Deby's partisans. In the end, a southerner close to Tombalbaye won the chairmanship. Another topic intensely debated was the competencies of the conference, for there were no juridical texts defining and specifying its mandate. According to delegates hostile to Deby's regime, the conference had the power to overthrow him and to elect a new head of state that would lead the country till the adoption of a new constitution. Obviously, Deby's partisans did not share that view. It was finally agreed that Deby would remain the president of Chad during the transition; nevertheless, the conference would elect a prime minister and appoint a transitory government.

The transitory government, called the High Council for the Transition (Conseil supérieur de la transition), was to implement the resolutions adopted by the conference and to appoint a committee of specialists to draft a constitution. In 1996, the draft was submitted to the Chadian people for approval. The proposed constitution, as far as civil liberties and rights were concerned, followed very much the orientations set by the conference; however, the opinion was not satisfied with its distribution of power—especially the powers attributed to the president—(May and Massey 2000). Despite that, many opposition leaders campaigned for the "Yes." They reasoned that the victory of the "No" would prolong an already tiresome transition period; it was a better strategy, in their eyes, to save their strengths for the upcoming presidential battle which they thought would be easily won because of Deby's unpopularity (Buijtenhuijs 1996). That argument received the support of the voters, and the constitution was adopted (with 71.19 % of the electorate in its favor). However, contrary to the prediction of many opposition leaders, Deby won the presidential election that followed. Later in 2005, the 1996 Constitution underwent major amendments; among other things, the presidential term limit was lifted up, the senate was suppressed, and another constitutional body was instituted (the Economic, Social and Cultural Council).

The current Cameroonian constitution was adopted in a context similar in many extents to that of Chad. As mentioned earlier, Cameroon's first constitution was an adaptation of French 1958 constitution nonetheless with some noticeable presidentialist deformations (Bouopda 2008). Ahidjo[7] pushed, at the time, for a strong executive arguing that the parliamentary system experimented in Cameroon before the independence was a source of instability and political deadlocks. In 1961, the reunification of French Cameroon and a part[8] of British Cameroon into a federation prompted for a new constitution. That new constitution saw the increase of presidential powers. In 1963, with a dose of ruse and "force," President Ahidjo united all the political parties of the country under the banner of *Union Nationale Camerounaise* establishing de facto a unique-party system.

Afterward, Ahidjo would use the rhetoric of fight against the "rebellion" to embellish his authoritarian drifts. In the early days of the independence, he launched a crusade against *Union des Populations du Cameroun* (UPC), the independentist party known for its strong opposition to the former colonial master. Although the leaders of UPC vowed to keep fighting Ahidjo's regime which they viewed as the continuation of the French government, UPC was no longer very much of a threat. The French army, just prior the independence, had already seriously weakened UPC by killing most of its important figures and many of its followers.[9] For the following years, almost until early 1970s, Ahidjo managed to maintain in the country an artificial atmosphere of "civil war" which made it easy for him to take "exceptional" measures and to strongly repress any form of opposition. Ahidjo quickly acquired the reputation of an autocrat; he was feared and even revered[10] throughout the polity.

On May 20, 1972, the country adopted, through a referendum, a new constitution establishing a unitary state. To justify that change, Ahidjo's government put forth the necessity to end inefficiencies and wastes caused by the federalism in place since 1961. In fact, the passage from a federal republic to a unitary one was the ultimate phase of his power concentration agenda: "The unification of the country" ended the "inconvenient" diarchal executive[11] of the former federal republic and weakened the powers of the Anglophone state. The 1972 Constitution was amended later in 1975 and 1979; when Ahidjo stepped down in November 1982, it became obvious that those amendments aimed at preparing his succession.[12] Ahidjo's prime minister, Paul Biya, then became the country second presi-

---

[7] The first president of Cameroon.

[8] British Cameroon was made up of two entities: South British Cameroon and North British Cameroon. The former joined the French Cameroon, while the latter joined Nigeria.

[9] For further historical details, see Chatain et al. (2012).

[10] See for example Médard (1979) or Mbembe (1990).

[11] Under the Cameroonian federalism, there was a rule according to which the vice president should be Anglophone.

[12] The 1975 amendment established the office of prime minister and that of 1979 made the prime minister the constitutional successor of the president upon vacancy.

dent. In the early years of his presidency, Biya would struggle to impose his authority over Ahidjo's regime *barons* and over Ahidjo himself[13]; in 1984, a coup was attempted against him. The same year the 1972 Constitution was again amended: The office of prime minister was suppressed, and more discretion was given to the president to choose a successor in case of incapacity.

Cameroon did not escape the wind of democratization that blew on sub-Saharan Africa in the early 1990s. Indeed, in 1990, protests for multipartyism broke out throughout the country, and despite the government yielding to that demand, the political climate during the next two years would remain tense: civil disobedience, general strike, etc. Leaders of newly created political parties, just like in Chad, asked for a Sovereign National Conference. Biya's government refused and instead convened the Tripartite Conference that sat from October 30, 1991, to November 17 of the same year. Contrary to what happened in Chad (and in many francophone countries where the Sovereign National Conference was experimented), Biya's government arranged to make the Tripartite Conference a simple consultative body. Furthermore, he limited the orders of business of that conference to two items: the drafting of an electoral code (elections bill) and the modalities of an equitable media access to all political parties even though the opposition also wanted the theme of constitutional reform to be included (Fodouop 2010: 280). In the view of several observers at the time, delegates close to Biya represented more than half of the total of delegates attending (Fodouop 2010: 278–279), a non-surprising outcome since Biya's Prime minister,[14] who also chaired the Tripartite Conference, unilaterally selected the participants. In the Tripartite Conference final declaration, delegates asked for the creation of a technical committee to reflect on a new and modern constitution. Afterward, the president appointed an experts committee (known as the Technical committee) to do just that; however, the upcoming legislative and presidential elections would push the issue of constitutional reform in the background.

Indeed, amidst an important economic and political crisis, legislative and presidential elections were held in March and October 1992, respectively. Biya's party won 88 of the 180 seats in the National Assembly and had to coalesce with *Mouvement démocratique pour la Défense de la République* (MDR) in order to have a majority necessary to run the government. The presidential election was as disputed as the legislative election: Biya defeated John Fru Ndi by a thin margin: 39.9 % for Biya versus 35.5 % for Fru Ndi. It was after those elections that the constitutional reform debate was brought back on the table. In 1994, Biya appointed a consultative committee of 57 members (representing political parties, religious leaders, tribal chiefs, and experts) to advise him on constitutional reform proposals submitted years earlier by the technical committee. Instead of calling a referendum for the adoption of a new constitution, Biya chose to submit a bill to

---

[13] Ahidjo stepped down as president of the country but remained president of the unique party and wanted to maintain a control over his successor. For Further details, see Bouopda (2008).

[14] The office of prime minister had been restored earlier in 1991.

amend the 1972 Constitution. The scope of the amendment was so large that many Cameroonian public law experts[15] simply refer to the "*Law No. 06 of 18 January 1996 to amend the Constitution of 2 June 1972*" as the Constitution of 1996. It is reported that during the twenty-day debate of the bill in the National Assembly, the topics most discussed concerned:

- the voting system in presidential election: the opposition favored the two-round system, while the majority supported the one-round system used for the 1992 election;
- the majority system in presidential election: the opposition advocated the absolute majority system;
- the designation method of senators and regional executives (Owona 2012: 82).

The National Assembly finally adopted the *Law No. 06 of 18 January 1996 to amend the Constitution of 2 June 1972* with 160 votes for, only 2 votes against, and 8 abstentions. That law would be amended as well in 2008: The amendment mostly concerned the office of president and the successoral mechanism in case of vacancy.

After this look into the background of Cameroonian and Chadian constitutions, we now turn to their analysis in terms of power relations as stipulated by the VOIP framework.

2 Chad and Cameroon Constitutions in Terms of Power Relations

The constitutional corpus used in our analysis for Cameroon is made up of the *Law No. 06 of 18 January 1996 to amend the Constitution of 2 June 1972,* also known as the Constitution of 1996: The 2008 amendment was not included. For Chad, we used only the initial 1996 Constitution (the subsequent amendment of 2004 was therefore excluded). We used the official French version of the aforementioned texts. Reading Chadian and Cameroonian constitutions in terms of power relations involves first *unitizing* and second *coding.*

2.1 Description of Constitutions in Terms of Power Relations

Unitizing here is the process of identifying power relations in the constitutional text under analysis. A power relation in that process is understood as a discursive structure that links an agent with a capacity (Imbeau and Jacob 2012). In the

[15] See Olinga (2006).

Table 1 Power relations in Chadian and Cameroonian constitution: summary statistics

	Words	Power relations	Density
Cameroon	7,814	415	53.1
Chad	10,917	541	49.6
VOIP mean	12,625.4	564.6	46.7

VOIP mean *K* alpha 0.92

Chadian and Cameroonian constitutions, we found, respectively, 541 and 415 units of analysis or power relations with an average Krippendorf statistics[16] of 0.92, well above the commonly accepted threshold of 0.80. In relative terms, however, we found the Chadian constitution less dense than the Cameroonian one: 49.6 power relations per thousand words versus and 53.1. Of the 16 constitutions analyzed in the VOIP, the two African constitutions are above the mean density of 46.7 (Table 1).

The Cameroonian constitution has a preamble and 69 articles distributed in thirteen parts. Interestingly, we found 38 power relations in the preamble. Moreover, parts with most power relations are part 4 which treats the relationship between legislative and executive, part 3 which deals with legislative powers and part 7 on the Constitution Council: 87, 80, and 45 power relations, respectively. On the other hand, the sections with the least power relations are part 6 on treaties and international agreements, part 9 on The Economic and Social Council with both no power relations at all, and part 8 on the court of impeachment that has only 6 power relations. Table 5 in Appendix gives us in detail the number of power relations in each section of the Cameroonian constitution.

The 1996 Chadian constitution is made up of a preamble and 239 articles arranged in fifteen sections or parts. Like in the Cameroonian case, we found power relations in the preamble: 25. The sections with outstanding number of power relations are as follows: part 3 on executive power with 139 power relations, followed by the section on the relationship between the executive and legislative power which has 92 power relations and finally, part 2 on the fundamental rights and liberties and duties which has 60 power relations. Sections with the least power relations are part 12 on traditional chiefs, part 8 on the Court of impeachment, and part 14 on the amendment with, respectively, 4, 6 and 9 power relations.

In summary, unlike the Cameroonian constitution, the Chadian constitution has at least a power relation in every section. Like in the Cameroonian case, we found a relatively important number of power relations in the preamble of the Chadian constitution. Furthermore, we found, both in the Cameroonian and Chadian cases, that the relationship between the executive and legislative branches was an area filled with power relations; however, in the case of Chad, the section on the relationship between the legislative and the executive is behind the section on the executive branch in terms of number of power relations. This presentation of

[16] See Imbeau and Jacob (2012), for details on the computation of that statistics.

Chadian and Cameroonian constitutions already gives us some clues on the areas of uncertainty at the time of the drafting/adoption of those texts. We need to characterize the power relations extracted to make some inferences.

2.2 Characterization of Power Relations

Coding here is understood as the process of characterizing power relations according to the source, the type, and the direction of the power involved. The source of power is the resource that an agent can mobilize to "perform the action he has the capacity to perform or to make another perform [that] action" (Imbeau and Jacob 2012); that resource can be authority, wealth, or knowledge. Of the 415 power relations extracted in the Cameroonian constitution, we found that authority is the resource mobilized by agents 314 times, versus 1 and 38, respectively, for wealth and knowledge. In the Chadian constitution, the power resource used by an agent is authority in 401 power relations over 541, which represents a proportion close to that found in the Cameroonian case. Also in the Chadian constitution, wealth and knowledge are mobilized by an agent only 10 and 48 times, respectively. These results are consistent with the VOIP first hypothesis according to which power relations found in constitutions would be more political than economic or preceptorial. Tables 2 and 3 provide a characterization of power relations found in Chadian and Cameroonian constitutions according to the source of power.

Table 2 Source and type of power relations in the Cameroonian constitution

		Type of power		Total
		Social power	Instrumental power	
Source of power	Authority	167	147	314
	Wealth	1	0	1
	Knowledge	21	31	52
	Indeterminate	22	26	48
Total		211	204	415

Table 3 Source and type of power relations in the Chadian constitution

		Type of power		Total
		Social power	Instrumental power	
Source of power	Authority	193	208	401
	Wealth	7	3	10
	Knowledge	27	21	48
	Indeterminate	17	65	82
Total		244	297	541

Table 4 Direction of power Cameroonian and Chadian constitutions

	Cameroon	Chad
Positive	411	521
Negative	4	20
Total	415	541

Power relations in the VOIP framework can be of two types: social and instrumental. They are coded as social when the exercise of a capacity by the influencing agent can alter the choice set of another explicitly identified agent. They are coded as instrumental when the influencing agent is said to have the capacity to act on things or events, and they are coded as indeterminate when the text does not provide us with enough information to unequivocally characterize a power relation according to the two types just mentioned. In the Chadian constitution, we found 297 instrumental power relations and 244 social power relations. In the Cameroonian constitution, we found 211 social power relations versus 204 instrumental ones. Tables 2 and 3 show the total number of power according to the type of power involved in the Chadian and the Cameroonian constitutions.

In both cases, the difference between the number of social and instrumental powers is small. It is therefore with a dose of caution that we say VOIP second hypothesis according to which social power will dominate instrumental power is not verified in the Chadian case, but it is, loosely, in the Cameroonian case. Even when we cross the type and the source of power, we still cannot say decisively for each categories of source of power whether social power dominates instrumental power.

Power relations can also be characterized according to their direction which can be either positive when the text ascribes agents with a capacity or negative when it denies agents the capacity to do something. We found in the Chadian constitution 521 positive power relations and in the Cameroonian constitution a similar overwhelming number of positive power relations: 411 which represent about 99 % of all power relations extracted. Clearly, the VOIP third hypothesis that constitutions would tend to restrict rather than ascribe power is rejected. Table 4 presents power relations extracted in the Cameroonian and Chadian constitution according to the direction.

In summary, the results presented here confirm the VOIP first hypothesis in the Cameroonian and Chadian cases. The second hypothesis is rejected in the case of Chad, but it is not firmly accepted in the case of Cameroon. Finally, the third hypothesis is unequivocally rejected in both cases. What can be made of these results? Can we tell whether or not Cameroonian and Chadian Constitutions were adopted behind a veil?

3 Discussion

Only unambiguous consistency between the results of our three tests of the VOIP hypotheses would have allowed us to affirm that the Cameroonian and Chadians constitutions were written behind a veil. Looking at the origins of the two documents, we saw how, throughout time, the office of the president became the center of political and institutional life in Chad and Cameroon. The first presidents of these countries succeeded in obtaining several constitutional powers thanks to the repressive resources at their disposal. This gradual concentration of powers in the office of the president eventually made it the most sought after and coveted political office those countries. Even during the popular conferences held in Chad and Cameroon in the early 1990 supposedly to discuss the general reform of the state and to provide new economic and social orientations, the rules concerning the office of the president remained the actors' main focus. It therefore comes as no surprise that constitutions adopted in those contexts dealt essentially with political power as we found. That political power is the primal concern of these constitutions indicates according to the VOIP, the presence of a veil at the time of their making.

In the case of Chad and Cameroon, using only public records, there is no easy way to determine the level of uncertainty faced by the actual drafters of the Chadian and Cameroonian constitutions. Nonetheless, because of their central role throughout the making process, we are not losing too much by looking at uncertainty from the standpoint of Deby and Biya who were, respectively, president of Chad and Cameroon at the time. In the light of the context surrounding the making of Chadian and Cameroonian constitutions, one can say that Deby and Biya faced some uncertainty in regard notably to their political powers in the early 1990s, but that uncertainty quickly faded out as the process advanced. Indeed, in the early 1990s, for the first time and even the only time since their independence, the presidents of Chad and Cameroon faced a sort of "*social revolt*": openly confrontational and critical protests against their governance. However, both Biya and Deby, despite that threat to the stability of their regime, skillfully managed to mitigate the uncertainty they faced. In the midst of social contestations, they feigned yielding to the people's demand, but they subtly made sure to remain in control. In the case of Chad, Deby ensured his control over the Sovereign National Conference during the participants' selection process. For example, the prefects of his administration were in charge of selecting the 168 delegates to represent the Chadian people (tribal chiefs, sultans, etc.). Another thing that helped Deby stay in control was probably the lengthening of the constitutional making process. The process started in 1991 in the midst of social protests, but ended up only in 1996: This certainly contributed to wear the opposition out.

In the case of Cameroon, although Biya promulgated a set of laws allowing and extending some civil liberties[17] to ease up the tensions, he never yielded to the demand of a Sovereign National Conference and proposed a mild form instead: the Tripartite Conference. Moreover, his government selected the participants and he himself fixed the agenda of that Tripartite Conference. Also, Biya choose to amend the 1972 Constitution instead of proposing a new Constitution. As we said earlier, the scope of the amendments and the orientations of the Law of 1996 were such that the option of a new constitution was probably more suitable. However,

[17] The Law on Freedom of Association (Law No. 90/053 of 19 December 1990) is a prominent example of this series of laws; it allowed people to freely create political parties or political associations.

having faced strong social protests in 1990–1991 and having almost lost the 1992 presidential election, it was not in Biya's interest to seek Cameroonian people approval for a new constitution which favored a strong presidency. Passing the amendment through the National Assembly was a better option: Although his party did not have the absolute majority, the main opposition party (SDF) was not represented in the Assembly during that term, for it had boycotted the 1992 legislative elections and the rest of the political parties were ideologically close to Biya's CPDM. Finally, like in Chad, the making process was somehow unnecessarily lengthened with the same consequence: the weariness of the opposition. In 1996, when the amendment was passed in the Assembly, the country was back on pre-1990 routine tracks: The bill was passed almost without any opposition. All this showed that we could not reasonably expect Cameroon and Chad Constitutions to mark high on uncertainty measures developed by the VOIP. The measure on sources of power is contrary to that expectation; however, the results on the two other measures tend to support it.

Assuming that our reading of the historical context was correct (that there was little uncertainty toward the end of the making process), we expected more instrumental power relations than social ones in the Chadian and Cameroonian constitutions. This was the case for Chad but not for Cameroon, with a dose of caution though. These results raised a question not explicitly addressed in the VOIP. Since unitizing and coding were done by humans, the VOIP provided us with an overall measure of reliability: The Krippendorf alpha statistics mentioned above. The VOIP, however, failed to present results adjusted for a probability of error. This adjustment is very important when the call is really close like in the Cameroonian case where we had 211 social power relations versus 204 instrumental power relations. Some form of adjustment is needed to tell whether or not the difference between the numbers of social power relations found in a constitution is statistically different than that of instrumental power relations found in the same constitution. At first, the VOIP second hypothesis is confirmed in the case of Cameroon; however, if we were to take into account possibilities of wrong unitizing/coding, we are not sure to confidently make the same call. It is only with adjusted results that we could make strong interpretations of the uncertainty measured developed by the VOIP.

When looking at direction of power, the adjustment is not very much a big deal because the difference between the number of positive and negative power relations in both constitutions was important. That we find such a big number of positive power relations is in line with our expectations after reading the context of the making of the Chadian and Cameroonian constitutions: These numbers indeed suggest the absence of uncertainty at the time of the making. However, even here, we are unable to say it confidently. It might be the case that we found more positive power relations simply because writing in positive form is tradition in legal and juridical drafting. Indeed, Ard (2010) make the point on the existence of a legal writing tradition. He explained that in many legislative bodies like the US Senate or the Congress, there are explicit writing rules provided to drafters that definitely affect their legal writing style. On a US government Web site, one can read the following instruction on drafting legal documents:

> 6. Write positively: If you can accurately express an idea either positively or negatively, express it positively. DON'T SAY: The Governor may not appoint persons other than those qualified by the Personnel Management Agency. SAY: The Governor must appoint a person qualified by the Personnel Management Agency.[18]

These drafting instructions are not peculiar to US legislative bodies, they can be found on several legislative bodies' Web sites around the world: in France, Australia and New Zealand, to name a few. It seems also that those who have studied law at some point in their curriculum have encountered a legal drafting manual since there are so many of them in the field. All this suggests that there might indeed be a tradition among lawyers to "write positively" when it comes to drafting legal texts. If it is the case, we could not interpret the big number of positive power relations found in Chadian and Cameroonian constitutions as indication of the absence of uncertainty at the time of the making of those texts.

4 Conclusion

The goal of this case study was to apply the VOIP framework to the Chadian and Cameroonian constitutions. Specifically, we wanted to know whether or not those constitutions were made under the settings described by the theoretical literature on constitutional choices: a setting marked by uncertainty. The VOIP first step consists in identifying the major events that led to and prevailed during the making of the texts under analysis. In the second step, we use that information to interpret three measures of uncertainty: the source, the type, and the direction of power. The source of power in a constitution written under uncertainty will be political, while the type will be social and the direction negative. Our interpretation of the context of the making of our two texts led us to believe that incumbent presidents faced little uncertainty at the time. We therefore expected the uncertainty measures to be consistent with that intuition. However, results on source of power indicated the presence of uncertainty, results on type of power indicated the presence of uncertainty in the case of Cameroon but not in the case of Chad, and results on direction of power in both cases indicated the absence of uncertainty at all. This inconsistency in our results prompted us two remarks: first, in VOIP, we need to present extracting and coding results adjusted for errors; second, lawyers' legal writing style more than the presence/absence of uncertainty can be a better explanation of the direction of power in constitutions.

[18] See for example, "Drafting Legal Documents", http://www.archives.gov/federal-register/write/legal-docs/clear-writing.html.

Appendix

Table 5 Power relations in the Cameroonian constitution per section

Section number and title (articles)	Number of power relations
Preamble	38
Part 1: State and Sovereignty (1–4)	22
Part 2: On executive power	
Chapter 1: the president (5–10)	25
The government (11–13)	7
Part 3: On legislative powers	
Article 14	15
Chapter 1: National Assembly (15–19)	35
Chapter 2: The Senate (20–24)	30
Part 4: Relationship between the executive and legislative powers (25–36)	87
Part 5: Judicial power (37–42)	24
Part 6: Treaties and international agreements (43–45)	0
Part 7: Constitutional Council (46–52)	45
Part 8: The Court of impeachment (53)	6
Part 9: The Economic and Social Council (54)	0
Part 10: Regional and local authorities (55–62)	41
Part 11: Amendment of the Constitution (63–64)	11
Part 12: Special provision (65–66)	18
Part 13: Transitional and final (67–69)	7

References

Ard BJ (2010) Interpreting by the book: legislative drafting manuals and statutory interpretation. Yale Law J 120(1):185–200

Bouopda P (2008) Cameroun du protectorat vers la démocratie. 1884–1992. L'Harmattan, Paris, 447pp

Buijtebhuijs R (1993) La conférence nationale souveraine du Tchad: Un essai d'histoire immédiate. Karthala, Paris

Buijtebhuijs R (1996) 'Le Tchad est inclassable': Le référendum constitutionnel du 31 mars. Politique Africaine, p 62

Chatain J, Epanya A, Moutoudou A (2012) Kamerun, l'indépendance piégée: De la lutte de libération à la lutte contre le néocolonialisme. Harmattan, Paris, France

Fodouop K (2010) Une expérience démocratique pluraliste unique. In: Fodouop K (dir) Le Cameroun. Autopsie d'une exception plurielle en Afrique. L'Harmattan, Paris, pp 273–297

Imbeau L (2009) Testing the 'Veil of Ignorance' hypothesis in constitutional choice: a 'walk-talk' approach. J Public Choice Public Finance 26(1):3–21

Imbeau LM, Jacob S (2011) Is the 'Veil of Ignorance' in constitutional choice a myth? An empirical exploration informed by a theory of power. In: Marciano A (ed) Constitutional mythologies: new perspectives on controlling the state. Springer, New York, pp 53–69

Imbeau LM, Jacob S (2012) Codebook of the Veil of ignorance project. Département de Science politique de l'Université Laval (on line). http://www.fss.ulaval.ca/cms_recherche/upload/veil_ignorance/fichiers/codebook__jan_2012.pdf (last consulted 19 Aug 2013)

Imbeau LM, Jacob S (2015) Measuring the opacity of the 'Veil of ignorance' in constitutions: theory, method and some results. In: Imbeau LM, Jacob S (eds) Behind a veil of ignorance? Power and uncertainty in constitutional design. Springer, New York
May R, Massey S (2000) Two steps forward, one step back: Chad's protracted 'Transition to Democracy'. J Contemp Afr Stud 18:1
Mbembe A (1990) Le Cameroun après la mort d'Ahmadou Ahidjo. Politique africaine, vol 37. pp 117–123
Médard JF (1979) L'Etat sous-développé au Cameroun. L'Année africaine. Pedone, Paris, pp 39–55
Olinga AD (2006) La constitution de la république du Cameroon. Presse de l'UCAC, Yaoundé
Owona J (2012) Droits constitutionnels et institutions politiques du monde. L'Harmattan, Paris, p 730

Chapter 14
Conclusion

Cristine de Clercy

As demonstrated in the preceding twelve chapters, this work presents two different approaches to considering uncertainty in constitutional design. First, the subject of constitutional design is engaged. In Chaps. 2–4, the authors introduce this project's theoretical foundation and delineate its intellectual inheritance and development. For the second approach, key propositions drawn from Buchanan and Tullock's work then are tested in nine independent case studies. So, to this point, the analysis has moved from the abstract level to concrete and specific analysis. To sum up this work, however, there is merit in reviewing the comparative findings generated in the nine case studies, and then considering these in the light of the original theory concerning how uncertainty influences constitutional creation. This is helpful particularly given Stefan Voigt's observation, in Chap. 2, that the "veilonomics" literature has leaned heavily in favour of studying Rawlesian interpretations of the veil of uncertainty (Voigt 2015: 10). Buchanan and Tullock's view, however, has remained largely unexamined in empirical analysis. Similarly, Christine Rothmayr Allison notes in her review of the socio-legal literature that there has been much more attention paid to constitutional norms than constitution drafting per se (Rothmayr 2015: 35).

1 Empirical Findings

The nine case studies have generated an impressive amount of data that, taken as a whole, represents the most extensive testing of Buchanan and Tullock's hypotheses to date. As Imbeau and Jacob (2015: 55) note in Chap. 4 above, this study is unique in its objective: to measure the prevalence of uncertainty in constitution-making. This marks a significant contribution to several academic literatures.

C. de Clercy (✉)
Department of Political Science, The University of Western Ontario, London, Canada
e-mail: C.Declercy@uwo.ca

L.M. Imbeau and S. Jacob (eds.), *Behind a Veil of Ignorance?*,
Studies in Public Choice 32, DOI 10.1007/978-3-319-14953-0_14

These analyses provide rich insight into each case as well as a wealth of comparative knowledge. Considered as a group, the nine constitutions under study contain a broad range of examples that illuminate three key variables. The variable of time is particularly well represented here. From the early cases of the 1787 United States constitution and Belgium's 1831 constitution to the postwar constitutions of Italy and Germany, and then Niger's 2010 constitution, the analysis spans more than two centuries. Such temporal breadth allows us to avoid basing conclusions on a narrow window of time, such as examining only the late 1700s or the mid twentieth century period. Interestingly, in many of the cases, the key hypotheses are supported despite the varying dates of each constitutional exercise.

For example, the first hypothesis proposes that owing to uncertainty, "There are more concerns for political power than for economic or preceptoral power in a constitution" (Imbeau and Jacob 2015: 67). As Imbeau and Jacob observe in Chap. 4, the results of the content analysis suggest there is some cross-country variation in constitutional references to authority as the source of power: the highest value for the manifestation of uncertainty among constitutional drafters is located in the case of the United States (0.85) and the lowest value among the cases is found in Switzerland (0.62). Ingold and Varone (2015), in summing up their findings for the Swiss case, note several unique factors that work to reduce uncertainty and therefore may help to explain Switzerland's outlier position among the nine cases. However, at the same time, it is worth noting that all the constitutions studied here contain a fairly large proportion of references to authority as the source of power despite vastly different temporal contexts. The case with the lowest value still records content above fifty per cent of all references, in support of the first hypothesis. So, the comparative temporal results of the analyses can be interpreted to suggest constitutions generally are veiled by uncertainty, although the opacity of each is variable.

The frequency of constitutional revision is a second variable that is highlighted in the comparative findings. In some cases, the constitution has remained largely unchanged since first drafting; the United States being the notable example here. In other studies, the original constitutional document has been significantly amended a few times, or undergone an extensive reworking. Because the analysts consider a nation's constitution currently in force as of 2011, as well as precedent constitutions, for several cases, the results illustrate the role of uncertainty across multiple constitutional iterations. The cases of Belgium and Canada exemplify this type, as constitutions created in the nineteenth century were recast in the twentieth century (Imbeau and Eboutou 2015). In the case of Greece, however, the analysis concerns six distinct constitutional documents as well as three major revisions. The variation in the frequency of constitutional reconstruction that is represented in these nine cases is an important aspect of the entire study. As Imbeau and Jacob (2015: 65) note above, "Because constitution choices last longer, the uncertainty of decision-makers is more prevalent than in in-period choices."

Viewing the findings across the cases, it appears there is a negative correlation between the frequency of revision and the level of uncertainty. Several authors such as Tridimas (2015) point to this relationship as part of the explanation for variation in the tests of the second hypothesis, which posits there are more concerns for social power than instrumental power in a constitution. It appears there is support for the argument that shorter time horizons do not generally serve the preferences of the median voter because the more frequently a constitution is revised, the less uncertainty permeates the minds of decision-makers. This finding is quite striking, and it presents a new set of opportunities to investigate further the role of political elites in constitutional review and reform.

A third variable revealed in the case studies concerns the condition of national economies. Economists tend to distinguish among developed, developing and under developed economies. The nine cases represent several types of economies in different conditions. Constitutional construction in the case of Germany, for example, occurred in a period when postwar reparations and restoration costs were extremely large, and the nation's sophisticated industrial infrastructure was shattered. Contrast this with the cases of Switzerland and Belgium concerning constitution-making in advanced, stable industrialized countries. A few cases, such as that of Estonia, Niger and Cameroon (Eboutou 2015), concern transitional or underdeveloped economies. The research is enriched by the variety of economic contexts that are engaged. These cases help to illuminate the role of economic contexts in the generation of constitutional texts. The findings here are a step in a promising direction, owing to the influence of contextual economic uncertainty on decision-makers' constitutional choices as discussed in more detail below.

So, considered as a group, the nine constitutions under study here contain a broad range of examples that illuminate the effects (or lack thereof) of three key variables: time, frequency of constitutional revision and the economic context. These studies are helpful, "real-world" analyses that have tested Buchanan and Tullock's core theoretical insights and so sharpened our understanding of how uncertainty affects constitutional choice. Consideration of the variable political and economic contexts surrounding each constitutional exercise helps us to focus attention on a second key contribution of these nine chapters: they present a set of complex and sometimes contradictory interpretations of uncertainty on the part of the authors.

2 Theoretical Insights

The concept of uncertainty is understood in a variety of ways within the social sciences, and the nine country-level studies exemplify this multiplicity. Some authors, such as Strauss (2015: 135) writing about the German case, treat uncertainty in the classic sense: it is a lack of information among constitutional drafters about the future. Other authors, such as Tridimas (2015: 183), adopt this view but suggest the Greek case shows uncertainty may be mitigated by the past experience of drafters who experienced the adverse effects of particular constitutional rules.

Other authors similarly highlight conditions that shape and influence the uncertainty held by key decision-makers. Some analysts clearly link the uncertainty held by political elites to the conditions extant at the time of constitutional founding. In analysing Estonia's 1992 constitution, for example, Raudla (2015) emphasizes its creation took place in a context of high uncertainty, owing mainly to the manifold societal transitions that were unfolding at this time. Similarly, de Clercy (2015: 87) underscores the highly uncertain economic and political context of the 1780s as key to analysing the development of the 1787 American constitution. In the Belgian case, Schiffino and Jacob (2015: 121) find that here the constitution-making process has "consistently remained in a state of uncertainty" across time which emanates from a very clear source: social cleavage. Moreover, and in contrast to the Greek case, Schiffino and Jacob find the veil of uncertainty has continued to pervade Belgium's constitution-making despite the potential benefits provided by path dependency and past learning.

Some analysts in this collection move beyond the classic assumption that uncertainty concerns a lack of knowledge about the future on the part of national political elites and consider how uncertainty may affect a broader group. Ingold and Varone find, in the Swiss case, it is impossible to distinguish among the drafters and adopters of the 1999 constitution. The mandatory referendum on constitutional revision introduces a unique source of uncertainty for the dominant political coalition (Ingold and Varone 2015: 193). And because the referendum process inserts Swiss citizens into the constitution-making process, analysing their degree of uncertainty seems to be crucial when investigating constitutional power relations. In their discussion of the role of uncertainty in Italian constitution-making, Galli and Grembi (2015: 155) emphasize that it is not only uncertainty at the national level that matters; the regions matter too. So, while several authors adopt the classic view of uncertainty in constitution-making, others have amended it to fit their specific studies to capture factors that are revealed as important within their chapters.

There are a variety of ways that uncertainty is treated here, in short, and this helps to flesh out the real-world implications of the original theoretical abstractions. Buchanan and Tullock (1962: 35) suggest uncertainty inheres in political processes when "the individual participant has no way of knowing the final outcome, the social choice, at the time he makes his own contribution to this outcome." But this can be interpreted narrowly, to mean someone who literally engages in constitutional drafting such as James Madison, or more broadly, to include people such as senior administrative elites who shape and inform the political actors' efforts. Put another way, is uncertainty located in the minds of the actual drafters only? Or is it salient if it exists among the larger group of elites who inform the views of the drafters? Is it germane to consider it if it exists among the citizenry, as in the case of Switzerland? And what about the drivers of uncertainty? Are there a finite number of sources of uncertainty, such regional war or deep economic recession, that perennially clearly shape the drafters' perceptions and hence their calculations? Or should we understand uncertainty as a generalized context that may be sharpened, or reduced, by each polity's particular socio-political arrangements and institutional configuration?

These questions, and many others, emanate from each author's specific case study in this volume. They are particularly salient given Stefan Voigt's conclusion that the central conjectures of veilonomics are unsatisfactory at the theoretical level and empirically unsupported. They challenge us to reconsider and perhaps refine the project's overarching theory, as well as pursue further knowledge gleaned from careful, comparative empirical analysis. At the same time, this substantive project has made a significant contribution towards focusing analytic attention on constitutional drafting and the role of uncertainty in social choice.

References

Buchanan JM, Tulluck G (1962) The calculus of consent: logical foundations of constitutional democracy. The University of Michigan Press, Ann Arbor

De Clercy C (2015) USA—uncertainty and the general interest in the American constitution: testing the "Veil of Ignorance" hypothesis in constitutional choice. In: Imbeau LM, Jacob S (eds) Behind a veil of ignorance? Power and uncertainty in constitutional design. Springer, Dordrecht

Eboutou TC (2015) Chad and Cameroon—constitutional choices turned into simple in-period choices: a power relations reading of the Chadian and Cameroonian constitutions. In: Imbeau LM, Jacob S (eds) Behind a veil of ignorance? Power and uncertainty in constitutional design. Springer, Dordrecht

Galli E, Grembi V (2015) Italy—different veils for different governments: the veil of ignorance in shaping the Italian decentralization. In: Imbeau LM, Jacob S (eds) Behind a veil of ignorance? Power and uncertainty in constitutional design. Springer, Dordrecht

Imbeau LM, Eboutou TC (2015) Canada—constitution-making Process under Uncertainty: The case of Canada. In: Imbeau LM, Jacob S (eds) Behind a Veil of Ignorance? Power and Uncertainty in Constitutional Design. Springer, Dordrecht

Imbeau LM, Jacob S (2015) Measuring the opacity of the 'Veil of Ignorance' in constitutions: theory, method and some results. In: Imbeau LM, Jacob S (eds) Behind a veil of ignorance? Power and uncertainty in constitutional design. Springer, Dordrecht

Ingold K, Varone F (2015) Switzerland—is the swiss constitution really constitutional? Testing the "Veil of Ignorance" hypothesis over time. In: Imbeau LM, Jacob S (eds) Behind a veil of ignorance? Power and uncertainty in constitutional design. Springer, Dordrecht

Raudla R (2015) Estonia—the thickness of the veil of uncertainty and its effects on constitution-making in post-communist transition: the 1992 constitution of Estonia. In: Imbeau LM, Jacob S (eds) Behind a veil of ignorance? Power and uncertainty in constitutional design. Springer, Dordrecht

Rothmayr C (2015) Law in books vs law in action: a review of the socio-legal literature. In: Imbeau LM, Jacob S (eds) Behind a veil of ignorance? Power and uncertainty in constitutional design. Springer, Dordrecht

Schiffino N, Jacob S (2015) Belgium—uncertainty and cleavages at stakes: do the belgian constitutions of 1831 and 1993 stabilize political power? In: Imbeau LM, Jacob S (eds) Behind a veil of ignorance? Power and uncertainty in constitutional design. Springer, Dordrecht

Strauss A (2015) Germany—testing the "Veil of Ignorance" hypothesis in constitutional choice: evidence from the German *Grundgesetz*. In: Imbeau LM, Jacob S (eds) Behind a veil of ignorance? Power and uncertainty in constitutional design. Springer, Dordrecht

Tridimas G (2015) Greece—constitutional convulsions in modern Greece. In: Imbeau LM, Jacob S (eds) Behind a veil of ignorance? Power and uncertainty in constitutional design. Springer, Dordrecht

Voigt S (2015) Veilonomics: on the use and utility of veils in constitutional political economy. In: Imbeau LM, Jacob S (eds) Behind a veil of ignorance? Power and uncertainty in constitutional design. Springer, Dordrecht

MIX
Papier aus verantwortungsvollen Quellen
Paper from responsible sources
FSC® C105338

If you have any concerns about our products,
you can contact us on
ProductSafety@springernature.com

In case Publisher is established outside the EU,
the EU authorized representative is:
Springer Nature Customer Service Center GmbH
Europaplatz 3, 69115 Heidelberg, Germany

Printed by Libri Plureos GmbH
in Hamburg, Germany